Frommer's

Copenhagen day by day®

2nd Edition

by Chris Peacock

FrommerMedia LLC

Contents

Published by:

Frommer Media LLC

ISBN 978-1-62887-290-3 (paper), 978-1-62887-291-0 (e-book)

Editorial Director: Pauline Frommer
Editor: Holly Hughes
Production Editor: Heather Wilcox
Photo Editor: Meghan Lamb
Cartographer: Elizabeth Puhl

Front cover photos, left to right: Raspberry cake at Royal Smushi: Courtesy of Royal Smushi; Nyhavn district: © S-F/shutterstock.com; Passing by the Danish Playhouse on a harbor tour: © Audrius Merfeldas/Shutterstock.com

Back cover photo: © Mikhail Markovskiy / Shutterstock.com
For information on our other products or services, see www.frommers.com.

Frommer Media LLC also publishes its books in a variety of electronic formats. Some content that appears in print may not be available in electronic formats.

Manufactured in China

5 4 3 2 1

About This Guide

Organizing your time. That's what this guide is all about.

Other guides give you long lists of things to see and do and then expect you to fit the pieces together. The Day by Day guides are different. These guides tell you the best of everything, and then they show you how to see it *in the smartest, most time-efficient way*. Our authors have designed detailed itineraries organized by time, neighborhood, or special interest. And each tour comes with a bulleted map that takes you from stop to stop.

Hoping to sample the best in modern Danish design and architecture? Seeking glimpses of Denmark's storybook past, from *Hamlet* to Hans Christian Andersen? Looking for canal boat rides, shopping expeditions, or a night in Tivoli Gardens? Whatever your interest or schedule, the Day by Days give you the smartest routes to follow. Not only do we take you to the top attractions, hotels, and restaurants, but we also help you access those special moments that locals get to experience—those "finds" that turn tourists into travelers.

The Day by Days are also your top choice if you're looking for one complete guide for all your travel needs. The best hotels and restaurants for every budget, the greatest shopping values, the wildest nightlife—it's all here.

Why should you trust our judgment? Because our authors personally visit each place they write about. They're an independent lot who say what they think and would never include places they wouldn't recommend to their best friends. They're also open to suggestions from readers. If you'd like to contact them, please send your comments our way at feedback@frommers.com, and we'll pass them on.

Enjoy your Day by Day guide—the most helpful travel companion you can buy. And have the trip of a lifetime.

About the Author

London-born **Chris Peacock** has nearly a decade of experience in travel journalism and is a former contributing editor for *National Geographic* Traveller and *ABTA Magazine* in the U.K. He's now a freelance travel writer and editor living in Copenhagen and specializing in all things Scandinavia for several newspapers, magazines, websites, and guides. He resides in Copenhagen.

An Additional Note

Please be advised that travel information is subject to change at any time—and this is especially true of prices. We therefore suggest that you write or call ahead for confirmation when making your travel plans. The authors, editors, and publisher cannot be held responsible for the experiences of readers while traveling. Your safety is important to us, however, so we encourage you to stay alert and be aware of your surroundings.

Star Ratings, Icons & Abbreviations

Every hotel, restaurant, and attraction listing in this guide has been ranked for quality, value, service, amenities, and special features using a *star-rating system.* Hotels, restaurants, attractions, shopping, and nightlife are rated on a scale of zero stars (recommended) to three stars (exceptional). In addition to the star-rating system, we also use a **kids** *icon* to point out the best bets for families. Within each tour, we recommend cafes, bars, or restaurants where you can take a break. Each of these stops appears in a shaded box marked with a coffee-cup-shaped bullet.

The following abbreviations are used for credit cards:

AE	American Express	DISC	Discover	V	Visa
DC	Diners Club	MC	MasterCard		

Frommers.com

Now that you have this guidebook to help you plan a great trip, visit our website at **www.frommers.com** for additional travel information on more than 4,000 destinations. We update features regularly to give you instant access to the most current trip-planning information available. At Frommers.com, you'll find scoops on the best airfares, lodging rates, and car rental bargains. You can even book your travel online through our reliable travel booking partners. Other popular features include:

- Online updates of our most popular guidebooks
- Vacation sweepstakes and contest giveaways
- Newsletters highlighting the hottest travel trends
- Online travel message boards with featured travel discussions

A Note on Prices

In the "Take a Break" and "Best Bets" sections of this book, we have used a system of dollar signs to show a range of costs for 1 night in a hotel (the price of a double-occupancy room) or the cost of an entree at a restaurant. Use the following table to decipher the dollar signs:

Cost	Hotels	Restaurants
$	under $100	under $10
$$	$100–$200	$10–$20
$$$	$200–$300	$20–$30
$$$$	$300–$400	$30–$40
$$$$$	over $400	over $40

An Invitation to the Reader

In researching this book, we discovered many wonderful places—hotels, restaurants, shops, and more. We're sure you'll find others. Please tell us about them, so we can share the information with your fellow travelers in upcoming editions. If you were disappointed with a recommendation, we'd love to know that, too. Please write to: Contact@FrommerMedia.com

17 Favorite **Moments**

17 Favorite Moments

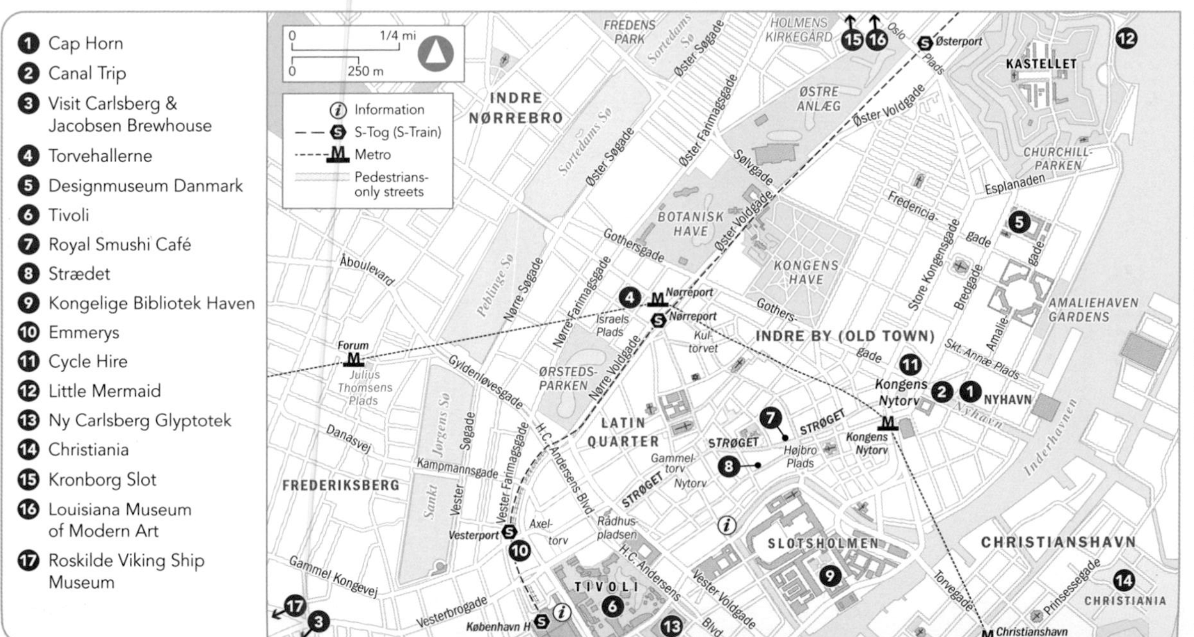

Previous page: Nyhavn district.

Copenhagen just may be that rarest of all rare things—a perfect holiday destination. It's compact and easy to navigate, yet bursting with royal palaces, innovative design museums, great shops, and vast green parks. Add to that a wealth of hip and plentiful bars, cafes, and restaurants, not to mention fascinating daytrips—it's a complete and enticing package. Here are some of my favorite things to do in the booming Danish capital and environs.

❶ **Lunching canal-side in the sun at Nyhavn,** preferably at Cap Horn for its excellent organic dishes and superb langoustines. If it's cold, wrap up in a blanket and huddle under one of the outside heaters. *See p 95.*

❷ **Exploring the canals by boat,** cruising by some of Copenhagen's most famous sights to get your bearings in the city. *See p 162.*

❸ **Making a fuss of the handsome Jutland horses** in the stables at Carlsberg (p 50) and afterwards enjoying a glass of chilled lager at the Jacobsen Brewhouse. *See p 107.*

❹ **Grazing the bustling food stalls of Torvehallerne,** a glass-covered gourmet market full of mouthwatering snacks, meals, and treats. Try the duck confit sandwich at Ma Poule. *See p 81.*

❺ **Getting a taste for Danish decorative arts** at the Designmuseum Danmark. Admire the sleek avant-garde chairs of Finn Juhl or explore a vast 3,000-piece collection of beautiful porcelain. *See p 27.*

❻ **Zooming at high speed around the Tivoli roller coasters** and afterwards grabbing the famous gourmet hot dog from Andersen Bakery. *See p 33.*

❼ **Joining the elegant ladies of Frederiksberg** for delicately constructed "smushi" (a mixture of sushi and smørrebrød) at the Royal Smushi Café (p 100), followed by a browse around the Royal Copenhagen flagship store to buy the famous blue-and-white china. *See p 76.*

❽ **Shopping in Strædet.** The cobbled streets and vintage and antique stores of Læderstræde and

The Demon roller-coaster at Tivoli Gardens.

Exploring Copenhagen on two wheels.

Kompagnistræde are ideal for bargain hunters. *See p 77.*

❾ **Kicking back with a book in Kongelige Bibliotek Haven** (Royal Library Gardens) on a bench just by the fountain. Perfect for reflecting on your visit to the Danske Jødisk Museum (Danish Jewish Museum). *See p 19.*

❿ **Buying rough-hewn bread and organic picnic supplies** from Emmerys, a store with several branches throughout Copenhagen. Those delicious smells! *See p 79.*

⓫ **Cycling around the city.** Traveling on two wheels is the best way to get around, thanks to scenic cycle-friendly roads and cool bike routes like the elevated Cycle Snake. *See p 162.*

⓬ **Walking off a Nyhavn lunch along Langelinie** on a Sunday afternoon to admire the Lille Havfrue (Little Mermaid, p 59) and her less attractive friend, the Mutant Mermaid, in Østbassin. *See p 17.*

⓭ **Admiring the vast sculpture collections** at Ny Carlsberg Glyptotek and strolling among the lush palms in its domed Winter Garden. *See p 14.*

⓮ **Wandering the famous Freetown of Christiania** with its eclectic locals, craft shops, crazy DIY homes, and clutch of tasty eco-restaurants. *See p 65.*

⓯ **Walking around the battlements at Kronborg Slot** (p 146) on its wild and remote headland in the north of Zealand, before settling in for some French-inspired cuisine at nearby Brasserie 1861 and watching the sun slip into the Øresund. *See p 102.*

⓰ **Catching sight of the glittering waters of the Øresund** from the glass-walled galleries at Louisiana Museum of Modern Art; walk in the rolling grounds after pleasantly overdosing on contemporary art. *See p 154.*

⓱ **Getting down to some serious rowing** on the fjord in a replica longboat at Roskilde's Viking Ship Museum. Afterwards visit the original longboats, dating from the 11th century. *See p 138.* ●

The iconic Little Mermaid statue wistfully gazes out to sea.

1 The Best **Full-Day Tours**

The Best in One Day

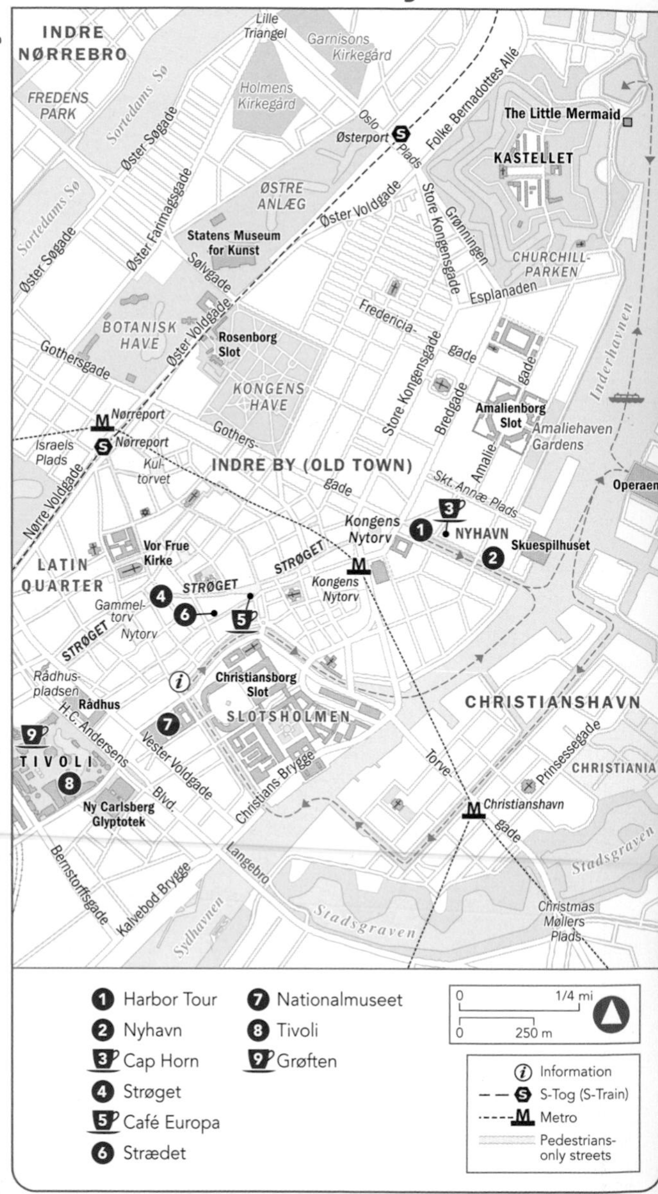

Previous page: The entrance to Tivoli.

Time to immerse yourself in romantic, chic Copenhagen. This city is about more than fabulous art collections and serious museums, although it has its fair share. Take to the cobbled streets to get right to its laid-back heart. See the city from the sea on a harbor cruise, then savor the casual vibe in the restaurants of Nyhavn. Discover the shopping streets of the old town, or delve into Danish history in Copenhagen's biggest museum. Wind up your day at the iconic pleasure gardens of Tivoli to scream around roller coasters and feast on the finest Danish cuisine. **START: Kongens Nytorv.**

1 ★★★ kids Harbor Tour. Boat tours leave up to six times an hour from the top of Nyhavn Canal, and I highly recommend taking one—not just to get your bearings, but also to understand how the city has developed from its medieval infancy to the cutting-edge destination of today. Take the Red Line boat trip to the north of the harbor and sit at the front of the boat if you want to catch the English commentary. As you leave Nyhavn, look left for the much-celebrated and handsome **Det Kongelige Teater Skuespilhuset (**Royal Danish Playhouse, p 121). Right across the water you'll spy the innovative **Opera House** (p 119), with a curving four-story foyer and cantilevered roof, floating on its man-made island. On the left and just downstream from the Queen's palace at **Amalienborg** (p 40) there's a photo opportunity at the **Little Mermaid** statue (p 59), who sits on an empty shoreline gazing wistfully out to sea. On the return journey through the canals of **Christianshavn** (p 64) get cameras ready for the gold-topped **Vor Frelsers Kirke**, which appears on the left (p 64), and the sparkling **Den Sorte Diamant** (Black Diamond), housing part of Denmark's royal library (p 29), which looms up as you turn out of Christianshavn Canal. Before returning to Nyhavn, the boat putters around the islet of **Slotsholmen** (p 39), site of Copenhagen's first palace, built by Bishop Absalon, who founded the city in 1167 A.D. *1 hr. Canal Tours, Nyhavn 1433 (at head of canal). ☎ 45 3296 3000. www.stromma.dk. Book in advance at Copenhagen Visitor Service, Vesterbrogade 4a. ☎ 45 7022 2442. www.visitcopenhagen.com. Tickets 80DKK adults, 40DKK kids; free with a Copenhagen Card (p 163). Daily June 27–Aug 16 9:30am–9pm, 6 tours per hour; Mar 12–June 26 & Aug 17–Sept 13 9:30am–6pm, 1–4 tours per hour; rest of year trips*

Passing the Danish Playhouse on a harbor tour.

leave at 10am, 11:20am, 12:40am; 2pm & 3:20pm. Metro: Kongens Nytorv.

2 ★★★ kids **Nyhavn.** Built in the 17th century to connect Copenhagen to the sea, Nyhavn street is bisected by a canal and lined with crooked, brightly painted gabled houses. Once home to sailors and dockworkers, the street was notorious for seedy drinking dens. Today the crowds and venues are still here but they've both gone up-market. Welcoming cafes, bars, and restaurants offer cold beers and (mostly) excellent local dishes at tables spilling into the street. Choose somewhere to eat and settle down to watch the world go by—my preferences are Cap Horn (see p 95), Leonore Christine (p 98) and Heering (p 97), for quality seafood and piled-high *smørrebrød.* ⏱ *45 min. Nyhavn. Metro: Kongens Nytorv.*

3 ★★ **Cap Horn.** My first choice at Nyhavn for a leisurely lunch plate of three open-faced sandwiches. If the sun is shining, grab a table in the street-side bar and order a chilled dark lager. *Nyhavn 21.* ☎ *45 3312 8504. www.caphorn.dk. $$.*

Shopping on Strøget, Europe's longest pedestrianized street.

4 ★★★ **Strøget.** Europe's longest pedestrianized shopping street runs 1.8 km (1.1 mi) from Kongens Nytorv down to the Rådhuspladsen, moving progressively downmarket as it goes. At the top end, have credit cards at the ready for Cartier, Gucci, Mulberry, and Chanel as well as department store **Illum** (p 76), beloved of wealthy Copenhagen matrons, and its delightful sidekick design emporium, **Illums Bolighus** (p 78), with its color-coordinated displays. Acclaimed silversmith Georg **Jensen**'s flagship store (p 81) is here too, next door **to Royal Copenhagen** (p 76), doing a roaring trade in

Save Money with a CPH Card

Copenhagen Card: don't go out without it. This brilliantly conceived card gives free entrance to 74 museums and attractions (all the major ones, including Tivoli, but not the Roskilde Viking Ship Museum, see p 138) plus free travel on public transport (bus, metro, train, and harbor bus, see p 162) throughout Copenhagen and beyond. At the time of writing, a 24-hour CPH Card cost 359DKK, a 48-hour card 499DKK, a 72-hour card 589DKK and a 120-hour card 799DKK. When ready to use your card, sign and date it, and write in your starting time; it's valid from that point. Two children go free with one adult card. Buy the card online (www.visitcopenhagen.com), from the visitor center at Vesterbrogade 4a (☎ **45 7022 2442**), or at the airport.

The modern atrium lobby of Nationalmuseet.

its famous blue-and-white pottery. Among the chain stores popping up further down Strøget (Topshop, H&M, Urban Outfitters), **Bodum** stands out for selling quality Danish design at sensible prices. 🕓 *1½ hr. Strøget. Metro: Kongens Nytorv. Short stroll from Nyhavn.*

5 ★★ kids **Café Europa.** At the heart of pedestrianized Strøget, Café Europa boasts an award-winning barista (coffee expert) and a selection of sinful teatime cakes. See p 94. *Amagertorv 1.* ☎ *45 3314 2889. $.*

❻ ★★★ **Strædet.** Discover the romantic tangle of narrow cobbled streets to the south of Strøget, often referred to as the Latin Quarter. You couldn't do better for hip boutiques, dusty old vinyl-record shops, and bustling cafes overflowing with students. Læderstræde and its continuation Kompagnistræde are lined with basement antique shops selling silverware, porcelain, and delicate glass (not many bargains to be found here). 🕓 *1 hr. Latin Quarter. Metro: Kongens Nytorv. Stroll from Strøget to Rådhuspladsen.*

❼ ★★ kids **Nationalmuseet (National Museum).** It's time for a whistle-stop tour of Danish history at the National Museum, housed in an 18th-century palace with a new atrium just off Rådhuspladsen. The collection is broken down into themes (ethnographic, coins and medals, Middle Ages and Renaissance, Prince's Palace) but don't try to see too much in one go; the collection is vast, and navigating around it is time-consuming. I advise you to choose one of several

Monday Closing

Don't get caught out: many museums and attractions in Copenhagen close on Monday, including most of those mentioned in this chapter. There's still lots to do; take a harbor trip past the Little Mermaid, enjoy *smørrebrød* (open sandwiches—they're so much more enticing than they sound) overlooking the canal at Nyhavn, wander around Christianshavn (p 64), or visit the Viking Ship Museum at Roskilde (p 138).

The Shop Signs of Copenhagen

Strolling around the Latin Quarter, you may be tempted to spend all your time gazing in shop windows—but don't forget to look up as well, to see the colorful painted-iron signs projecting over the street at right angles. Relics of long-ago eras when many people couldn't read, their symbols instantly tell what sorts of wares are sold within the premises. They're now cherished by design-conscious Danes—in fact, alongside the authentically medieval signs you'll notice plenty of hip modern versions.

60-minute audio-guides (find near the ticket desk) to steer you through the highlights. If you're travelling *en famille*, there's an interactive children's museum to spark little imaginations (p 34). Especially good are the ethnographic collections (ground floor, Rooms 151–172) where you can see an Inuit snow suit, an eerily beautiful Edo period golden screen decorated with frolicking horses, and a collection of Samurai costumes. Tour the state rooms of 1743, complete with fine Flemish tapestries (Rooms 127–134 on the ground floor) and don't miss the mystical Iron Age Gundestrop Cauldron, decorated with carved Celtic warriors and dogs, the symbol of death, just off the atrium. ⏲ *1 hr.*

Ny Vestergade 10. ☎ *45 3313 4411. www.nationalmuseet.dk. Free admission. Tues–Sun 10am–5pm. Closed Dec 24–25, 31. Bus 1A, 2A, 9A. 10-min. walk from Strædet.*

8 ★★★ kids **Tivoli.** Bewitching Tivoli weaves its magic after dark, when all its pavilions, pagodas, follies, and intricately landscaped boating lakes are brightly floodlit. Founded in 1843, the pleasure gardens are as Danish as bacon and maintain a sweetly old-fashioned appeal, pulling daily crowds by the thousand. You'll find over 30 rides to choose among, from adrenaline-pumping coasters to gentle diversions specially aimed at young kids (p 33). But there's so much more to Tivoli than fairground rides—see mini-tour on p 11. Food and drink options abound, whatever your budget: Grab a hot dog on the hoof, sink a pint of lager in the Beer Garden, or sit down for a formal dinner in one of Tivoli's pricey restaurants (p 90). ⏲ *3 hr. Vesterbrogade 3.* ☎ *45 3315 1001. www.tivoli.dk. Admission 99DKK Mon–Thurs; 110DKK Fri–Sun; free entry children under 8. Multi-ride tickets 209DKK Mon–Thurs; 220DKK Fri–Sun. Apr–Sept Sun–Thurs 11am–11pm; Fri–Sat 11am–12am; reduced hours rest of year. Closed Jan to early Apr. Bus 2A, 5A, 9A. 10-min walk from Nationalmuseet.*

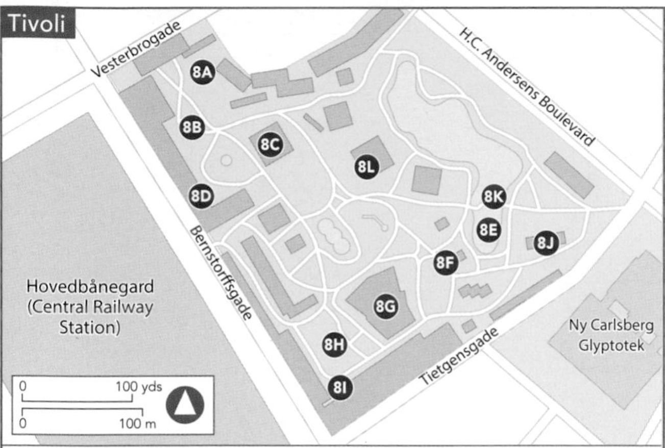

8A Pantomimeteatret
8B Promenade Pavilion
8C Plænen
8D Nimb Palace
8E Tivoli Lake
8F Trolley Bus
8G Tivoli Concert Hall
8H Rides
8I Amusement Arcade
8J Demon roller coaster
8K Wooden bridge
8L Tivoli Glass Hall Theatre

8A ★★★ kids **Pantomimeteatret.** The Chinese pavilion (p 117) to the left of the main entrance stages nightly performances of mime and panto. Opposite is the 8B ★ **Promenade Pavilion,** home to the Tivoli Promenade Orchestra. There's rock music at the 8C ★★ **Plænen (Open-Air Stage Tivoli),** where local kids hang around looking for action (p 120).To your right, 8D ★★★ **Nimb** has a trendy restaurant, bar, and hotel (p 132). Walk to the ornamental lake and on the left is 8E ★★★ kids **Tivoli Lake,** with Dragon Boats (p 33) for children. Take toddlers on the 8F ★★ kids **Trolley Bus** to explore the rest of the gardens—it stops by the Illums Bolighus store (p 78) on your left. Straight ahead the 8G ★★ **Tivoli Concert Hall** provides music by the resident symphony orchestra (p 118) and mainstream concerts. Around the hall to the right are 8H ★★★ kids **Rides** including Bumper Cars, Nautilus and the Star Flyer for the brave (p 33). The 8I ★★ kids **Amusement Arcades** provide old-fashioned fun and cotton candy. A scary 8J kids **Demon Roller Coaster** has high-speed inversions, while the Golden Tower boasts high-velocity drops of up to 63m (207 ft). Cross the 8K ★ **Wooden bridge** over the floodlit lake and follow the shore around to 8L ★ kids the **Tivoli Glass Hall Theatre,** where variety shows are held. Up ahead is the exit.

9 ★★★ **Grøften.** The 40-plus food outlets in Tivoli range from hotdog stands to haute cuisine. Choose from all the smørrebrød classics. *Tivoli. Vesterbrogade 3. ☎ 45 3375 0675. www.groeften.dk. $$.*

The Best **in Two Days**

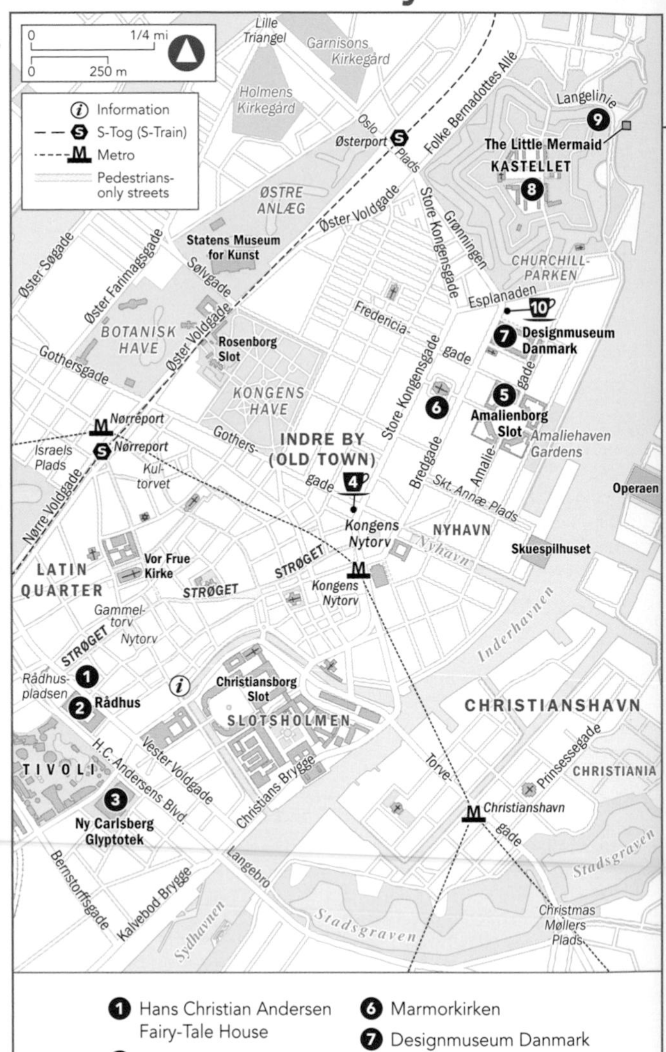

1. Hans Christian Andersen Fairy-Tale House
2. Rådhus & Astronomical Clock
3. Ny Carlsberg Glyptotek
4. Bistro Royal
5. Amalienborgmuseet
6. Marmorkirken
7. Designmuseum Danmark
8. Kastellet
9. Langelinie
10. Café Petersborg

Today's the day to ingest a little more culture. You'll see a rare and immense collection of antiquities and the very best of Danish decorative arts. Between times, visit the Royal Family at home and introduce your kids to the fairy-tale world of Hans Christian Andersen. There's even a chance to stretch your legs along the seafront, maybe even see a mermaid or two. START: **Rådhuspladsen.**

1 ★ kids Hans Christian Andersen Fairy-Tale House. If you are traveling with young kids or have a keen interest in the works of Denmark's favorite storyteller, this is a good option to start the morning, with a series of tableaux illustrating Andersen's fairy-cum-morality tales, plus letters, newspaper clippings, and photographs to appeal to older visitors. *1 hr. Rådhuspladsen 57. ☎ 45 3332 3131. www.ripleys.com/copenhagen. Admission 60DKK, 40DKK kids 4–11, free with Copenhagen Card. Mid-June to Aug daily 10am–10pm. Rest of year Sun–Thurs 10am–6pm; Fri–Sat 10am–8pm. Closed Dec 24–25 & 31, Jan 1. Bus 10, 12, 26, 33, 2A, 5A, 6A.*

2 ★ Rådhus & Astronomical Clock. If whimsical fairy stories are not your thing, head straight for the monumental architecture of the Rådhus (city hall), which dominates the eastern end of its busy square. It was built at the turn of the 20th century by Martin Nyrop (1849–1921), Scandinavia's leading romantic architect. Influenced by the Palazzo Pubblico in Siena, the city hall is studded with carvings of mythical creatures and its 106m **tower** gives great views over the city and Tivoli (p 33). In a room off the main foyer, you can see Jens Olsen's **World Clock:** Completed in 1955, it has 14,000 moving parts,

Jens Olsen's immense World Clock, with 14,000 moving parts, can be viewed in the lobby of the Rådhus.

The Palm Garden atrium of the NY Carlsberg Glyptotek museum.

perfectly exhibited in a double-sided glass case. There are guided tours of the impressive mock-Gothic interior, and separate trips up the tower. *30 min. Rådhuspladsen 1. ☎ 45 3366 3366. www.kk.dk. Guided tours in English (tower) 30DKK; (city hall) 50DKK. Tower tours Mon–Fri 11am & 2pm; Sat noon. City hall tours Mon–Fri 1pm; Sat 10am. Bus 10, 12, 26, 33, 2A, 5A, 6A.*

3 ★★★ NY Carlsberg Glyptotek (Carlsberg Collection). Cross over Hans Christian Andersen Boulevard to an unsurpassable collection of antiquities and 19th-century French and Danish paintings donated to Copenhagen in 1897 by scions of the Carlsberg brewing dynasty (p 50). The ancient sculptures, gathered from Egypt, Greece, and Rome, are laid out in two light-filled neoclassical galleries built around a charming sculpture-and-plant-filled courtyard garden. Make a point of seeing the gilded sarcophagus of Aurelia Kyrelia (300AD), the impassive head of Roman goddess Juno (she's had a nose job), and the evocative Greek statue of an actress holding the head of Dionysus, dating from 200AD. For a change of pace, Helge Carlsberg's collection of Danish and French art hangs well in local architect Henning Larsen's minimalist three-story gallery extension. Highlights include Van Gogh's stark 1889 *Landscape from Saint-Remy*, several of Gauguin's Tahitian women, and a series of Degas's ballet-dancer bronzes. There's a delicious but pricey cafe in the palm-filled Winter Garden (p 94). *2 hr. Dantes Plads 7. ☎ 45 3341 8141. www.glyptotek.dk. Admission 95DKK adults, free for kids under 18, free with Copenhagen Card. Tues–Sun 11am–6pm; Thurs 11am–10pm. Closed Dec 24–25, Jan 1. Bus 1A, 2A, 5A, 6A, 9A, 10, 12, 33, 37, 250S. 2-min. walk across Rådhuspladsen from Hans Christian Andersen Fairy-Tale House.*

4 ★★ Bistro Royal. Cross town to Kongens Nytorv to find this bustling bistro serving quick and affordable classics such as burgers and steaks—perfect for a lunchtime pit stop. When the weather is good, grab a table outside for great views over the plaza. See p 93. *Kongens Nytorv 26. ☎ 45 3841 4164. www.madklubben.dk/bistro-royal. $$.*

5 ★★ Amalienborgmuseet (Amalienborg Museum). Walk off lunch to the rococo palaces of the Amalienborg complex, built in the 1750s by Nicolas Eigtved (1701–1754, who also played a role in

The grand domed Marmorkirken, part of the Amalienborg palace complex.

building the palace at Christiansborg). Ranged around an immense central plaza, they are still used by the Royal Family today. With your back to the imperious equestrian statue of Frederik V, look towards the dome of the Marmorkirken (p 15). The palace immediately to the left serves as luxury accommodation for visiting diplomats; there are guided tours between June and September. The next palace on the left is the winter home of the present Queen, Margrethe II. The first palace on the right was the home of Crown Prince Frederik and his Tasmanian-born wife Princess Mary until 2011 but they now live in the remaining fourth palace. Their former home is partly open to the public; a series of royal apartments house royal jewels, paintings, and costumes, plus fascinating family portraits. A recreation of Frederik VIII's opulent study from 1869 is dominated by a very non-PC polar bear skin.

🕓 1 hr. Christian VIII's Palace. ☎ 45 3315 3286. www.amalienborgmuseet.dk. Admission 90DKK, 60DKK students, free under 18, free with Copenhagen Card. Nov–Apr Tues–Sun 11am–4pm; May–Oct daily 10am–4pm. Closed Dec 23–26, 31. Bus 1A, 26.

6 ★ Marmorkirken (Marble Church). Properly called Frederiks Kirke and designed as part of the Amalienborg palace complex (see p 56) in the 1750s, this Baroque church was eventually inaugurated in 1894. The 31m dome was to be clad in marble (hence its nickname), but, alas, the budget didn't stretch to that. Still, they made up for it inside; the decorative dome is gilded and smothered with representations of the prophets and cherubim. Choral concerts are

Keep the Change

Most museums won't allow bags and backpacks to be taken into the galleries: all baggage has to be deposited in lockers before entry so I make sure to carry 10DKK and 20DKK coins with me to operate the lockers. The coins are refundable when you reclaim your belongings.

held here in summer. ⏲ *30 min. Frederiksgade 4. ☎ 45 3315 0144. www.marmorkirken.dk. Church admission free; open Mon–Thurs & Sat 10am–5pm, Fri–Sun noon–5pm. Tours of dome 35DKK, 20DKK under age 18; tours June–Aug & Oct 11–19 Mon–Fri at 1pm, Sat–Sun at 1pm & 3pm; rest of year Sat–Sun at 1pm & 3pm. Bus 1A, 26. 5-min. walk from Amalienborgmuseet.*

Royal Copenhagen porcelain on display at the Designmuseum Danmark.

❼ ★★★ kids **Designmuseum Danmark.** This impressive collection of decorative arts is set in a former hospital backing on to tranquil lawns. Where else can you find blue-patterned drinking cups and tulip vases from the Golden Age of the Dutch and Danish guilds, Chinese and Japanese ceramics, embroidery, and avant-garde contemporary Danish design under the same roof? The late, great Arne Jacobsen and Scotland's Charles Rennie Mackintosh are given floor space alongside an extensive lace collection, temporary exhibitions, and the Design Studio, where kids can handle ceramics and other crafts. ⏲ *2 hr. Bredgade 68. ☎ 45 3318 5656. www.designmuseum.dk. Admission 100DKK, free students & under 26, free with Copenhagen Card. Tues–Sun 11am–5pm (Wed until 9pm). Closed Dec 24–26, 31, Jan 1. Metro: Kongens Nytorv. 5-min. walk from Marmokirken.*

❽ ★ kids **Kastellet.** Built by Christian IV in 1626 as a star-shaped fortress to strengthen the city walls, Kastellet suffered damage during both the Swedish Siege of Copenhagen (1658–60) and by the British in 1807 during the Napoleonic Wars. Today the buildings inside the fortress are occupied by the army although the public

Military barracks at the harborside Kastellet fortress.

can still enjoy a stroll outside and watch swans swim about the moat. *45 min. Churchilparken.* ☎ *45 3311 2233. Admission free. Metro: Kongens Nytorv. 5-min. walk from Designmuseum Danmark.*

9 ★ kids **Langelinie.** Join Copenhageners on an afternoon's promenade along Langelinie, following the shoreline along Øresund. The walkway starts by the bronze statue of mythical Gefion ploughing up land to create Denmark, atop a fountain next to the ramparts of the **Kastellet** (see above). A couple of hundred meters along Langelinie, look for Edvard Eriksen's iconic *Little Mermaid* (p 59), perched on her rocky island since 1913. Carry on up Langelinie Quay to the cruise-liner port and turn left into Østbassin for another intriguing pile of stones with a mermaid atop. Dubbed the *Mutant Mermaid,* this sculpture is twisted like a figure in a Mannerist painting and sits opposite a sinister group sculpture called *Paradise Genetically Altered*, a distorted vision of the Holy Family; both are by anarchic artist Bjørn Nørgaard. From here walk back past Kastellet and follow Bredgade into the city center, or catch the number 26 bus. *15 min. Bus 26. 1-hr. round-trip walk to & from to Bredgade.*

10 ★★★ **Café Petersborg.** In atmospheric basement premises, this cafe is a real treat, serving the best herring in town, presented three ways: marinated, pickled, or curried. See p 95. ***Bredgade 76.*** ☎ ***45 3312 5016. www.cafe-petersborg.dk. $$.***

The Best in Three Days

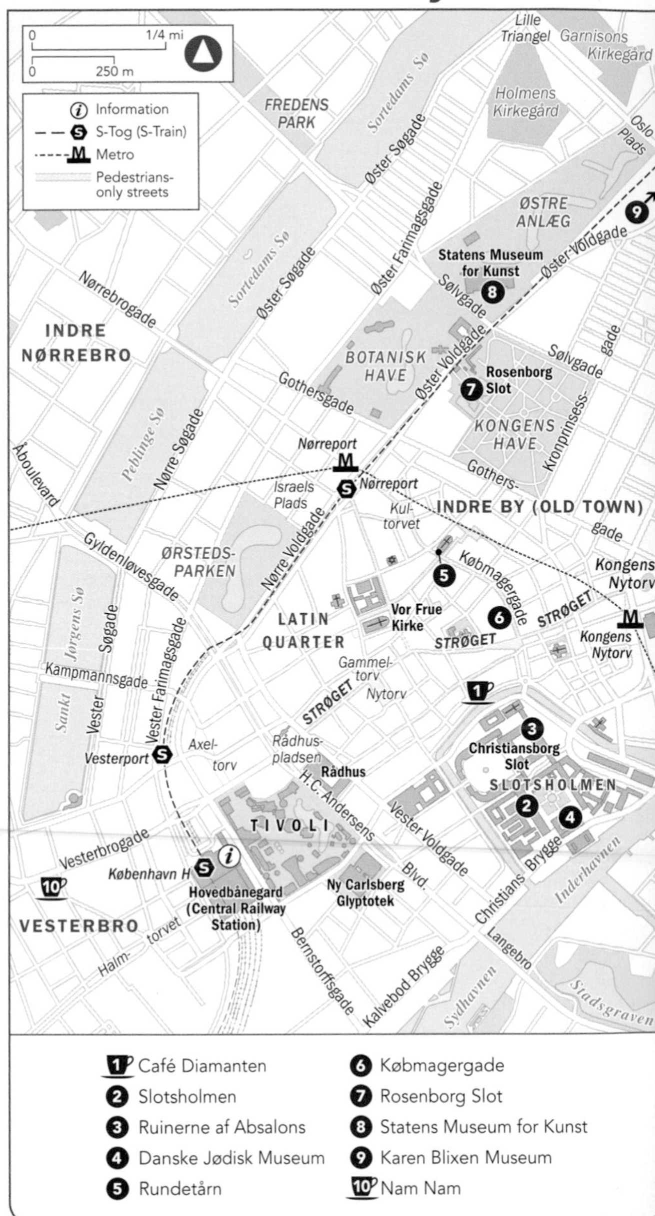

1 Café Diamanten
2 Slotsholmen
3 Ruinerne af Absalons
4 Danske Jødisk Museum
5 Rundetårn
6 Købmagergade
7 Rosenborg Slot
8 Statens Museum for Kunst
9 Karen Blixen Museum
10 Nam Nam

Along with more art and history, today offers a chance to peer across the Copenhagen skyline—obviously you will see more if you choose a clear day. Take a look at Slotsholmen, the island power-base of Danish politics for a thousand years, and visit a couple of unusual museums, one up the coast near the marina in Rungsted. Wear a pair of comfy shoes for walking along Copenhagen's cobbled streets! **START: Gammel Strand.**

1 Cafe Diamanten. Stop off for a frothy café au lait and chocolate croissant, or indulge in a hearty and heavy full Danish breakfast. *Gammel Strand 50. ☎ 45 3393 5545. www.cafediamanten.dk. $.*

2 Slotsholmen. Cross the bridge to the tiny island of Slotsholmen, the site of Bishop Absalon's Copenhagen in the 12th century and subsequent home to the Danish Royal Family in a series of ever-more flamboyant palaces. Today it houses the Danish Parliament in **Christiansborg Palace** (p 39), as well as a grand neoclassical church and no less than seven diverse **museums**. The two described below are my recommendations, for their unusual content.

3 ★★★ kids Ruinerne af Absalons (Absalon's Ruins). The foundations of Absalon's castle lie below Christiansborg Palace in an atmospheric little museum; entry is through the arched front gateway. See granite pillars from the chapel, remains of the castle's protective double walls, and the ruins of Absalon's Secret—a coy euphemism for the medieval bathrooms. *45 min. Kongeporten. ☎ 45 3392 6492. www.christiansborg.dk. Admission 50DKK, 40DKK students, 25DKK kids 4–17, free kids under 4, free with Copenhagen Card. May–Sept daily 10am–5pm; Oct–Apr Tues–Sun 10am–5pm. Metro: Kongens Nytorv. 5-min. walk from Gammel Strand.*

4 ★★ Danske Jødisk Museum (Danish Jewish Museum). Tucked away in a

Christiansborg Palace on Slotsholmen island nowadays houses the Danish Parliament.

Inside this former royal boathouse is the innovatively designed Danish Jewish Museum.

corner of the Kongelige Bibliotek (Royal Library), this little museum is worth a visit just to experience the startling slopes and angles of Daniel Libeskind's extraordinary design. The collection tells the 400-year-old story of Jewish life in Denmark through a series of interactive and clearly labeled exhibits, including ornate Chanukah candlesticks and illuminated Torah manuscripts. The tranquil, fountain-filled garden outside is a secret spot to take a few moments out. ⏱ *45 min. Proviantpassagen 6.* ☎ *45 3311 2218. www.jewmus.dk. Admission 50DKK, 40DKK students & seniors, free for kids under 18, free with Copenhagen Card. June–Aug Tues–Sun 10am–5pm; Sept–May Tues–Fri 1pm–4pm, Sat–Sun noon–5pm. Metro: Kongens Nytorv. 5-min. walk from Gammel Strand.*

A 17th-century astronomical observatory, the Rundetårn offers great city views from its top.

5 ★★★ kids Rundetårn (Round Tower). Head back to the city center to find the imposing brick Rundetårn, commisioned in 1642 by King Christian IV as an observatory for astronomer Tycho Brahe. It now hosts art exhibitions and concerts. Wend your way up the circular internal ramp to the top for the best views across Copenhagen's Latin Quarter (p 9). At 35m high, you'll see the Øresund, the rides of Tivoli, and the tower of Christiansborg Palace (p 39) as Copenhagen stretches into the distance. ⏱ *45 min. Købmagergade 52a.* ☎ *45 3373 0373. www.rundetaarn.dk. Admission 25DKK, 5DKK kids 5–15, free with Copenhagen Card. Tower open daily, May 21–Sept 20 10am–8pm, Sept 21–May 20 10am–6pm (Tues–Wed until 9pm mid-Oct to mid-Mar). Closed Dec 24, 25, Jan 1. Metro: Nørreport. 10-min. walk from Christiansborg Slot up Købmagergade.*

6 Buzzing **Købmagergade** and the surrounding streets offer plenty of food stalls selling hotdogs and burgers if you are after a quick snack. Croissant'en in Frederiksborggade does a roaring trade in tasty pizza slices.

7 ★★ Rosenborg Slot (Rosenborg Castle). A fairy-tale castle bang in the middle of Copenhagen, Rosenborg was built as the summer residence for Christian IV, who moved in about 1634. The opulent interior, largely untouched for the past 100 years, now houses the Danish Royal Collections. There are a few sights you cannot miss: fat little cherubs encrusted on the marble ceiling of room 5; Frederick IV's ornate ivory-inlaid mandolin in room 10; the strange mirrored floor of his dressing room (room 13a), and the majestic red, black, and white tiled Long Hall on the third floor. Downstairs in the Treasury, the Danish Crown Jewels sparkle in semi-darkness. The palace is surrounded with the lawns of **Kongens Have** (Royal Gardens, p 85), the perfect picnic venue on sunny days. ⌚ *1 hr. Øster Voldgade 4a.* ☎ *45 3315 3286. www.rosenborgslot.dk. Admission 90DKK, 60DKK students, free under 18, free with Copenhagen Card. Open mid-June to Aug daily 9am–5pm; May to mid-June & Sept–Oct daily 10am–4pm; Nov–Apr Tues–Sun 10am–2pm (until 3pm Feb 13–28, until 4pm Dec 27–30 & Mar 22–28). Closed Dec 23–26, 31, Jan 1. Metro: Nørreport. Bus 14, 26, 37, 42, 5 A, 6A, 184, 185, 173E, 150S, 350S. 10-min. walk from Rundetårn.*

A Dutch Baroque gem, Rosenborg Slot was built for King Christian IV.

8 ★★ kids Statens Museum for Kunst (National Gallery of Denmark). Spanning art from the 14th century to contemporary work, this glorious light-filled gallery began life in the 19th century. Renaissance works, portraiture, and Danish art plus a few Rembrandts and Rubens are housed in the original section of the museum, while modern works are in a modern glass extension, linked by a wide exhibition space called Sculpture Street. Look for quality paintings by Braque, Derain, Matisse, Dufy, and Modigliano as well as the odd Picasso and interesting contemporary Danish work. A massive patchwork quilt by Kirsten Roepstorff in 1972 pre-dates Tracey Emin's similar creations by decades. ⌚ *1½. Sølvgade 48-50.* ☎ *45 3374 8494. www.smk.dk. Admission permanent exhibitions free. Fees apply to special exhibitions, free with Copenhagen Card. Tues–Sun 10am–5pm (Wed until 8pm). Closed Dec 24–25, 28, 31, Jan 1. Metro: Nørreport. Bus 14, 26, 37, 42, 6A, 184, 185. 5-min. walk from Rosenborg Slot.*

9 ★★ Karen Blixen Museum. Jump in the train from Østerport (a 10-min walk from Statens Museum) and to go Rungsted to visit the ivy-covered family home of Karen Blixen (1885–1962), Denmark's

The Statens Museum for Kunst (Danish National Gallery) has an impressive modern art wing.

favorite lady of letters, best known to the rest of us by her pen name **Isak Dinesen,** author of *Out of Africa*. The coach house is now converted into an exhibition of prints, photos, letters, and manuscripts charting the story of her tumultuous life; witness the striking black-and-white portrait by Cecil Beaton and cartoons featuring her with Ernest Hemingway; they shared a mutual passion for Africa. Born at Rungstedlund in 1885, Blixen moved to Kenya in 1914 with her aristocratic Swedish husband Bror von Blixen-Finecke. Controversially they divorced in 1924 and Karen returned to Denmark in 1931 after her lover Denys Finch Hatton was killed in a plane crash. Living quarters in the main house are virtually unchanged since Blixen's death in 1962. Off the hallway is a gallery hung with her paintings; the two Kikuyu portraits shine out. The rooms are pleasantly but plainly furnished, with great wood-burning stoves and Kenyan furniture. A short film showcases Blixen's life, and there are tapes of her reading her stories. The Corona typewriter she used is in the study at the front of the house. Outside, Blixen is buried at the bottom of Ewald's Hill in the 14-acre garden. Follow the path from the museum through the orchard and her grave is under the beech tree. ◷ *1 hr. Rungsted Strandvej 111, 2960 Rungsted Kyst.* ☎ *45 4557 1057. www.karen-blixen.dk. Admission 75DKK, under age 14 free, free with Copenhagen Card. May–Sept Tues–Sun 10am–5pm; July–Aug also Mon noon–7pm. Oct–Apr Wed–Fri 1pm–4pm, Sat–Sun 11am–4pm. Guided tours in English by appointment. Train: from Østerport to Rungsted departs every 20 min.; trip takes 25 min. It's a 20-min. hike to the museum, or take bus 388 from station. Return to Hovedbanegården (Central Station) in Copenhagen.*

10 **Nam Nam.** Round off a long sightseeing day back in Vesterbro, just behind Central Station. Order delicious hoisin-marinated spareribs or a slow-cooked chicken curry; there's even take-away service if you want to head straight back to your hotel. See p 98. *Vesterbrogade 39.* ☎ *45 4191 9898. www.restaurantnamnam.dk. $$.* ●

2 The Best Special-Interest Tours

Copenhagen Art & Design

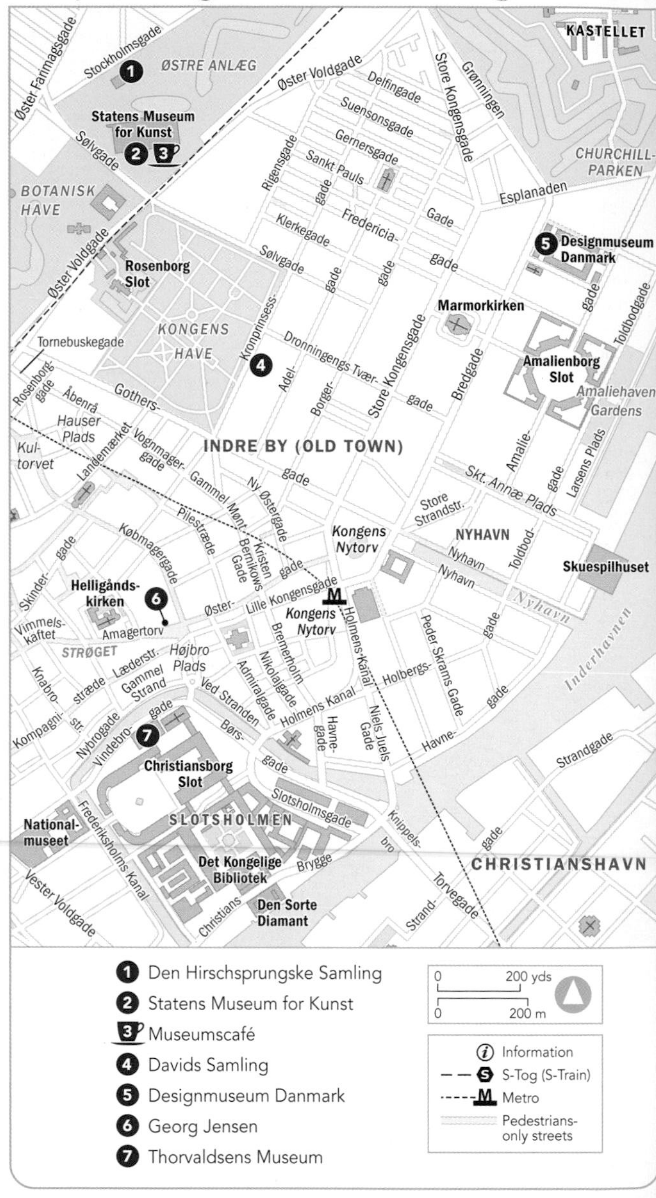

Previous page: Changing of the guards on the square at Amalienborg Castle.

If you ever doubted Copenhagen's flair and commitment to the best of art and design, this tour will make you think again. You'll see some inspiring art from the Golden Age of the late 19th century, contemporary industrial design, and a whole swathe of work by iconic designers. **START: Metro or S-Tog to Nørreport and a 5-minute walk up Øster Voldgade.**

❶ ★★ Den Hirschsprungske Samling (The Hirschsprung Collection). This unsung little salon, specializing in Danish art from the 19th and early 20th centuries, to my mind deserves more attention. Tobacco magnate Heinrich Hirschsprung bequeathed his collection to the nation in 1911; it's housed in a porticoed pavilion behind the Statens Museum (see p 21). Ranging through a series of elegantly decorated rooms, you'll see in Room 1 portraits by CW Eckersberg (1783–1853), an influential art professor of the era, and in Room 2 a fine portrait by his student Christen Købke (1810–48). Early rooms record works by artists on the Grand Tour, later pastoral paintings depict scenes of rural bliss. For me the gallery's highlights include Kristian Zahrtman's (1843–1917) irreverent royal portraits in Room 13 and the fabulous body of work by Peder Severin Krøyer (1851–1909) in Room 21. He was the shining light of the Skagen Painters, a colony of artists who went to north Jutland to paint the soft light there; Hirschsprung was his patron. Catch his dreamy *Summer Evening at the Beach at Skagen*, which includes the artist, his wife, and dog. *⏲ 1 hr. Stockholmsgade 20. ☎ 45 3542 0336. Admission 90DKK; 80DKK students; kids under 18 free. Free with Copenhagen Card. Open Tues–Sun 11am–4pm. Guided tours arranged in advance. Metro: Nørreport & 5-min. walk up Øster Voldgade.*

The little-known Hirschsprung Museum has a rich trove of art from Denmark's late-19th-century Golden Age.

Abstract mobile in the lobby of the Statens Museum for Kunst.

❷ ★★ kids **Statens Museum for Kunst.** Across Østre Anlæg park, Copenhagen's National Gallery showcases a wealth of Danish art through the ages. Rooms 218-229 display a strong collection o f paintings and sketches from Golden Age artists such as CW Eckersberg, Abildgård (1743–1809), and Hammershøi (1864–1916). Work by CoBrA Group artists, a 1950s pan-European group centered on Copenhagen, Brussels, and Amsterdam, celebrate Denmark's continuing significance in the art world. Look in Room 208 for abstracts by Asger Jorn (1914–73, see p 155), inspired by the darker side of Norse mythology. ⏱ *45 min.* *See p 21,* ❽.

❸ ★★ **Museumscafé.** In the delightful modern extension to the Statens Museum, this airy, sun-filled cafe has views across Østre Anlæg gardens to a small lake. Refuel here on organic coffees and pastries, salads, and various open sandwiches. *Sølvgade 48-50.* ☎ *45 2552 7236www.smk.dk. $–$$.*

❹ **Davids Samling (David Collection).** On the other side of Kongens Have gardens, this gallery features Scandinavia's largest collection of Islamic art, gathered by wealthy barrister Christian Ludvig David (1878–1960), along with a splendid collection of Danish decorative arts from the 18th century onwards—a trove of silverware, porcelain, glassware, and portraits by Jens Juel (1745–1802) as well as Golden Age paintings by CW

Innovations in modern chair design at the Designmuseum Danmark.

Taking Them Home

Serious design addicts can indulge their fancy in Copenhagen's avant-garde style shops: **Hay Cph**, **Illums Bolighus**, **Normann Copenhagen**, and trusty old **Kartell** (p 78) all have on-trend designs for sale at sometimes reasonable prices. Art lovers can explore the galleries on **Bredgade,** but don't expect any bargains!

Eckersberg. *Kronprinsessegade 30-32. ☎ 45 3373 4949. www. davidmus.dk.*

❺ ★★★ kids **Designmuseum Danmark.** My favorite museum is the best place to see the development of Danish applied arts and industrial design through the years. If you have been before, bypass the porcelain, lace, and Chinese embroidery (p 16) to concentrate on what Danes do best; create beautiful and functional designs. There is iconic cutlery made by Arne Jacobsen (1902–71) for the Radisson Blu Royal Hotel (p 132), the Platypus Dish by Henning Koppel (1918–81), Finn Juhl (1912–89) chairs, lots of functionalist furniture, and lighting by Verner Panton (1926–98). Temporary exhibitions often include jewelry by young local designers. 🕔 *1 hr. See p 16, ❼. Metro: Kongens Nytorv. 10-min. walk down Dronningens Tværgade, left on Bredgade.*

❻ ★★ **Georg Jensen.** On your way back toward through Kongers Nytorv, pop into Georg Jensen on Strøget (p 81) to nose around the museum in the basement, with its roll call of silversmiths from 1904 to the present day. As well as letters and designs by Jensen (1866–1935) himself, there are exhibits by Arne Jacobsen, Henning Koppel, Søren Georg Jensen (1917–82), and Jensen senior's main associate, Johan Rohde (1856–1935), whose designs influenced the functionalist movement of the 1930s. 🕔 *30 min. Amagertorv 4. ☎ 45 3311 4080 www.georgjensen.com. www. georgjensen.com.*

❼ ★ **Thorvaldsens Museum.** What appears like a colorful Greco-Roman mausoleum is in fact a museum dedicated to one man's obsession with sculpture. Danish sculptor Bertel Thorvaldsen (1770-1844) spent more than 40 years in Rome and was one of the most renowned artists among his contemporaries in Europe. Heavily influenced by mythology after his time in Rome, Thorvaldsen returned to Copenhagen and in 1838 donated his large private collection to the Danish public. In return, his native city constructed one of its finest buildings next to the parliament building and canal to house Thorvaldsen's remarkable collection—paintings, plaster molds, and marble statues together with thousands of objects from classical antiquity. 🕔 *1 hr. Bertel Thorvaldsens Plads 2. ☎ 45 3332 1532. www.thorvaldsensmuseum.dk. Admission 40DKK, under age 18 free. Free with Copenhagen Card. Tues–Sun 10am–5pm; free admission Wed. Guided tours in English by prearrangement from 695DKK. 8 min. from Kongens Nytorv to Slotsholmen island.*

Icons of Modern Architecture

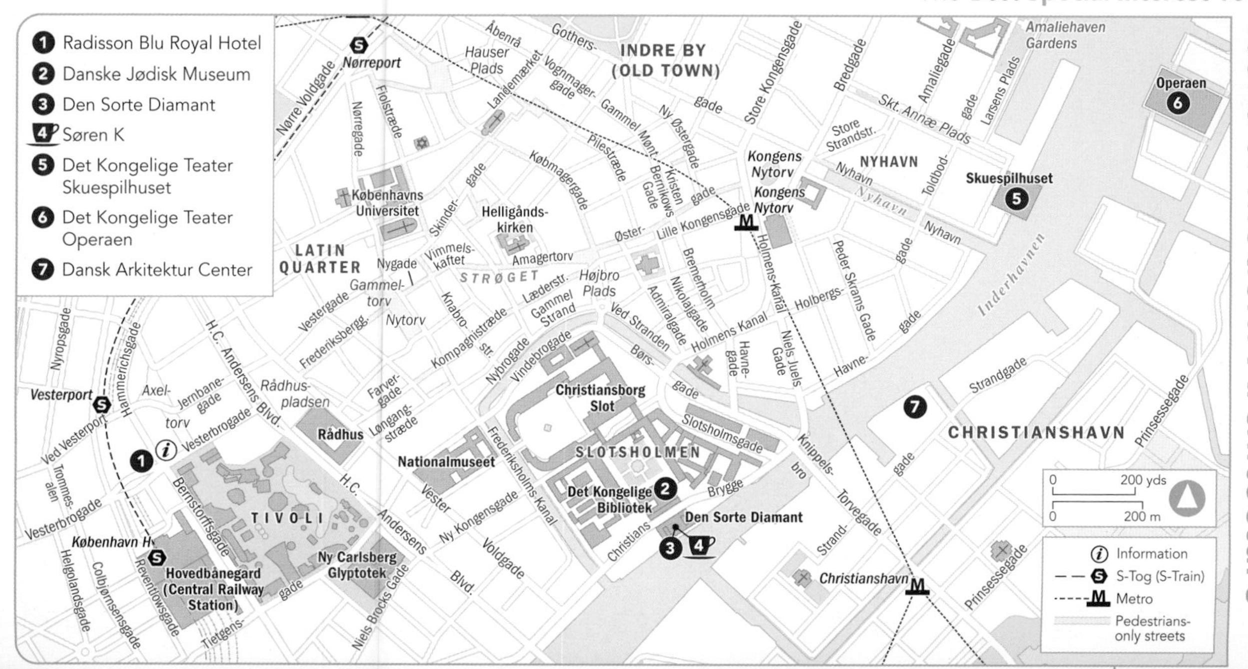

Ever since Arne Jacobsen changed the face of Copenhagen with his radical Radisson Hotel, the city has been proud to embrace innovative architecture. New buildings have been springing up all over, especially around the revitalized waterfront; here's a chance to tour the highlights of this thoroughly 21st-century city. **START: Bus 2A, 10, 12, 26, 33 to Rådhuspladsen.**

1 ★★ Radisson Blu Royal Hotel. What better place to kick off a tour of Copenhagen's contemporary architecture than at the city's original boutique hotel (p 132) and local landmark? In 1956, Arne Jacobsen, Denmark's most famous designer, had a hand in it all from the architecture (square, functional, it's not an attractive building) to the furniture and the cutlery, and so doing revolutionized Danish design concepts. At 22 stories, the Radisson was briefly Scandinavia's tallest building, and the windows stretch around the rooms like ribbons, giving views over Copenhagen's rooftops. Jacobsen moved into room 606 for a while, before taking a violent dislike to his handiwork and moving out. Following renovations, few elements of his original designs remain, but room 606 has been preserved (ask at reception if you want to have a look at it). Nevertheless, his Swan, Pot, and Egg chairs, cutlery, and crockery are regarded as timeless classics; they have been copied by several hotels and are sold in many Copenhagen shops (p 78). ◷ *40 min. Hammerichsgade 1. 5-min. walk from Rådhuspladsen.*

2 ★★ Danske Jødisk Museum (Danish Jewish Museum). Designed by American architect Daniel Libeskind (b. 1946), this museum occupies what was originally the Royal Boat House of Christian IV, who invited Sephardic Jews to Denmark from Portugal in 1622; the boathouse was subsequently enveloped in the Kongelige Bibliotek (Royal Library), built in 1906. Behind that traditional exterior, however, the interior of the Jewish Museum, opened in 2004, is boldly innovative. Interconnecting wooden passageways tip at crazy angles, conflicting with the display cases, which point in all directions. The pod-like interconnections between museum sections represent the close relationship between the Danes and the Jews, after they were helped to flee Denmark in WW2. ◷ *30 min. 20-min. walk up Frederiksbergade to Strøget; look at the diverse architecture as you go. See p 19, 4.*

3 ★★★ Den Sorte Diamant (Black Diamond). One of Copenhagen's most spectacular sights, this iconic building is best seen by boat as you emerge from Christianshavn Kanal (p 64). Sitting in the same complex as the Jewish Museum, the Black Diamond bends over the sparkling Øresund, with a glass and granite-clad frontage

Den Sorte Diamant (the Black Diamond), built in 1999 to house the Royal Library.

Opened in 2005, the Royal Opera House is at its most spectacular lit up at night.

reflecting the waves and boats as they pass by. Built by architects Schmidt, Hammer, and Lassen, it opened in 1999 and now houses part of the Royal Library, the largest in Scandinavia. The library has 4.5 million books accessible to the public, with rare manuscripts by national treasures Karen Blixen, Hans Christian Andersen, and Søren Kierkegård. There's also a bookshop, concerts in the Queen's Hall, exhibition space, and a highly rated restaurant **Søren K** (see below). *1 hr. Søren Kierkegårds Plads 1. ☎ 45 3347 4747. www.kb.dk. Admission to library free. Exhibitions 40DKK; 25DKK students; free for kids under 16. Exhibitions: Mon–Sat 10am–7pm. Library: Mon–Sat 8am–10pm (July–Aug closes at 7pm).*

4 Søren K. Expensive but worth it for the views over the Øresund from the first floor of the Black Diamond (see above), this tony restaurant with minimalist gray décor serves international cuisine of the highest level (see p 101). Enjoy a late lunch or book for dinner. *Søren Kierkegaards Plads 1. ☎ 45 3347 4949. www.soerenk.dk$$$.*

5 ★★★ Det Kongelige Teater Skuespilhuset (Royal Danish Playhouse). A triumphant success for Danish architects Lundgård and Tranberg, this national center of dramatic art opened in 2008. Personally the Playhouse (p 121) reminds me of a squat glass box with a wooden-clad brick sitting on top of it, albeit a box with splendid vistas of the Øresund and Operaen across the water. Despite its bulky appearance, the people of Copenhagen have taken the theater to their hearts; its wooden waterfront pier and walkway is a great place to stroll. *45 min. See p 121. 10-min. wander along the waterfront.*

6 ★★★ Det Kongelige Teater Operaen (Opera House). With first performances in 2005 on a man-made island at Dokøen, directly opposite Amalienborg (p 40), the Opera House (p 119) wasn't an immediate success with the Danish public, but as the infrastructure improved around it, the building became more popular. Its cantilevered roof and semicircular frontage, designed by Henning Larson, looks spectacular when lit up at night. To explore

Other Places to See

Copenhagen's newest quarter of Ørestaden has risen phoenix-like from an industrial wasteland between the motorway and railway. With a concept initially conceived by Daniel Libeskind (p 29), highlights include two curved 20-story high-rises surrounding a central square, apartments, offices, restaurants, bars, and shops; it's Copenhagen's answer to the Western Harbor development in Malmö (p 150). One Metro stop away on the island of Amager, Jean Nouvel's revolutionary **DR Koncerthuset** (p 117) has quickly established itself as a world-class concert hall. Take bus route no. 388 from Rådhuspladsen to Vilvordevej to see the striking Zaha Hadid-designed gallery extension at the **Ordrupgaard Museum** or cycle over Olafur Eliasson's **Cirkelbroen** (The Circle Bridge), a new landmark pedestrian bridge spanning Christianshavn canal.

inside, book a guided tour in advance (☎ 45 3369 6933, www.operaen.dk). They run Sat–Sun 9:30am and 4:30pm and cost 100DKK to see the spacious interior. ⏲ *45 min.* ☎ *45 3369 6933, www.operaen.dk. See p 119. Movia harbor boat service from Nyhavn.*

❼ ★ Dansk Arkitektur Center. Still on the island of Holmen, but further south in Christianshavn, this venue provides an overview of Danish architecture through a series of temporary exhibitions and publications; the center is publicly funded and calls itself a "visionarium." The bookshop is fabulous for lovers of architecture. ⏲ *45 min. Strandgade 27B.* ☎ *45 3257 1930. www.dac.dk. Admission 60DKK; 40DKK students; free under age 15; free with Copenhagen Card. Daily 10am–5pm (Wed until 9pm, free admission 5–9pm). 15-min. walk from Operaen.*

Exhibits at the Dansk Arkitektur Cente showcase new architecture.

Copenhagen for Kids

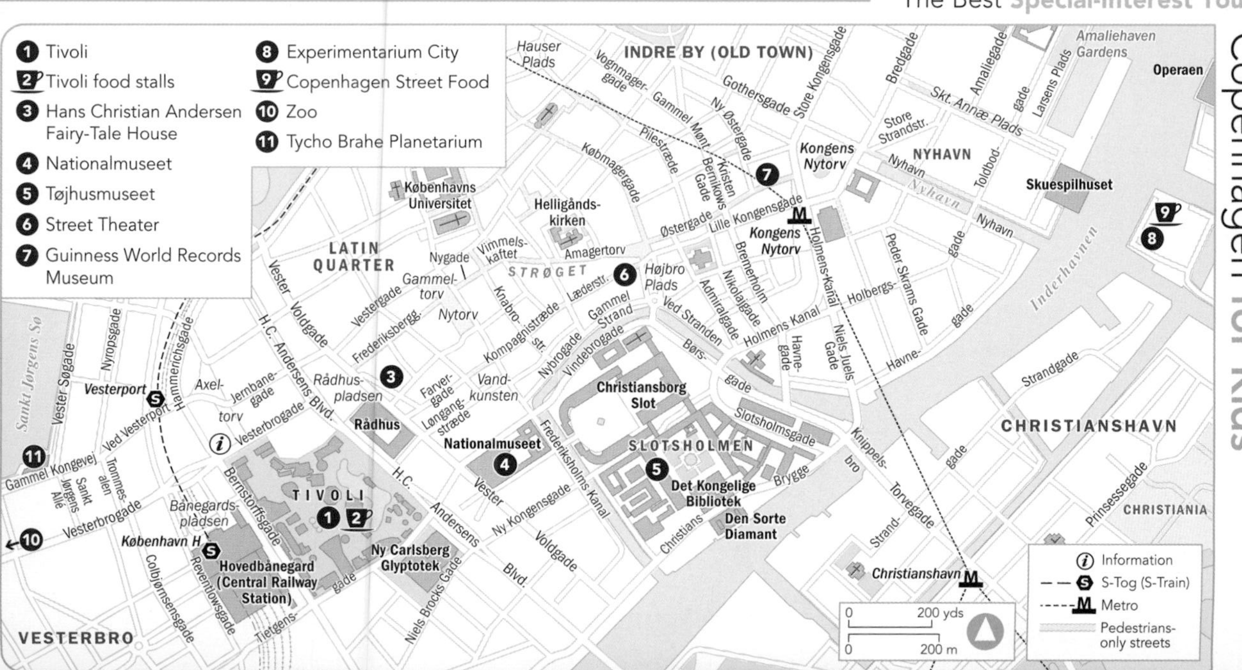

Copenhagen's an easy place to get around, with light traffic, a pedestrianized center, and a fairly laid-back pace. But there are many other reasons why it's ideal for families: storybook streetscapes, lots of museums with kid appeal, plenty to do outdoors, and of course Tivoli, with its arcades and roller coasters. The packed list below may be too much for one day, pick and choose according to your kids' ages and interests. START: **Bus 2A, 10, 12, 26, 33 to Rådhuspladsen.**

Chinese lanterns hang along the entrance walk at Tivoli Gardens.

1 ★★★ kids **Tivoli.** Where all children will want to start, Tivoli is as enticing by day as it is by night (p 88). Get there for 11am to see the Tivoli Boys Guard Parade (Wed, Sat, Sun) playing "oompah" music. There are several places in the park to buy multi-ride tickets (see p 10 for prices), which allow you to try the rides as often as you want. If shooting through the pitch black on the Roller-Coaster is too extreme, take toddlers for a gentle underwater adventure with Nemo on the Nautilus carousel or putter around on the Dragon Boats. A slow underground trundle past dragons and mice in The Mine is perfect for little ones, but most teenagers determinedly head straight for The Star Flyer, which rises to spin 80m above Copenhagen. Try it if you dare; if you can keep your eyes open the views of Copenhagen are spectacular. *2 hr. See p 10, 8.*

2 **Tivoli food stalls.** With all the choice Tivoli offers, a mid-morning ice cream or cotton candy from any stall around the fairground rides will be easy to find.

3 ★ kids **Hans Christian Andersen Fairy-Tale House.** An experience aimed directly at kids. Born in Odense in 1805, Andersen arrived in Copenhagen in 1819 determined to be an actor (p 44). He didn't get his big theatrical break but in 1835 wrote his first whimsical fairy tale, *The Tinder Box*. In this museum you'll find scenes from his early life and tableaux of his stories *Thumbelina* and *The Tin Soldier* for children to enjoy, alongside the original manuscript for *The Stone of the Wise Man*, the museum's most costly purchase and found in the Legacy Room. This attraction is unfortunately in the

Thumbelina is one of many storybook characters at the Hans Christian Andersen Fairy-Tale House.

same building as the rather ghastly Ripley's Believe it or Not! which should be avoided at all costs. (Two-headed cow? No thanks.) ⏲ *45 min. See p 13, ❶.*

❹ ★ **Nationalmuseet.** Denmark's National Museum is Scandinavia's largest, set within a vast, rambling former palace. In the Children's Museum (rooms 51–55), younger kids can attend a 1940s' Danish school, try on clothes worn when their grandparents were young, clamber over a full-size model of a Viking ship, or try on a medieval knight's boots and helmet. Elsewhere in the museum, there's a well-labeled prehistoric

Reading ancient runestones at the Nationalmuseet.

collection, housing a fabled Iron Age Sun Chariot, a Bronze Age girl's grave, and musical instruments. Entry to the museum is free so there's no need to feel you have to see everything at once—stay just as long as their attention spans last. ⏲ *2 hr. See p 9, ❼.*

❺ ★ kids **Tøjhusmuseet (Royal Danish Arsenal Museum).** Part of the **Slotsholmen museum complex** (p 39), this is a winner for kids who are fascinated by military paraphernalia. Stored in the vaulted palace arsenal opened by Christian IV in 1604, cannons, machine guns, and mortars line the walls. Upstairs in the Armory Hall, there are uniforms, ceremonial swords, and guns, together with all sorts of other military weapons and accessories, spanning the 19th century to present day—even a German V-1 flying bomb from World War II. ⏲ *1 hr. Tøjhus 3. ☎ 45 3311 6037. www.thm.dk. Admission free. Tues–Sat 10am–5pm (Wed until 8pm), Sun noon–4pm.*

❻ ★★★ kids **Street Theater.** Most days see some sort of entertainment along pedestrianized Strøget, be it mime artists, jugglers, or musicians. Even watching the rickshaw peddlers and cyclists steer around the crowds on Hojbrø Plads is amusing. ⏲ *15 min.*

❼ ★ kids **Guinness World Records Museum.** You may love it or hate it, but the sight of the world's tallest man standing outside the museum makes it irresistible to kids. The well-trodden formula here (man with longest moustache, most prolific sow) is at least enlivened by a sports gallery, in which various games test physical strength; there's a truly awful waxwork of the Danish Royal Family that made me giggle too. ⏲ *45 min. Østergade 16. ☎ 45 3332 3131. www.topattractions.dk. Admission 90DKK, 50DKK kids 4–11, free under age 4. Free with Copenhagen Card. Mid-June to Aug daily 10am–10pm, rest of year Sun–Thurs 10am–6pm, Fri–Sat 10am–8pm. Closed Dec 24–25 & 31, Jan 1.*

❽ ★★★ kids **Experimentarium City.** Cross the Knippelsbro

Hands-on learning at Experimentarium City.

Playing Outdoors

Need to let off some steam? There are loads of open green spaces in Copenhagen. **Kongens Have** (p 85) and **Frederiksberg Have** (p 87) have play areas for toddlers, and the **Lakes** (p 86) are good for afternoon strolls. **Canal tours** (see p 85) always are a hit, as are the artificial beach at **Havnebadet** (p 85), and the grazing deer at **Dyrehaven** (p 87). Older children are perfectly safe getting around the city-center cycle lanes by **bike;** younger ones will enjoy **rickshaw rides**—pick one up at the north end of Nyhavn on Kongens Nytorv.

bridge to Christianshavn to find this kid-friendly science museum, a whole warehouse full of hands-on exhibits, activities, and experiences for curious minds. Its permanent exhibition contains over 300 different displays, including such time-honored classics as the hall of mirrors and test of strength, as well as 3D math puzzles, smell tests, reaction games, and even an experiment to see if you can ride a reverse steering bike. Special temporary exhibits offer interactive technology fun, with flashing lights, beeping noises, and plenty of opportunities to touch and try. *1 hr. Trangravsvej 10-12. ☎ 45 3927 3333. www.experimentarium.dk. Admission 160DKK adults, 140DKK students, 105DKK kids 3–11. Daily 10am–5pm (Nov–Mar closes 4pm Mon–Fri). Bus 9A.*

9 ★★★ kids Copenhagen Street Food. Next door to the Experimentarium, the city's first genuine street food market offers over 30 food trucks and stalls, dishing up everything from Turkish mezes and Korean barbecues to fresh salads, authentic shawarma, juicy burgers, and of course smørrebrød. Simply follow your nose. *Papirøen, Trangravsvej 14, hal 7 & 8. www.copenhagenstreetfood.dk. $–$$.*

10 ★★ kids Zoo. Although the greatest attractions at the Zoo are the Norman Foster elephant house and polar bear Arctic Ring, those are just the beginning for youngsters. With over 3,000 animals, the zoo is divided into zones (Africa, Birds, etc.) so kids can understand where animals come from and the

Petting pygmy goats at the Children's Zoo.

Young at Art

Many Copenhagen museums and galleries have children's workshops, including **Statens Museum for Kunst** (p 21) and the **Designmuseum Danmark** (p 27), where there are lots of opportunities for hands-on learning. Perhaps the most extensive, though, is at the **Louisiana Museum of Modern Art** (p 154), 25 miles north of Copenhagen. There, children get an entire three-story wing of their own, featuring a computer room, a story-telling center, and several active workshops related to current exhibitions.

conditions they inhabit naturally. Climb the observation tower to get your bearings and you'll be rewarded with fine views over Frederiksberg Have and beyond to the city center. The Children's Zoo has pygmy goats and a small pony track for toddler rides, plus an enclosure for cuddling rabbits. There are shows on the Zoo Stage every day during school holidays. Feeding times are also popular attractions: to see when the chimps, seals, and birds of prey get fed, check at the entrance gate for times. ⌚ *2 hr. From Experimentarium City take bus 9A to Vesterport then bus 6A.*

⓫ ★★★ kids **Tycho Brahe Planetarium.** Round off a long day relaxing under the stars (literally) in the Planetarium's Space Theatre. With up to 10 shows a day (last shows at 8:50pm), the IMAX and 3D shows begin with a presentation of the night sky—perfect for budding astronomers. There's a small science exhibition on the ground floor, as well as a changing choice of superb short 3-D films in the cinema off the foyer. I sat through the fantastic *Cosmic Coaster* film twice, as it took the audience on a high-velocity dash across the galaxy. ⌚ *1 hr. Bus 6A or 26 to Rådhuspladsen & 5-min. walk. See p 119.*

Making Waves

Not far from the city center, in the coastal suburb of Kastrup Havn, you'll find **Den Blå Planet (The Blue Planet),** northern Europe's largest aquarium (Jacob Fortlingsvej 1, Kastrup. ☎ **45 4422 2244;** www.denblaaplanet.dk). Designed to look like a giant whirlpool, this eco-friendly aquarium is divided into climactic and geographic zones such as The Ocean, where hammerhead sharks swim with stingrays and moray eels in over a million gallons of seawater. To get there, take the M2 Metro to Kastrup station (one stop before the airport), or take Bus 5A. Bonus: Once you've finished the aquarium, you can hit the shore yourselves on the soft sands of **Amager Beach,** just the other side of Kastrup harbor.

Royal Copenhagen

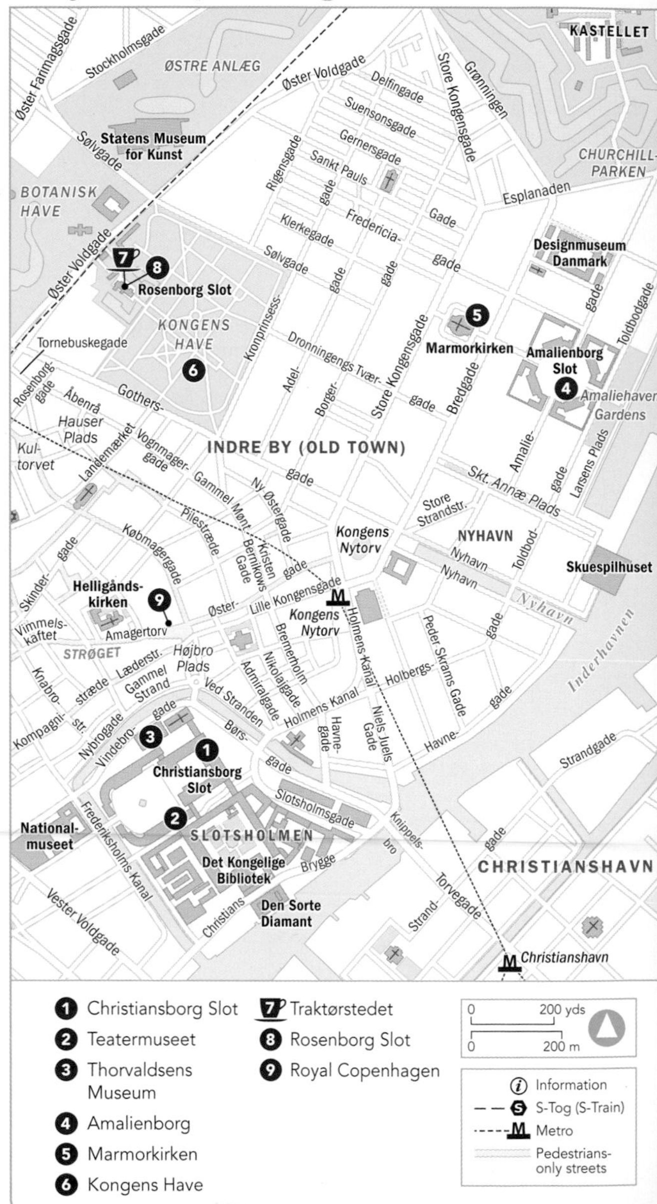

Never a family to settle down anywhere for long, the Danish Royals built castles the way some women collect handbags. The extraordinary legacy left by generations of kings eager to make their mark is felt all over Copenhagen, in their splendid palaces, polished museums, and priceless collections of heirlooms. START: **Metro to Kongens Nytorv.**

The ornate Royal Reception Rooms at Christiansborg Palace.

❶ ★★ **Christiansborg Slot.** On the island of **Slotsholmen**, where **Bishop Absalon** founded Copenhagen in 1160–67 and built his first stronghold, Christiansborg Palace serves as the ceremonial headquarters of the Danish Royal Family. as well as being the seat of the Folketinget, Danish parliament. There were four previous buildings on the site. Absalon's Palace went up in smoke in 1367; visit the remains under the present palace (p 19). Its replacement, fortified Copenhagen Castle, was demolished by King Christian VI in 1731 to make way for his flamboyant baroque statement palace; sadly that did not see the century out before burning down in 1794. A second, even more splendid palace was destroyed by fire in 1884, although the chapel survived unscathed until 1992 before itself succumbing to fire. Today's palace dates from 1928 and at one time had the tallest tower in the city, at 106m. The grand **Royal Reception Rooms** on the second floor are the scene of gala dinners, presidential visits, and ambassadorial meetings. Tapestries and murals adorn some walls, others are covered in historical oil paintings, while marble busts and fine furniture fill every room. ⏲ *50 min. Prins Jørgens Gård 1* ☎ *45 3392 6492. www.christiansborg.dk. Admission 120DKK, 100DKK students; 60DKK kids 4–17. May–Sept daily 10am–5pm. Oct–Apr Tues–Sun 10am–5pm. 10-min. walk from Kongens Nytorv.*

Neoclassical sculpture at Thorvaldsens Museum, in the former Royal Coach House.

❷ ★ Teatermuseet (Theater Museum). After the 18th-century Christiansborg Palace was finished by German architect Elias David Häusser (1687–1745) in 1745, the space above the Royal Stables was converted into a theater for the Court, which opened in 1767. It was refurbished in 1842, and still contains plush red stalls and leather seats. There's not a huge amount to see; programs and posters, a few costumes and an old wind machine that still works, but you can wander the auditorium and go backstage to watch some black-and-white film footage. ⌚ *30 min. Christiansborg Ridebane 18.* ☎ *45 33 11 51 76. www.teatermuseet.dk. Admission 40DKK, 30DKK seniors & students, free under 18. Free with Copenhagen Card. Tues–Thurs 11am–3pm; Sat–Sun 1–4pm. In the courtyard of the palace.*

❸ ★ Thorvaldsens Museum. Bertel Thorvaldsen (ca.1770–1844) was born in Denmark but spent much of his working life as a much-praised neoclassical sculptor in Rome. In 1837 he returned to Copenhagen a wealthy man and bequeathed his art collection and many of his sculptures to the city. His collection is housed in an elegant neoclassic-influenced building designed by Gottlieb Bindesbøll and opened in 1848 on the site of the old Royal Coach House. The side facing Gammel Strand is decorated with scenes of Thorvaldsen's triumphant return to Copenhagen; spot his contemporary Hans Christian Andersen raising his hat in the crowds. The three-story museum is arranged around a courtyard containing Thorvaldsen's grave. Hundreds of neoclassical busts, marble statues, and relief work are on view, along with an assortment of religious and romantic paintings. Although the collection is phenomenal, to my mind the most special element of the museum is the intricate plasterwork and decoration covering the interior. On the second floor, stand at the end of one of the long galleries to admire the blue ceiling and plaster work, the ornate marble floors, and the sun flooding in onto the sculptures lining the walls. ⌚ *1 hr. Bertel Thorvaldsens Plads 2.* ☎ *45 3332 1532. www.thorvaldsensmuseum.dk. Admission 40DKK, under age 18 free. Free with Copenhagen Card. Tues–Sun 10am–5pm; free admission Wed.*

❹ ★★ Amalienborg. Take a stroll through Kongens Nytorv—the King's Square—and down Bredgade to Amalienborg, a complex of four virtually identical palaces bordering a massive octagonal cobbled square. The Royal Family. They took a fancy to these palaces in 1794 after Christiansborg burned down again (p 39), which was

The changing of the royal guards at Amalienborg Castle.

unfortunate for the aristocratic families who had them built by Nicolas Eigtved in the 1750s. To the left as you enter the square, Christian VIII's palace is partly open to the public (p 39). To its left, the interior of Brockdorff's Palace was designed by Bertel Thorvaldsen (p 27) in his early career. The statue in the square depicts Frederik V, posing as a Roman emperor; it was sculpted by French artist JJ Saly. Frederik's son, Christian VII, unveiled it to the public in 1771; the same Christian VII later halted construction work on the **Marmorkirken** (see p 15) when the coffers ran dry on Frederik's master plan to aggrandize the palace complex. Royal Guards parade in two-hour shifts outside all four palaces. *30 min. See p 41,* ❺.

Stately Marmorkirken, where the queen attends church.

❺ ★ **Marmorkirken (Marble Church).** A step away from Amalienborg, this circular church's massive copper dome (p 15) is a local landmark. When in residence, the Queen attends services here. Drop by to look at the painted ceiling and fine altar or at the weekend join the climb to the top of the dome. It's worth the struggle up 150 steps for the views over the

Royal treasures on display at Rosenborg Slot.

palace complex, the golden onion domes of the Russian Orthodox church next door, and Rosenborg Slot in the distance. Not suitable for those afraid of heights. *30 min. See p 15, ❻.*

❻ ★★ kids Kongens Have. A 5-minute walk up Dronningens Tværgade brings you to this perfect spot for relaxing on a sunny day. These formal gardens were commissioned by Christian IV in the 17th century to surround his summer palace, Rosenborg (see p 21). Otto Heider drew up the original plans, but fashions in landscaping changed over the years; a lane of trees has been planted leading to the castle and the formal parterres in front of the castle now serve as parade ground for the soldiers living in barracks next door. There is an adventure playground for kids and a puppet theater on the edge of the gardens. *45 min. See p 85, ❺. 5-min. walk along Dronningens Tværgade.*

Royal Connections

The royals certainly liked their creature comforts; other homes include **Kronborg Palace** in Helsingør (p 146), **Fredensborg,** the Queen's summer home (gardens open to the public in July, see www.ses.dk for details), and romantic **Frederiksborg Palace** at Hillerød (p 142). **Roskilde Cathedral** (p 141) is the traditional burial place of kings and queens. Back in Copenhagen, the 18th-century summer palace at **Frederiksberg** (p 52) has landscaped gardens that make an ideal spot for a stroll in the summer sun.

Family & Friends

The Danes are sweetly sentimental about their Royal Family and don't appreciate criticism of the Queen. On her birthday (April 16), you can join the crowds gathering in their thousands under the balcony of her palace to cheer her and sing happy birthday as she waves grandly from above. Whenever Queen Margrethe is in residence at Amalienborg, soldiers stationed at Rosenborg Slot (p 21) march regally between the two castles to change the guards at midday.

7 ★★ **Traktørstedet.** Grab a table on the pretty terrace for regal views of Rosenborg Castle over coffee and freshly baked cakes or a glass of wine. There's also an excellent lunch menu with a range of smørrebrød, salads, and steaks. It's the only restaurant I know where the candles come in little coronets. *Øster Volgade 4a. ☎ 45 3315 7620. $–$$.*

Royal Copenhagen China, so called because of its connection to the royal household.

8 ★★ **Rosenborg Slot.** Partly built by Hans van Steenwinckel, Christian IV's architect, the Rosenborg Castle continued to grow over many years. With the engaging Royal Danish Collection, the interior of this ornate red-brick castle brims with royal paintings, fine furniture, and tapestries in rooms decorated in Renaissance and rococo styles. Royal Copenhagen fans can head to room 23 to see rare Flora Danica porcelain. In the Treasury, you'll be impressed by Christian IV's ostentatious saddle and the Crown Jewels, encrusted with vast diamonds, sapphires, and garnets. *1½ hr.* *See p 21, 7.*

9 ★ **Royal Copenhagen.** If you fancy taking home a piece of modern Flora Danica china (the original flower-patterned service was commissioned in 1790, see p 145), stroll back to Strøget and pop into the Royal Copenhagen store. Upstairs there is a fine collection, but you might be taken aback by the price—it's possibly the world's most expensive china. Best to make do with some of Royal Copenhagen's timeless blue-and-white pattern. *130 min.* *See p 76.*

Hans Christian Andersen Walk

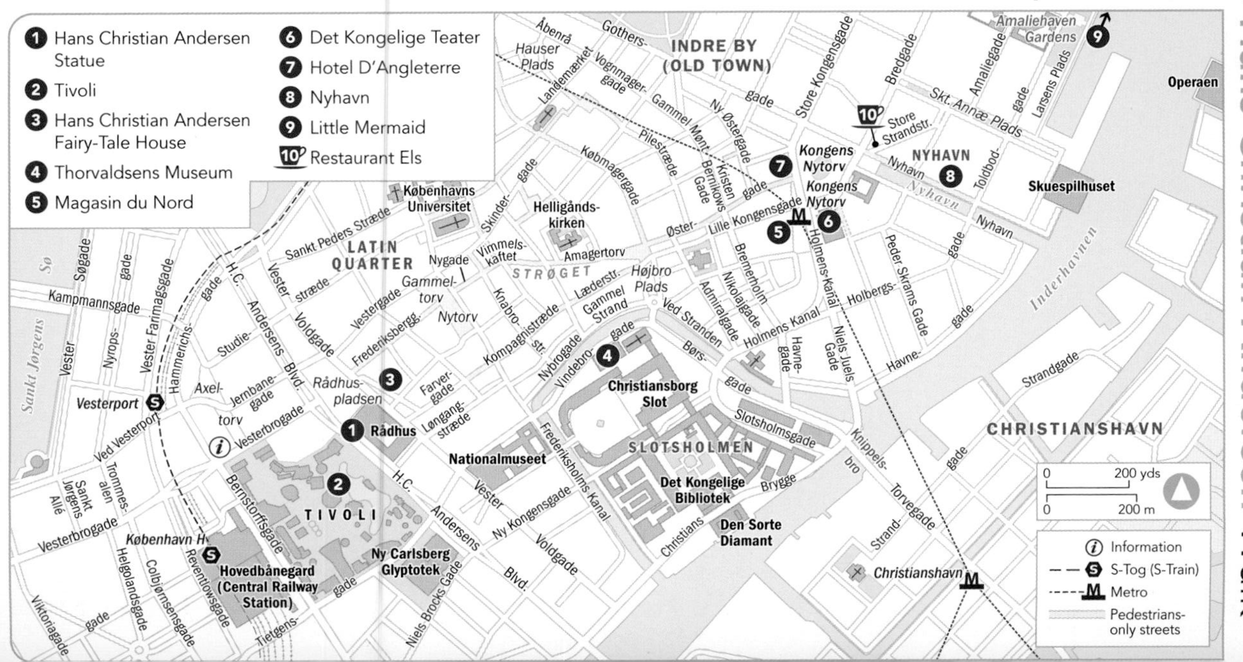

Denmark's favorite literary son was born in Odense in 1805 but lived in Copenhagen for many years in between European jaunts and sojourns with aristocratic Danish friends. He arrived in the city in 1819 to seek his fortune as an actor; when that career stalled he turned to writing, landing a hit in 1829 with *A Journey on Foot from Holmen's Canal to the East Point of Amager,* before scoring wild success with *Fairy Tales* in 1835. Oddly enough, he never bought a property, despite the immense wealth brought to him from his fairy tales, but moved around a series of apartments in town. His influence is everywhere; in statues, his own museum, in Tivoli, and on the blue plaques that mark his many homes. **START: Rådhuspladsen.**

H. C. Andersen statue near Tivoli Gardens.

❶ ★★ Hans Christian Andersen Statue. Sandwiched between the Rådhus (p 13) and Tivoli, Andersen sits ruminatively gazing towards Tivoli, attired in top hat and formal clothes, on the boulevard that now bears his name. ⏲ *5 min.*

❷ ★★★ kids Tivoli. It's only fitting that Tivoli amusement park should have a ride dedicated to Andersen's memory: The Flying Trunk, which presents 32 scenes from his stories. Kids can have fun guessing what they are. ⏲ *20 min. See p 10, ❽.*

❸ ★ kids Hans Christian Andersen Fairy-Tale House. A must for all young (and old) Andersen fans for the simple way his life is portrayed in tableaux. Despite the apparent gentleness of his fairytales, Andersen was reputedly a bit of a curmudgeon; look at the haughty demeanor he wears in his portraits. ⏲ *45 min. See p 13, ❶.*

❹ ★ Thorvaldsens Museum. Andersen and Bertel Thorvaldsen (ca 1770—1844) were leading lights in the Danish Golden Age (p 169). The storyteller is depicted in the frieze on the museum's outside wall, raising his hat in greeting to his old friend. ⏲ *10 min. See p 40, ❸.*

❺ ★ Magasin du Nord. Now a vast, multi-level department store, Du Nord was a prime hotel in Andersen's day. He lived there in the attic, writing his salutary tales and gaining recognition, from 1838 to 1847. ⏲ *30 min. See p 76.*

❻ ★★★ Det Kongelige Teater. Despite never realizing his

Andersen Between the Lines

After Andersen died of cancer, his funeral at Vor Frue Kirke (Copenhagen Cathedral, see p 61) on August 11, 1875, was attended by thousands; King Christian IX declared a day of national mourning. His final resting place, marked by a simple tombstone, is at plot 31 in **Assistens Kierkegård** (Kapelvej 4, Nørrebro. Bus 5A from Rådhuspladsen).

To learn more about Andersen's life, take a day trip to his childhood home in **Odense** on the island of Funen. Here a small **cottage** where he lived from 1807 to 1819 paints a picture of the writer's poverty-stricken childhood. It's at Munkemøllestræde 3-5 (☎ **45 6551 4601;** www.museum.odense.dk)

adolescent dreams to be an actor, Andersen had 28 plays performed here and *The Little Mermaid* was performed as a ballet. The Royal Theatre was the center of his world; during his time in the Hotel du Nord his rooms overlooked it. A marble bust in the foyer of the theater marks his influence. 🕓 *10 min. See p 121. Opposite Magasin du Nord.*

7 ★★★ Hotel D'Angleterre. Andersen stayed several times in this opulent hotel; in 1860 he occupied ground-floor rooms on the corner of Østergade, where he could see his beloved Royal Theatre across Kongens Nytorv. He returned in 1869 and 1871, using the hotel as a stop-gap before moving in with aristocratic friends. 🕓 *10 min. See p 130. Opposite Royal Theatre.*

8 ★★★ kids Nyhavn 18, 20 & 67. Several houses along Nyhavn hosted Andersen as a lodger. In 1834 he moved to number 20, settling for four years before moving to Hotel du Nord. 1848 saw him back on Nyhavn at number 67, where he remained for 17 years. Later in life he spent another two years at number 20, leaving in 1873. Numbers 20 and 67 have commemorative plaques. 🕓 *20 min. See p 8.*

9 ★★★ kids Little Mermaid. was Unveiled in 1913, this statue—paid for by brewing heir Carl Jacobsen and sculpted by Edvard Eriksen—pays homage to Andersen's sad tale *The Little Mermaid*, published in 1836. It's still Copenhagen's number-one tourist site 🕓 *10 min. See p 59,* **12***. 30-min. walk along Langelinie.*

10 Restaurant Els. In Andersen's time Els (p 100) was known as Grandjean's Patisserie, and he was so fond of the place that he wrote a poem about it. Little has changed inside since then, including the frescoes of dancing ladies on the walls. *Store Strandstræde 3. ☎ 45 3314 1341. www.restaurant-els.dk. $$$.*

3 The Best Neighborhood Walks

Vesterbro to Frederiksberg

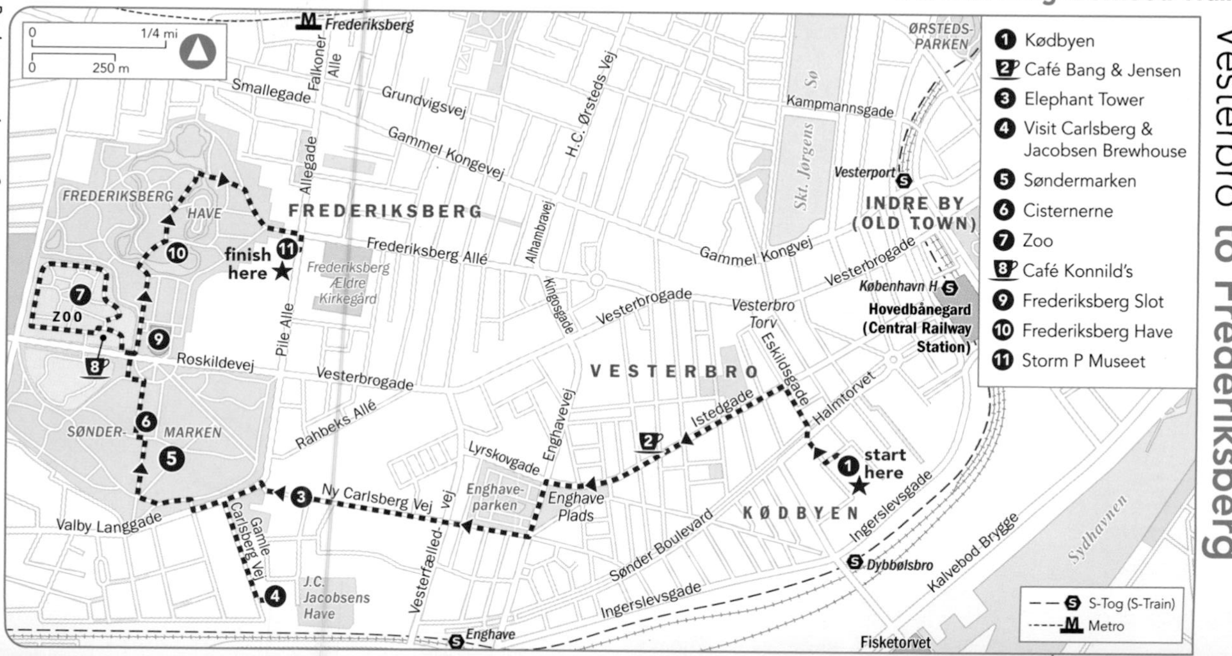

Previous page: Amager Square.

The once-gritty Vesterbro district west of the central train station has been transformed in the past few years, with a new wave of hipster bars and cafes, ethnic shops and restaurants. Around the Carlsberg Brewery, one of the oldest in the world, the atmosphere changes as you enter smart Frederiksberg, with its royal connections and expansive mansion-lined boulevards. **START: Bus 1A to Dybbølsbro St.**

1 ★★ Kødbyen (Meatpacking District). Vesterbro's rejuvenated Meatpacking District might be known for its hipster nightlife, packed with trendy bars, restaurants, and clubs, but it's also home to a cluster of independent art galleries and studios well worth exploring. These forward thinking galleries are largely gathered on **Flæsketorvet** square. One of the most established is **Galleri Bo Bjerggaard** (Flæsketorvet 85 A) with curated work focused on international contemporary art, photography, and film installations from the likes of Per Kirkeby, Georg Baselitz, and Jonathan Meese. Just next door, **V1 Gallery** (Flæsketorvet 69-71) is one of Copenhagen's most progressive art galleries, where some of the world's most legendary street artists, such as Banksy, Todd James and Lydia Fong, have exhibited. **Gallery Poulsen** (Flæsketorvet 24) is also good for a browse for its small collection of colorful prints and drawings. A block away, the high-ceilinged and beautifully-lit **Fotografisk Center** (Bygning 55, Staldgade 16) showcases everything from fine art photography to photo journalism through eight or so different exhibitions a year. *Free admission to Flæsketorvet galleries. Fotografisk Center admission 25DKK.*

2 ★ Café Bang & Jensen. Heading over the green belt of Sønder Boulevard and onto Istegade, it's time for a reviving coffee and continental brunch (served after 10am), or dishes from the all-day menu, in mellow surroundings (p 94). *Istedgade 130 ☎ 45 3325 5318. www.bangogjensen.dk. $.*

The Elephant Tower at the New Carlsberg Brewery.

What's That All About?

On the corner of Oehlenschlægersgade (try pronouncing that!) and Kaalundsgade, look for the bar called Art and Color, completely covered inside and out with riotous mosaics by the late Nigerian artist Mustapha Manuel Tafat. This mad mosaic-maker's work, which is reminiscent of Gaudí's flamboyant decorative tiling in Barcelona's Parc Guëll, features several depictions of Danish Queen Margrethe and Jesus—Tafat was a big fan of them both.

❸ ★★★ kids Elephant Tower. Walk past lots of ethnic shops and cafes down Istegade towards the red-brick Carlsberg brewery complex. Soon you'll trek up a long gradual hill towards the Elephant Tower at the New Carlsberg Brewery (not so new anymore, as it was founded in 1889 by Carl Jacobsen). The brewery's gatetower sits atop four life-size Bernini-esque granite elephants, one at each corner. Built in 1901 by Vilhelm Dahlerup, the elephants are a metaphor for Carl Jacobsen's loyalty and philanthropy towards his workers and his country. *Ny Carlsberg Vej.*

❹ ★★★ Visit Carlsberg & Jacobsen Brewhouse. Established in 1847 by Jacob Jacobsen, the famous Carlsberg Brewery was named after his son Carl, who later took over the business. For years the family has been a powerful force for good within Copenhagen, building housing for their workers and donating the fabulous Ny Carlsberg Glyptotek to the city (p 14). The complex consists of two breweries, offices, laboratories, an academy, plus a small museum on Carlsberg family history. Skip that museum and head instead to the **Visitor Centre,** established in the Old Brewery (built in 1847). The center provides a thoroughly up-to-date and interactive journey through the history of brewing at Carlsberg. Things kick off with a display of 13,000 bottles of limited

Interactive tours at Visit Carlsberg explain the brewing process.

The Cisternerne, an art space beneath Søndermarken's lawns.

edition beers; you'll rattle past steam engines, the cooperage (where the beer barrels were made), bottling displays, and a short film on cleaning the huge wooden barrels used to store the beer. In the stables, you'll see Carlsberg's answer to the Budweiser Clydesdales—contented chestnut Jutland horses that are still used to pull brewery drays around the city (they also travel the world promoting the brewery). The tour ends up at the **Jacobsen Brewhouse** (p 107), a vast pine-floored barn with a gleaming tear-shaped copper bar, where there is a choice of lagers for sale. We got there late in the afternoon and saw several parties that had clearly been there for some time! ⏱ *1½ hr. Gamle Carlsberg Vej 11. ☎ 45 3327 1282. www.visitcarlsberg.dk. Admission 85DKK, 60DKK ages 5–18, free for children under 5. Ticket includes 2 vouchers for beer or soft drink. Tues–Sun 10am–5pm. S-Tog to Enghave from Hovedbanegården (Central Station).*

5 ★★ kids Søndermarken. Pretty Søndermarken is a stretch of untamed greenery forming part of western Copenhagen's green lungs. Its grassy slopes are criss-crossed with paths, with part of the zoo taking up the far end of the gardens. Walk around the edge of the zoo to get free views of ostriches and antelopes.

6 ★★ Cisternerne. Housed underneath a glass pyramid in the middle of the Søndermarken lawns, this unique exhibition venue was once the underground cistern providing water to **Frederiksberg Slot** across the road (see p 52). It's now one of the city's most unusual and atmospheric art spaces, holding one major exhibition every year. Guided group tours cover not only the exhibition but also the underground geology and architecture of the cistern. A word of warning: water drips constantly over the floor, which can be a pain if you're wearing sandals. ⏱ *45 min. Søndermarken, Roskildevej 28. ☎ 45 3073 8032. www.cisternerne.dk. Admission 50DKK, 40DKK seniors & students, free for children under 18. Tues–Sun 11am–5pm. Closed Dec–Mar.*

7 ★ Café Konnild's. By the zoo's main entrance, Café Konnild's serves a simple menu of salads, burgers and curried meatballs, with up-close views of the camel enclosure. *In the Zoo. ☎ 45 3646 6060. $$.*

Elephants at the Copenhagen Zoo.

8 ★★ kids Zoo. Occupying both sides of Roskildevej, this is one of the oldest and largest zoos in Europe, with over 3,000 animals. Its reputation as a breeding center for rare species is second to none although sadly not all animals have got as much room to roam as they should have. The elegant glass-roofed Elephant House, built in 2008 by English architect Norman Foster, is a step in the right direction. *See p 36, 10. Free with Copenhagen Card.*

9 Frederiksberg Slot. Largely built by 1669 under the eye of King Frederik IV, and much expanded until it reached its present extent in 1735 during the reign of Christian VI, this splendid ocher-colored palace was the Royal Family's summer residence until 1852, when it was taken over as a military academy. It occupies a dramatic position overlooking the sloping landscaped lawns of Frederiksberg Have; in the distance you can see the rides of Tivoli. Getting inside the castle requires planning; opening hours are limited to the last Saturday of the month (11am–1pm by guided tour only) but it's worth the effort to see the ornate baroque interior of the palace chapel, hidden in the east wing. *Roskildevej 28. ☎ 45 3613 2611. www.frederiksbergslot.dk.*

10 ★★★ kids Frederiksberg Have. From the castle, head off through the bucolic delights of Frederiksberg's manicured English-style gardens (p 87). Once the playground of royalty, they now brim

Frederiksberg Slot, once the royal family's summer palace.

Rowing in Frederiksberg Garden by the Chinese Pavilion.

over with family life at the weekends; in summer take a lake tour by rowing boat from the front of the castle. Turn left towards the back of the zoo to the **Temple of Apis**, a mock-Palladian folly built in 1806—from here you can glimpse the **Chinese Pavilion** among the trees. Walking on, you get a cheat's preview of the zoo's Elephant House on the left and an artificial waterfall tumbling to the right. From here, meander along winding paths to the **Rose Garden** for a quiet, contemplative few moments, and then on to **Duck Island** to see the grey herons roosting there. Close by is the decidedly odd **Dummy Tree**, a live tree hanging with dummies; a local superstition held that bringing discarded dummies here eases a child's path through life. Turn off right here to the Chinese Pavilion (see p 87 for opening times) or continue on to the park's imposing main entrance **at Frederiksberg Runddel** (flooded to form an ice rink in winter) and the equally majestic **statue of Frederik VI**. *See p 87.*

⓫ ★ **Storm P Museet.** By the gates of Frederiksberg Have, this tribute to the much-loved Danish cartoonist and social campaigner Robert Storm Petersen (1882–1949) will bring a wry smile to most faces. Even if you don't understand the cartoons, the drawings are executed with compassion and his collection of pipes is sweetly endearing. ⏲ *30 min. Frederiksberg Runddel.* ☎ *45 3886 0523. www.stormp-museet.dk. Admission 45DKK, 40DKK seniors & students, free for children under 18. Free with Copenhagen Card. Tues–Sun 10am–4pm. To return to central Copenhagen, take bus no 26 from Frederiksberg Allé or take the S-tog from Fredericksberg station.*

A Waterfront **Walk**

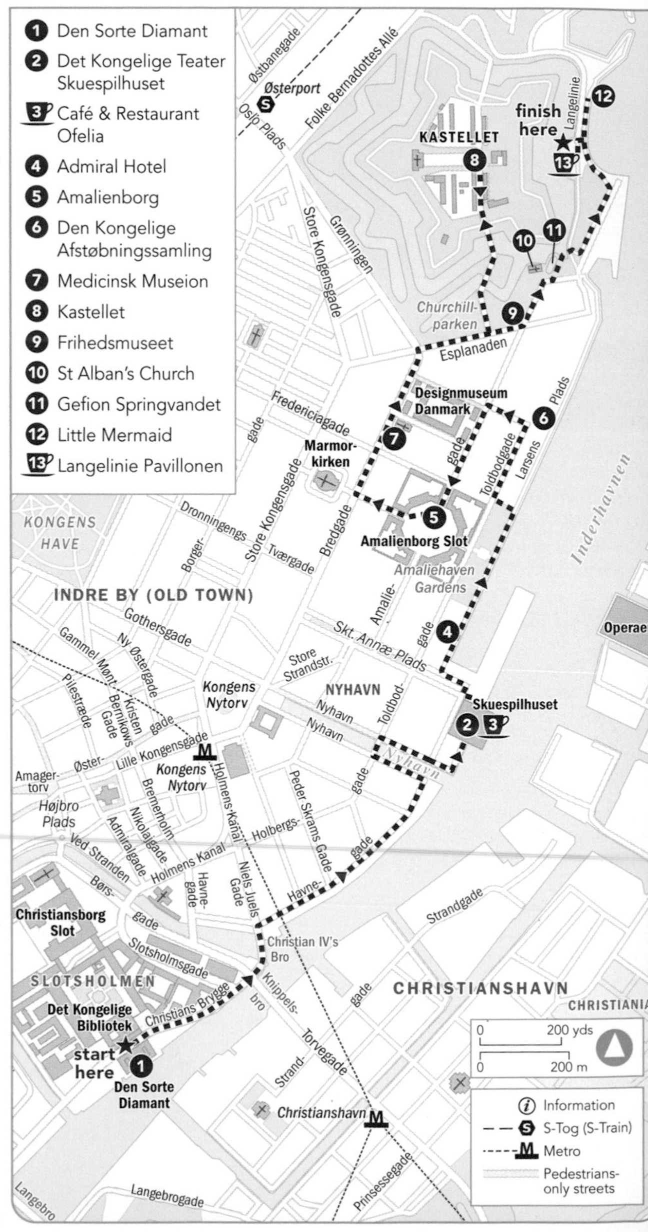

Copenhagen's long harborline has been transformed, with a gleaming new landscape of fabulous buildings replacing the old stretches of 17th-century industrial waterfront. You'll see architecture of all periods and styles, visit a couple of oddball museums, and recognize how the maritime commerce that brought the city its wealth is being replaced by 21st-century leisure and tourism. **START: Metro to Kongens Nytorv, 10-minute walk to Black Diamond.**

❶ ★★★ Den Sorte Diamant (Black Diamond). Spend a happy hour looking at the exhibitions in the Royal Library, known to all as the Black Diamond. There are often political caricatures in the **Museum of Danish Cartoon Art;** the **National Museum of Photography** is also well worth your attention. Elegantly laid out in sleek, minimal spaces, the images exhibited span the history of photography as well as featuring contemporary works. The **Montana Hall** is a softly lit circular glass space housing long-term exhibitions. Outside, wander around Søren Kierkegård Plads and marvel at the sunlight glinting of the Black Diamond's granite-coated glass facade as it leans over the Øresund. 🕓 *1 hr. Free admission.* *See p 29, ❸.*

Soaking in the sun beside the waterfront Royal Danish Playhouse.

❷ ★★★ Det Kongelige Teater Skuespilhuset (Royal Danish Playhouse). Walk left along the waterfront, crossing under Knippels Bridge, and pass Havnegade, a quiet street with pretty rows of houses. When you hit Nyhavn (p 8), cross the canal bridge amid all the hustle and bustle and the wooden boats, grab an ice cream from **Vaffelbageren** (Nyhavn 49, see p 102), and head for the **Royal Danish Playhouse** to dangle your feet from the wooden pier. Or you can stop off for refreshments at its smart in-house cafe, with views across the sound to the Opera House (p 119). 🕓 *1½ hr. if eating.* *See p 121.*

❸ ★★ Café & Restaurant Ofelia. Mix with the Copenhagen chattering classes over a mint tea or mid-morning coffee. If you get here at lunchtime, it's well worth splurging on a two-course lunch from th[e] Danish menu. Bag a table by th[e] endless smoked-glass windo[ws] back, and enjoy the view *Annæ Plads 36.* ☎ *45 www.skuespilhus.dk*

Colonial Denmark

Across the Øresund from the Royal Danish Playhouse, just to the right of Experimentarium City (see p 35), sits **Nordatlantens Brygge** (North Atlantic House). Set in an historic warehouse, it showcases the art and culture of Denmark's former North Atlantic colonies Greenland, the Faroe Islands, and Iceland. Four exhibition rooms are dedicated to all things Nordic through art, music, film, dance, and educational events. *Strandgade 91.* ☎ ***45 3283 3700.*** *www.bryggen.dk. Admission 40DKK, 20DKK students, children under 12 free. Mon–Fri 10am–5pm, Sat–Sun noon–5pm.*

❹ ★★ **Admiral Hotel.** Just past the square white box of Hotel Scandic FRONT (see p 133), the magnificently restored grey brick warehouse of the Admiral allows us to see what the Copenhagen waterfront would have looked like in the 1790s; a Copenhagen grown prosperous on overseas trade thanks to its strategic position on the Øresund. The industrial style of the Admiral juxtaposes neatly with the futuristic Opera House across the Øresund, and also with the fanciful rococo architecture of the Amalienborg complex beyond. 🕓 *10 min. See p 129.*

❺ ★★ **Amalienborg.** Continue along the waterfront of Larsens Plads to Christian IX's Palace on the

A copy of Michelangelo's David outside the Cast Museum.

left, the winter residence of Queen Margrethe II and the Prince Consort, part of a complex of four identical palaces earmarked by the Royal Family as their homes in 1794. Two of these are open to the public. If you wash up here at midday, stop off to see the changing of the guard. From the fountain at the entrance to the vast Amalienborg courtyard, the **Marmorkirken** (p 15) and the **Opera House** (p 119) appear to be exactly in line. Take a couple of minutes among the box hedges of the little gardens of Amaliehaven in front of the palace complex. *30 min. See p 40, 4.*

6 ★★★ Den Kongelige Afstøbningssamling (The Royal Cast Collection). Look for the vast cast of Michelangelo's *David* among the 17th-century warehouses and modern office blocks, some owned by the Danish Navy, which line the waterfront. (One time I spotted a massive Roman Abramovich-owned superyacht moored outside this eccentric museum; sometimes the Danish Royal Family's yacht can be seen here too.) It was opened in 1895 as a branch of the Statens Museum for Kunst (p 21) and contains plaster casts taken from over 2,000 famous sculptures dating from classical to Renaissance times. Worth a visit for its oddball charm although it's only open Tuesdays and Sundays. *1 hr. Vestindisk Pakhus, Toldbodgade 40. www.smk.dk. Free admission. Tues 10am–4pm; Sun 2–5pm. Guided tours Mon–Fri 10am–2pm (☎ 45 3374 8484, book 1 week in advance).*

7 ★★ Medicinsk Museion (Medical Museum). Hop round the back of the Cast Collection (see above) to another curiosity, and not one for the faint-hearted. Part repository for the medical collections of the university and part Victorian horror show, the museum collections feature saws used in early amputations, grisly bits of the human anatomy, and wooden prostheses. A fine lecture hall with domed roof is still in use, and many of the temporary exhibitions aim to educate. *1 hr. Bredgade 62. ☎ 45 3532 3800. www.mhm.ku.dk. Admission 50DKK, 30DKK seniors & students, kids under 16 free. Wed–Fri & Sun noon–4pm. Guided tours in English at 2pm (1:30pm Sun).*

8 ★ kids Kastellet. Head up Bredgade past the Designmuseum Danmark (p 27) (you may want to stop here if you haven't yet seen it). At the end of Bredgade, if you have kids with you, let them have a romp around in the grounds of this

A historic windmill catches the sea breezes at Kastellet.

17th-century star-shaped fortress, built to guard the waterfront. There's a windmill to spot and plenty of water birds; herons in particular are often hiding along the moat banks. *See p 16,* ❽.

❾ ★★★ **Frihedsmuseet (Museum of Danish Resistance).** Across the road from Kastellet, this intriguing branch of the Nationalmuseet (p 9) relates the story of the Nazi occupation of Denmark between 1940 and 1945. Photos depict the hardships suffered by the Danes and the gradual change from acceptance of their lot to the formation of resistance movements. Maps, weapons, uniforms, printing machines for producing underground newspapers, and even a German enigma-code machine are displayed; there's even a mock air-raid shelter set up just outside the museum. A series of short films features Resistance heroes recounting their experiences. For me the most touching exhibit was the rose fashioned from chewed bread made by a Polish prisoner in Ravensbrück womens' concentration camp in northern Germany. *Churchillparken 1263.* ☎ *45 3347 3921. Currently closed due to a fire but reopens late 2018.*

The very English St. Alban's Church at the foot of Langelinie.

The Little Mermaid poses for canal tour boat snapshots.

⑩ ★ **St. Alban's Church.** The "English church" has a wonderful setting by the side of Kastellet's moat. Copenhagen's only Anglican church, it was consecrated in 1887 and has an elegant, angular neo-Gothic spire. There are English-speaking services every Sunday at 10:30am. *Churchillparken 6.* ☎ *45 3962 7736. www.st-albans.dk.*

⑪ ★★ **Gefion Springvandet (Gefion Fountain).** A step past St. Alban's Church, the mythical Gefion is busily ploughing up Swedish soil to claim land for Denmark from King Gylfe; it is said she turned her sons into the four oxen, depicted in this flamboyant bronze with straining backs and flaring nostrils. Designed by Anders Bundgard in 1908, the fountain is built on a slight incline; look straight the Øresund for views over Amalienborg (p 40). *Churchillparken.*

⑫ ★ kids **Little Mermaid.** Just beyond Gefion, there is a lookout point on the seafront walkway Langelinie with views to the Little Mermaid. Copenhagen's world-famous Little Mermaid sculpture (p 46) might be small but she's definitely popular—she receives over one million visitors a year to her little boulder with its industrial backdrop. Sadly not everybody is kind to her; her head has been knocked off twice since she was unveiled in 1913. 🕓 *15 min. Langelinie.,10-min. walk from Gefion. From here, catch the no. 26 bus back into the city center from the shops at Langelinie Allé.*

⑬ ★ **Langelinie Pavillonen.** This glass-fronted pavilion has pole position looking out over the Øresund and its pretty terrace is just the thing for a long, cool lager on summer days. Inside there is an eclectic mix of furniture by design greats, including Arne Jacobsen, and a reasonable buffet menu in the pristine white dining room. *Langelinie 10.* ☎ *45 3312 1214. www.langelinie.dk. $$–$$$.*

Latin Quarter to Christiania

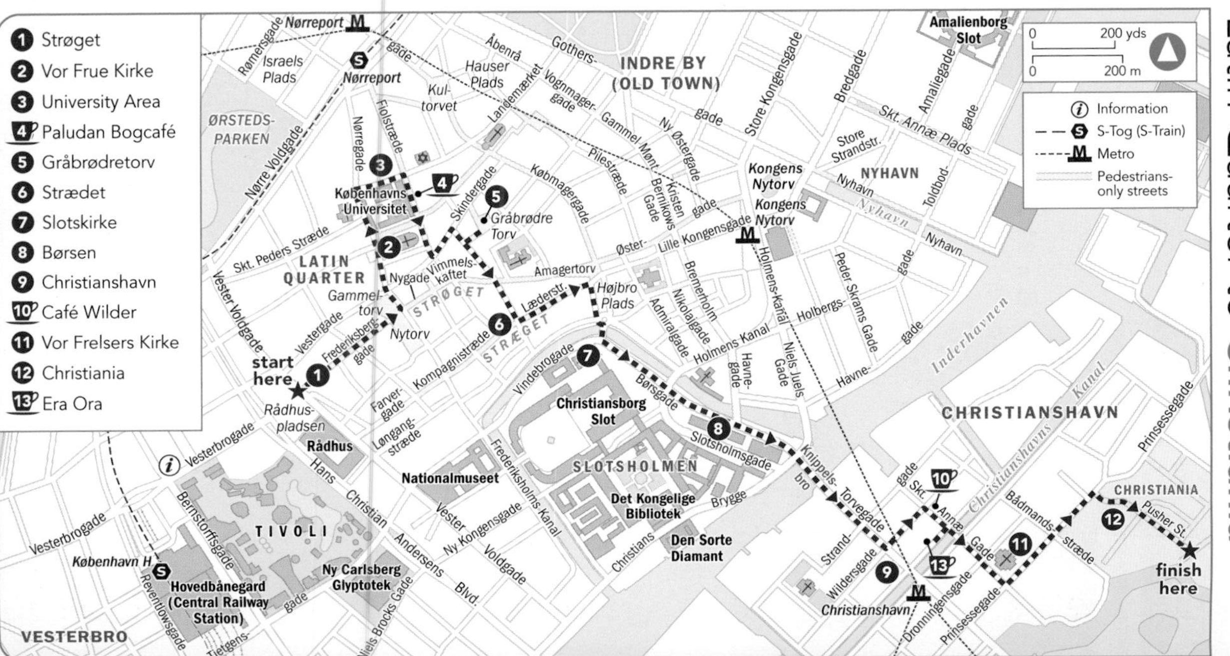

Today's the day to explore churches and historic buildings in the pedestrianized Latin Quarter and enjoy some individual interesting shops en route. Later explore a mini-Amsterdam in Christianshavn and leave Denmark altogether in boho Christiania. As always in this compact city, you'll notice the influence of the Danish Royal Family, particularly Christian IV, the king who sought to make Copenhagen the national capital in the 17th century.
START: **Bus to Rådhuspladsen.**

❶ ★★★ **Strøget.** I am powerless to walk up this shopping street without being tempted into some of the stores. Although things are a bit tatty around the Rådhuspladsen, there is plenty of color and some cut-price bargains to be had. Most mornings there is a tiny craft market in Nytorv, where stallholders sell unusual jewelry. It's a square to linger in; sit outside one of the cafes or nose around the adjoining Gammel Torv, with its neoclassical courthouse and imposing Caritas Fountain, the oldest in Copenhagen, built by our good friend Christian IV. In warm weather, people sit, drink and picnic on the steps around the fountain. 🕓 *45 min.* *See p 8.*

❷ ★ **Vor Frue Kirke.** Cut up Nørregade to the Church of Our Lady. Copenhagen's cathedral, with a nave 60m (198 ft.) long, has been the scene of several royal weddings, including Crown Prince Frederik and Mary Donaldson in

The neoclassical Von Frue Kirke, Copenhagen's cathedral.

2004. Founded by Bishop Absalon in 1209, this great church has had a checkered history. Like many medieval Copenhagen buildings, the cathedral burnt down in 1728; its replacement suffered damage under Nelson's siege in 1807, and

Five Streets in One

At 1.8km, Europe's longest pedestrianized shopping strip is actually five streets fused into one. Going north from Rådhuspladsen, you hit Frederiksberggade, then Nygade, Vimmelskaftet, Amagertorv, and Østergade before stepping into Kongens Nytorv. The street changes character along the way; around Rådhuspladsen the shops are less expensive and compete for custom with take-away international burger bars. Towards the top end you'll find designer shops and big prices.

A crafts fair on Frue Plads, by the cathedral and the university.

the present neoclassical version was completed in 1829. The interior is chiefly remarkable for the religious statuary by Bertels Thorvaldsen (p 27), and many visit just to look at the figure of Christ above the altar, with his hands splayed to reveal his stigmata. *20 min. Nørregade 8. ☎ 45 3337 6540. www.koebenhavnsdomkirke.dk. Free admission. Mon–Sat 8am–5pm.*

3 ★★ University Area. Just behind the cathedral is the site of the university's original campus, founded in 1479 but subsequently damaged in Nelson's siege of the city—much rebuilding took place in the latter half of the 19th century. Although most of the departments have now decamped to shiny new digs at Amager, the law faculty, the library, and a couple of residences remain. The oldest, Regensen, is opposite the Rundetårn (p 20), which was itself the university's observatory. The student population is responsible for the multitude of cafes, bookshops, and vintage stores that make this an attractive area to snoop around. *45 min.*

4 ★★ Paludan Bogcafé. Opposite the university library, this rambling bookshop (p 75) has a great cafe to enjoy delicious hot chocolate and a panini. There are sometimes book and poetry readings during the week (call to check). *Fiolstræde 10–12. ☎ 45 331 0675. www.paludan-cafe.dk. $.*

5 ★★ Gråbrødretorv. At the bottom of Fiolstræde, turn left and first right down Klosterstæde into Gråbrødretorv. This pretty square is dominated by a huge plane tree and was once site of a monastery. The 17th-century gabled houses lining the square are attractively painted in bright colors; in summer the cobbles are covered with tables from restaurants and bars. The best restaurant on the square is the traditional **Peder Oxe** (p 70), although **Jensens Bøfhus** (Gråbrødretorv 15, ☎ 45 3332 7800) runs a close second, with excellent open sandwiches. The normally low-key square transforms into a buzzing venue during the Copenhagen Jazz

Festival (see p 158). 🕓 *20 min. to wander around, longer if you eat.*

❻ ★★★ **Strædet.** Consisting mainly of the two pedestrianized streets of Læderstræde and Kompagnistræde south of Strøget, this chic area of Copenhagen has many shops. I love the piles of silver cutlery and the jewel-colored glassware in the basement windows of the antique shops. Danish womenswear staple **wettergren & wettergren** (p 77) and the sustainable but glamorous fashion shop **Ecouture by Lund** (Lædenstræde 5) are two places to head for, as well buying colorful and creative ceramics at **Liebe** (Kompagnistræde 23). *www. violasky.dk.* 🕓 *1 hr.*

❼ ★ **Slotskirke.** From Læderstræde, walk up to Amagertorv and right across the Højbro bridge to Slotsholmen. Here the Slotskirke forms part of the Christiansborg complex, the seat of Danish parliament (p 39). This squat neoclassical church was designed in 1826 by the classically influenced Danish architect CF Hansen as a mock-Greek temple with pediments and pillars at the entrance. Nowadays it is used for private occasions by the Royal Family; the State Opening of

The Dragon Spire atop the Børsen, Copenhagen's old stock exchange.

Parliament takes place here every October. The roof burnt down when a firework landed on it in 1992, but Hansen's classical motifs and plasterwork in the interior have all been carefully restored. 🕓 *15 mins. Prins Jørgens Gård 1.* ☎ *45 3392 6300. www.christiansborg.dk. Daily 10am–5pm.*

❽ ★★ **Børsen.** Just past the Slotskirke in the Christianborg complex, the amazing twisted copper tower of the Old Stock Exchange

A service at Slotsholmen's Slotskirke Church.

Houseboats crowd the narrow canals of Christianshavn.

(Børsen) sits atop a wonderful Dutch-baroque gabled civic hall commissioned by Christian IV in 1620 to rival Amsterdam's thriving money markets. Originally it had a similar set-up to an early department store, where anything from grain to household goods could be bought. The hall was built on pillars over the water and is surrounded on three sides by canals, which is probably why this is one of the few old buildings to have survived Copenhagen's frequent fires. The tower is fashioned from four intertwined dragon's tails, while the golden crowns on the spire represent the Nordic powers of Denmark, Sweden, and Norway. *10 min. Christiansborg Slotsplads.* ☎ *45 3374 6573. Not open to public. Visible from Slotskirke.*

9 ★★★ Christianshavn. Cross busy Knippels Bridge onto the island of Amager and the trendy, affluent area of Christianshavn, riven with canals packed with moored yachts, motorboats, and houseboats. It doesn't take long to recognize the Dutch influence; the pastel-colored 17th-century canal-side houses are tall and narrow, with gables and crane hooks for pulling goods onto the upper floors. Indeed, Christian VI encouraged Dutch immigrants to settle here in 1619 for their architecture skills, and he later fortified the island with ramparts. I recommend taking half an hour to stroll around the atmospheric streets, in particular Strandgade (first left over the bridge). The minute you leave Torvegade, the main thoroughfare, all is peace and tranquility. *65 min.*

10 ★★ Café Wilder. If you are in need of fortification, there are dozens of cafes and bars around Christianshavn. Café Wilder (p 95) is a great local option for a panini, beer, or glass of wine. *$–$$.*

11 ★★ Vor Frelsers Kirke. From Strandgade, take the first right down Sankt Annæ Gade, and cross Christianshavn Kanal to the Church of Our Savior, famed throughout the city for the gilded staircase that runs up the spire and

Taking a break at Café Wilder.

Fantastical wall murals adorn the counter-cultural Free State of Christiania.

the vast golden globe with a statue of Christ on top. This church is the handiwork of Scandinavian architect Lambert van Haven, who completed its baroque interior in 1696. Inside, you can't miss the gloriously over-the-top-altar, all flying figures and sunflares, or the massive three-story organ built by the Botzen brothers in 1696–98 (miraculously, not burnt down or destroyed by Nelson). The wooden spire was added in 1752, more than 50 years after the church was consecrated. Frederik V wanted a landmark tower for Christianshavn and Lauritz de Thurah, the bright light of Danish baroque architecture, was the man to do this for him. You can climb its 400 steps for great views to the city center and the Opera House (p 119), but be forewarned: It's 90m from the ground to the top of Christ's banner and there's not much protection. ⏲ *45 min. Sankt Annæ Gade 29.* ☎ *45 3254 6883 www.vorfrelserskirke.dk.*

⓬ ★ **Christiania.** Turn left out of Vor Frelsers Kirke and you're in a mini-state within the state; Christiania declared its independence from Copenhagen in the 1970s and has run itself as a separate country since then. People flock here on Sundays for brunch at one of the dozens of restaurants; Spiseloppen at Bådmandsstræde 43 has an ever-changing cuisine delivered by a variety of international chefs. Most visitors come to snoop at Pusher Street, its market stalls and occupants, who take grave exception to being photographed. Around 1,000 people live in Christiania and many of them have built their own homes, workshops, galleries and music venues. ⏲ *1 hr. From here, have dinner in Christianshavn or catch a performance at the Opera House on Holmen (p 119), the adjacent island.*

13 ★★★ **Era Ora.** Under the watchful eye of Elvio Milleri (p 96), Era Ora is the only Michelin-starred Italian restaurant in Denmark. Deservedly so; the decor is elegant, the terrace overlooks the canal, the wine list well chosen, and the light Italian dishes are a superb treat. Reservations required. *Overgaden Neden Vandet 33B.* ☎ *45 3254 0693. www.era-ora.dk. $$$.*

Nørrebro & the Lakes

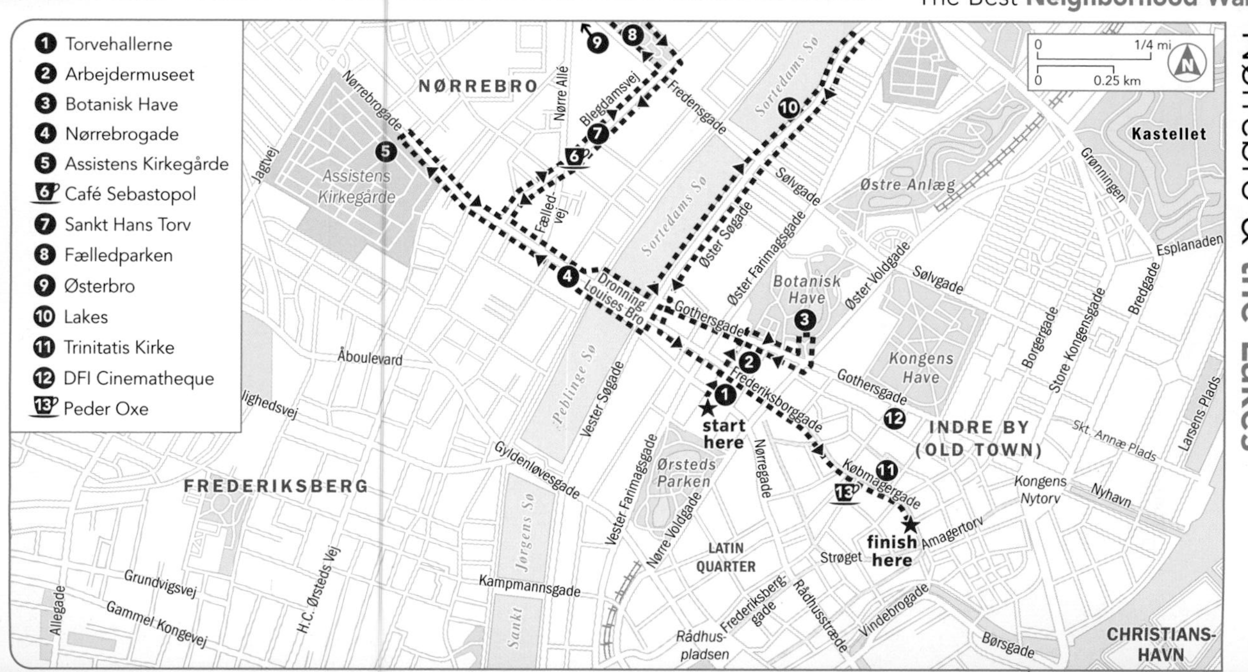

It's time to venture out of the city center to Nørrebro and Østerbro, two distinct areas where "real" Danish people live. One is bohemian and laid-back, the other lined with designer shops and expensive housing along wide streets. Be warned, there's a lot of walking, so wait for a sunny day and grab comfortable shoes. The route encompasses cemeteries, eccentric museums, the odd church, and lots of green spaces. At several points you can break off and return to the city center by bus or S-train. START: **Metro to Nørreport.**

❶ ★★★ **Torvehallerne.** Since opening in 2011, this glass-covered food market on Israels Plads has proved a huge success and firmly established itself on Copenhagen's culinary map. You'll find more than 60 stands and stalls showcasing fresh and seasonal produce with everything from smoked meats and artisanal coffees to stacks of seafood, *smørrebrød*, cheese, and chocolate. It's easy to while away a few hours here, grazing from stall to stall across its twin halls. Seek out **Ma Poule**, offering arguably the best sandwich in town, loaded with duck confit, mustard, and arugula. ⏲ *1 hr. Frederiksborggade 21.* ☎ *45 2763 1981. www.torvehallernekbh.dk. Tues–Thurs 10am–7pm, Fri–Sat 10am–8pm, Sun 11am–5pm.* *See p 81.*

❷ ★ **Arbejdermuseet (Workers' Museum).** Just across Frederiksborggade and first right up Rømersgade is an homage to the daily life of the Danish working classes over 170 years. It's hidden away in an historic townhouse built in 1879 and once used as a workers' union building. Permanent exhibitions include displays of machines and processes introduced during industrialization, and a somber reminder of the struggle of one family during the Depression of

A coffee bar in Nørrebro's sleek new Torvehallerne food hall.

The palatial Palm House conservatory in the Botanical Gardens.

1930s. Proceedings are considerably enlivened by the elegant, balconied assembly hall, where union meetings took place, and even more so by the well-restored beer hall Café & Ølhalle 1892, where there's a good selection of draught and bottled beers, some with original labels from the 1940s. ⌚ *1 hr. Rømersgade 22. ☎ 45 3393 2575. www.arbejdermuseet.dk. Admission 65DKK, 55DKK seniors & students, free for children under 18. Free with Copenhagen Card. Daily 10am–4pm.*

❸ ★ Botanisk Have (Botanical Museum and Gardens). On a sunny day, wander around the botanical gardens to see what's growing and listen to the ducks squabbling on the lake. If you bought a picnic at Torvehallerne, settle down on a bench here with views of the Palm House. There's a botanical museum in an elegant red-brick mansion just inside the gardens (entrance at Gothersgade 130); this isn't always open, so call ahead to check if this appeals to you. Anyone with a botanical bent should try to get in to view some of the millions of species squirreled away here for research. *See p 86,* ❻.

❹ ★★ Nørrebrogade. For a blast of full-on city life, leave the botanical gardens via Gothersgade and turn right. Cross over Dronning Louises Bridge, which separates Peblinge Sø and Sortedams Sø, the second and third links in the defensive chain of lakes laid around the western part of the city by Christian IV. Straight ahead is Nørrebrogade, the pivotal street of down-to-earth and classless Nørrebro. Here students and professionals, people of all nationalities and backgrounds brush along happily. The street is dynamic and buzzing, lined with chain stores, ethnic shops, and supermarkets but it's not without a coating or two of graffiti. ⌚ *30 min. Nørrebrogade. 10-min. walk.*

❺ ★ Assistens Kirkegårde. At the far end of bustling Nørrebrogade, I like to seek solace in the tree-lined pathways of this historic cemetery, burial place of philosopher Søren Kirkegård and Hans Christian Andersen (see p 44). Other eminent but less well-known Danes who languish in this quiet corner of Copenhagen include Hans Christian Ørsted, revered for his work in electromagnetism, who died in 1851 and lent his name to a pretty park (see p 87) and Nobel Prize-winning physicist Niels Bohr, who died in 1962. Guided tours of the cemetery are given by tour leaders in period costume; call in advance. There are sometimes concerts in the church and a weekend flea market lays itself out against the walls of the cemetery. *Kapelvej 2. ☎ 45 3366 9120. www.assistens.dk. Free admission. Apr–Sept 7am–10pm, Oct–Mar 7am–7pm.*

Serene Fælledparken is Copenhagen's largest park.

6 ★ **Café Sebastopol.** This Nørrebro institution serves French dishes all day long, with tables and heaters in the square during the summer. I like the big wooden bar for a late-night drink (open until 1am at the weekend). *2 Guldbergsgade, Sankt Hans Torv 32. ☎ 45 3536 3002. www.sebastopol.dk. $$.*

7 ★★ Sankt Hans Torv. Turn north off Nørrebrogade to meander along Elmegade, taking the time to explore its vibrant cafes, bric-à-brac shops, and bakeries. You'll soon reach Sankt Hans Torv, acknowledged as Nørrebro's trendsetting heart. All around this edgy square are bars, cafes, vintage shops, and one-off designer boutiques. 🕓 *1 hr. Sankt Hans Torv.*

8 ★★ Fælledparken. Follow Nørre Allé up to Østerbro's largest park, beautifully kept and full of secret pathways; it's a lovely place for a wander among the trees and it's home to Parken (p 120), where FC København play. There's a skate park, soccer fields, cycle lanes, and jogging paths, so if you are feeling energetic one day, this is the place to come and let off steam. 🕓 *30 min.*

9 ★★★ Østerbro. Cut through Fælledparken to Trianglen square, at the park's southeastern corner. Notice the dumpy, copper-roofed public bathrooms in the middle—known to locals as the 'soup tureen' because of its ungainly shape. If you want to give up here, bus 1A runs back into Kongens Nytorv. At Trianglen, five roads meet to form busy boulevards, the main shopping area of what are considered locally the preserve of "middle class" Danes, with quality shops like Emmerys (see p 79) and design icon **Normann Copenhagen** worth stopping off for. 🕓 *30 min.*

10 ★★ Lakes. Follow Østerbrogade back to the Lakes, where there are are a few cafes on the water's edge; these fill to bursting in the summer, especially on weekend lunchtimes, when the wealthy natives of the area are home from work. You may want to make a detour to skirt through deserted **Holmens Kirkegård,** with its neat tombs, then take the path alongside the left of Sortedams Sø to stroll back into the city center via Gothersgade. 🕓 *50 min. for the walk back into town.*

Baroque cherubs decorate the ornate altar of Trinitatis Kirke.

⑪ ★★★ **Trinitatis Kirke.** Cross Gothersgade, and take the next left back along Frederiksborggade, about a 10-minute walk to **Kultorvet**, a city-center piazza full of students and tourists chilling out in pavement bars. Take time out here or carry on to the **Rundetårn** (p 20) and its spectacular adjoining church, Trinitatis Kirke. This typically Danish church, built in 1637 at the behest of Christian IV, has a painted white interior, exotic carvings on the pulpit, and a flamboyant baroque altar installed by Friedrich Ehbisch (who also created the altar in Vor Frue Kirke, see p 61) in 1731. *Landemærket 12. ☎ 45 3337 6540. www.trinitatiskirke.dk. Free admission. Mon–Sat 9:30am–4:30pm, Sun 10:30am–4:30pm.*

⑫ ★★ **DFI Cinematheque.** Guaranteed to pique the interest of movie buffs and cinephiles, the Danish Film Institute's cinema center presents more than 60 films a month across three screens, many of which are in English or have English subtitles. It also holds a twice-monthly Danish on a Sunday event, presenting a new or classic Danish film with English subtitles. If you don't have the time or appetite to sit through a whole film then you can always browse the extensive library of film and TV literature, which is open to the public, together with a vast stills and poster archive. There's also a videotheque, featuring over 3,000 short films and documentaries, as well as a small shop and café restaurant. *Gothersgade 55. ☎ 45 3374 3400. www.dfi.dk. Admission 70DKK. Tues–Wed 2–10pm, Thurs–Fri 9:30am–10pm, Sat noon–10pm, Sun noon–7pm.*

⑬ ★★★ **Peder Oxe.** There are so many food choices in the pedestrianized city center. Try Peder Oxe (p 70) as a special treat—perfect for a last nostalgic Danish dinner in Copenhagen, or any of the cafes of Kultorvet, although this is quite a touristy area and prices will reflect that. If you are up for a long evening of Danish hospitality (hygge), head for the bars and restaurants of Nyhavn, a 15-minute walk away. *Gråbrødretorv 11. ☎ 45 33 11 00 77. www.pederoxe.dk. Open daily.* ●

4 The Best Shopping

Copenhagen **Shopping**

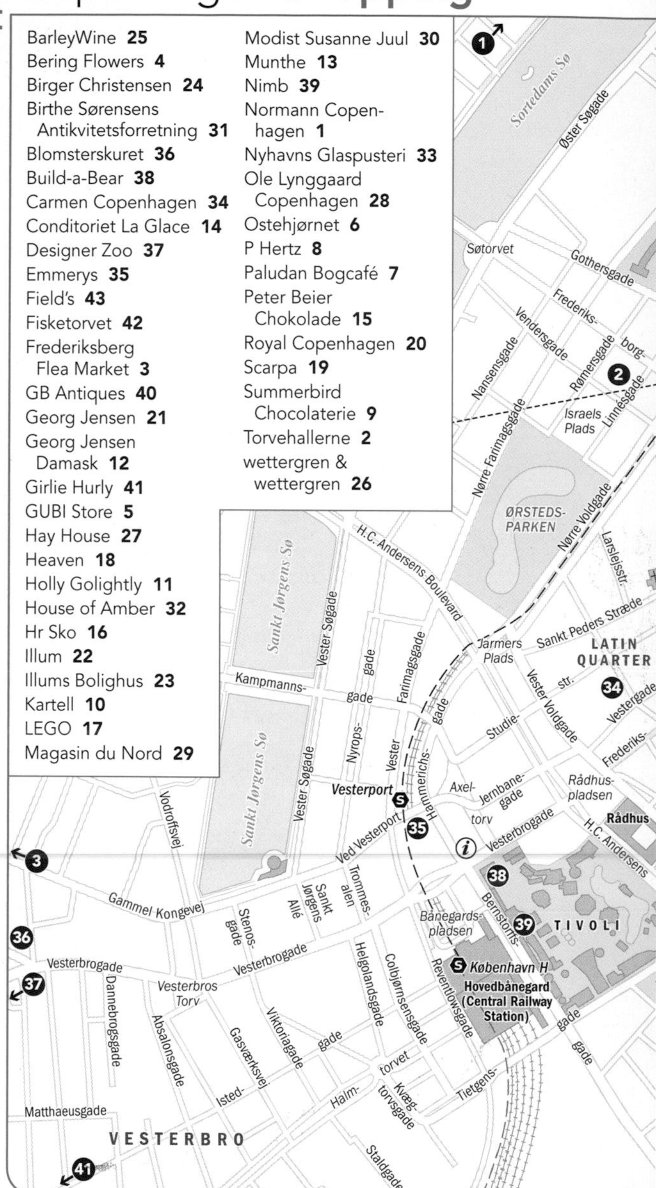

Previous page: Strøget shopping street.

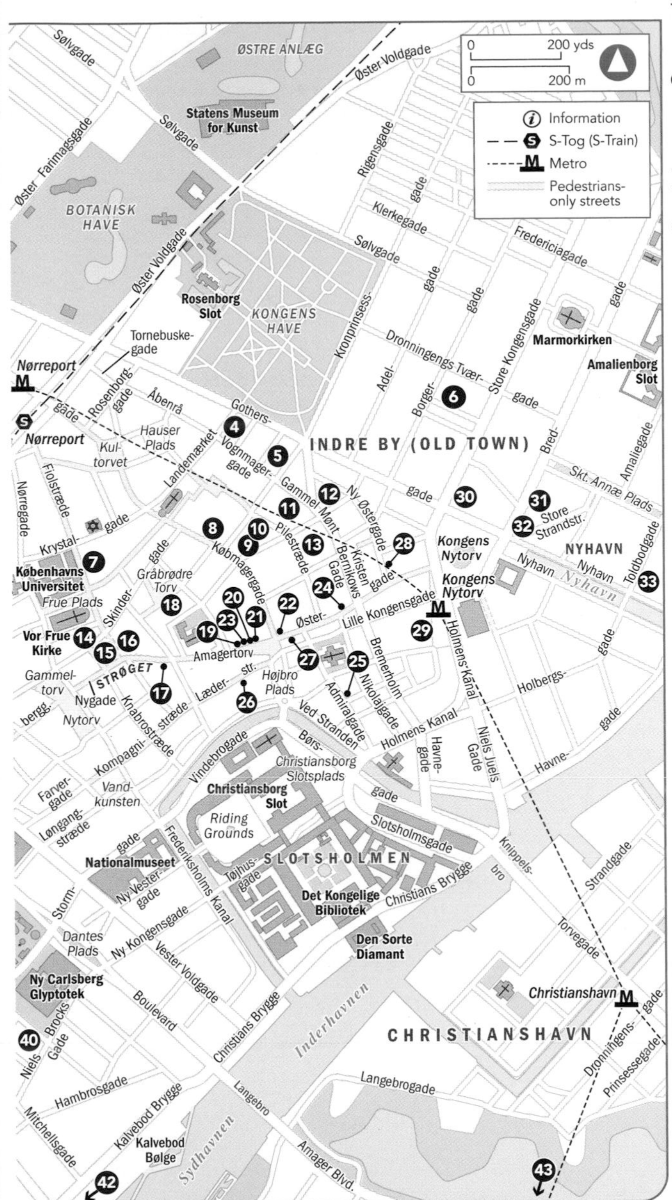
0 200 yds
0 200 m
Information
S-Tog (S-Train)
Metro
Pedestrians-only streets
ØSTRE ANLÆG
Statens Museum for Kunst
BOTANISK HAVE
Rosenborg Slot
KONGENS HAVE
INDRE BY (OLD TOWN)
NYHAVN
Marmorkirken
Amalienborg Slot
Nørreport
Kultorvet
Hauser Plads
Københavns Universitet
Frue Plads
Vor Frue Kirke
Gråbrødre Torv
Amagertorv
STRØGET
Gammeltorv
Nytorv
Højbro Plads
Kongens Nytorv
Christiansborg Slotsplads
Christiansborg Slot
Riding Grounds
SLOTSHOLMEN
Nationalmuseet
Det Kongelige Bibliotek
Den Sorte Diamant
Dantes Plads
Ny Carlsberg Glyptotek
Inderhavnen
Sydhavnen
Kalvebod Bølge
Christianshavn
CHRISTIANSHAVN
Sølvgade
Øster Farimagsgade
Øster Voldgade
Tornebuskegade
Rosenborggade
Åbenrå
Gothersgade
Vognmagergade
Landemærket
Fiolstræde
Nørregade
Krystalgade
Skindergade
Købmagergade
Pilestræde
Gammel Mønt
Ny Østergade
Kristen Bernikows Gade
Østergade
Lille Kongensgade
Lædergade
Nygade
Knabrostræde
Kompagnistræde
Farvergade
Vandkunsten
Løngangstræde
Vindebrogade
Børsgade
Ved Stranden
Admiralgade
Nikolajgade
Bremerholm
Holmens Kanal
Havnegade
Niels Juels Gade
Holbergsgade
Nyhavn
Toldbodgade
Amaliegade
Skt. Annæ Plads
Store Strandstr.
Bredgade
Store Kongensgade
Dronningens Tværgade
Borgergade
Adelgade
Kronprinsessegade
Rigensgade
Klerkegade
Fredericiagade
Øster Voldgade
Slotsholmsgade
Tøjhusgade
Frederiksholms Kanal
Christians Brygge
Knippelsbro
Strandgade
Torvegade
Ny Vestergade
Ny Kongensgade
Vester Voldgade
Stormgade
Boulevard
Brocks Gade
Niels
Hambrosgade
Kalvebod Brygge
Mitchellsgade
Langebro
Amager Blvd.
Langebrogade
Dronningensgade
Prinsessegade
4
5
6
7
8
9
10
11
12
13
14
15
16
17
18
19
20
21
22
23
24
25
26
27
28
29
30
31
32
33
40
42
43

Shopping Best Bets

Best **One-Stop Shopping**
★★★ Illum, *Østergade 52 (p 76)*

Best **Silversmith**
★★★ Georg Jensen, *Amagertorv 4 (p 81)*

Best **Hand-Blown Glass**
★★★ Nyhavns Glaspusteri, *Toldbodgade 4 (p 75)*

Best **Colorful Copenhagen Design**
★★★ Illums Bolighus, *Amagertorv 10 (p 78)*

Best **Antiques**
★★★ Birthe Sørensens Antikvitetsforretning, *Bredgade 10 (p 75)*

Best **Classic Jewelry Design**
★★★ Ole Lynggaard Copenhagen, *Ny Østergade 4 (p 80)*

Coolest **Household Design Shop**
★★ Designer Zoo, *Vesterbrogade 137 (p 77)*

Best **Leader of the Fashion Pack**
★★★ Munthe, *Grønnegade 10 (p 77)*

Best **Danish-Designed Shoes**
★★ Scarpa, *Amagertorv 14 (p 81)*

Best **Mad Hatter**
★★ Modist Susanne Juul, *Store Kongensgade 14 (p 76)*

Best **Retro Clothing**
★★ Carmen Copenhagen, *Larsbjørnsstræde 5 (p 82)*

Best **Toy Temple**
★★★ LEGO, *Vimmelskaftet 37 (p 82)*

Best **Gastronomic Souvenirs**
★★ Heaven, *Gråbrødretorv 7 (p 80)*

Best **Chocolatier**
★★★ Summerbird, *Kronprinsensgade 11 (p 76)*

Best **Gourmet Food Empire**
★★★ Nimb, *Bernstoffsgade 5 (p 80)*

Best Place to **Buy a Picnic**
★★★ Emmerys, *Ved Vesterport 3 (p 79)*

Best **Beer Sommelier**
★★ BarleyWine, *Admiralgade 21 (p 82)*

Copenhagen **Shopping A to Z**

Antiques & Art

★★★ Birthe Sørensens Antikvitetsforretning KONGENS NYTORV This lovely little shop sells affordable and colorful period glassware, porcelain collectables, silverware and some typically Danish painted wooden furniture. *Bredgade 10. ☎ 45 3311 7067. MC, V. Metro: Kongens Nytorv. Map p 72.*

★★ GB Antiques TIVOLI A vast emporium is crammed with blue-and-white Royal Copenhagen pottery, kitsch Bing and Grøndhal porcelain figurines, cutlery sets, collectible silver, and Little Mermaid plates. Not the most sophisticated antiques shop, but reasonably priced and close to Tivoli (p 10). *Ved Glyptotek 6. ☎ 45 2168 2529. www.gb-antiques.com. MC, V. Bus 1A, 2A, 5A. Map p 72.*

★★★ Nyhavns Glaspusteri NYHAVN Beautiful hand-blown glass in clean, pure lines and bright tones is all created on site by artist Christian Edwards. Watch him at work and buy a set of jewel-tinted *schnapps* glasses to take home. *Toldbodgade 4. ☎ 45 3313 0134. www.copenhagenglass.dk. AE, MC, V. Metro: Kongens Nytorv. Map p 72.*

Books

★★ Paludan Bogcafé LATIN QUARTER Across the road from the university library, this is the preferred haunt of student bookworms. Second-hand books are on the ground floor, with an extensive collection of fiction and coffee-table books upstairs. There's a little cafe in which to enjoy a mid-morning pastry, brunch, or dinner while reading your purchases, and a stall of old books to rummage through along the library wall. *Fiolstræde 10–12. ☎ 45 3315 0675. www.paludan-cafe.dk. MC, V. Metro: Nørreport. Map p 72.*

The Paludan Bogcafé bookstore.

Cakes & Chocolate

★★★ kids Conditoriet La Glace STRØGET Copenhagen's oldest confectioner has been making lacey, layered cakes, pastries, chocolates, and ice cream since 1870. Sample the goodies in the elegant two-story cafe or bag a box of buttery cookies for a picnic lunch. *Skoubogade 3-5. ☎ 45 3314 4646. www.laglace.com. MC, V. Metro: Kongens Nytorv. Map p 72.*

★★★ Peter Beier Chokolade STRØGET Right next door to Conditoriet La Glace (see above), the Bagger family have turned chocolate into a modern art form. Buy a selection of champagne truffles and multi-flavored pyramid- and heart-shaped chocs—the perfect present for back home. *Skoubogade 1. ☎ 45 3393 0717. www.peterbeierchokolade.dk. MC, V. Metro: Kongens Nytorv. Map p 72.*

★★★ Summerbird Chocolaterie STRØGET Pop in here for a fine range of simply packaged and truly delicious liqueur chocolates, spreads, marzipan bars, petit fours, gift boxes, and organic bars. They're pricey (the organic chocolate is reputedly the most expensive in the world) but worth it! *Kronprinsensgade 11. ☎ 45 3393 8040. www.summerbird.dk. AE, MC, V. Metro: Kongens Nytorv. Map p 72.*

China

★★★ Royal Copenhagen STRØGET Royal Copenhagen's famous blue-and-white patterned china sells at a remarkable rate from a wondrous gabled shop on Strøget. If you are shocked by the price tags on the Flora Danica pieces, have a look at the reasonably priced seconds in the basement. *Amagertorv 6. ☎ 45 3313 7181. www.royalcopenhagen.com. AE, DC, MC, V. Metro: Kongens Nytorv. Map p 72.*

Department Stores

★★ Birger Christensen STRØGET Sleek, cool, and expensive, this is the flagship store of Copenhagen's poshest chain of shops. You'll find menswear from the likes of Ralph Lauren, Lanvin, and Balmain, but the real strength is the women's fashions, including Alexander Wang, Prada, Valentino, Givenchy, Viola Sky, and the handmade jewelry of Anni Lu. *Østergade 38. ☎ 45 3311 5555. www.birger-christensen.com. AE, DC, MC, V. Metro: Kongens Nytorv. Map p 72.*

Royal Copenhagen's flagship store on Amagertorv.

★★★ Illum STRØGET Expertly laid out to highest Danish design ideals, exclusive Illum leads the way in Copenhagen for designer clothes (Acne Jeans, Ralph Lauren, Diesel, and Paul Smith), cosmetics, expensive jewelry, and quality accessories. *Østergade 52. ☎ 45 3314 4002. www.illum.dk. AE, DC, MC, V. Metro: Kongens Nytorv. Map p 72.*

★★ Magasin du Nord STRØGET Housed in an enormous multi-floored building first opened in 1868 as a draper's shop, you'll find clothing, accessories, household goods, books, and even a quality Mad & Vin supermarket alongside a Meyers deli. *Kongens Nytorv 13. ☎ 45 3311 4433. www.magasin.dk. AE, DC, MC, V. Metro: Kongens Nytorv. Map p 72.*

Designer Clothes & Accessories

★★★ Holly Golightly KONGENS NYTORV This on-trend boutique flogs top labels from Balenciaga and Marni to Marc Jacobs. Luxury leather accessories can be found around the corner in the Store Regnegade branch. *Gammel Mønt 2. ☎ 45 3314 1915. Also at: Store Regnegade 2. ☎ 45 3314 1911. www.hollygolightly.dk. AE, MC, V. Metro: Kongens Nytorv. Map p 72.*

★★ Modist Susanne Juul FREDERIKSSTRADEN Neat stylish headwear, fluffy angora berets,

Trendy decor items at Designer Zoo.

and felt pillbox hats come from one of Copenhagen's brightest talents. She also sells elegant gloves in vivid colors and the softest leather, made by Randers Handsker. *Store Kongensgade 14.* ☎ *45 3332 2522. www.susannejuul.dk. MC, V. Metro: Kongens Nytorv. Map p 72.*

★★★ Munthe STRØGET A Danish design leader, this boutique is a favorite among supermodels. Tucked away in an attractive courtyard, it's spacious and calm and always somehow one step ahead of its rivals. The clothes are glam and superbly made; the prices reflect this. *Grønnegade 10.* ☎ *45 3332 0312. www.munthe.com. AE, MC, V. Metro: Nørreport. Map p 72.*

★★ wettergren & wettergren STRÆDET In this cluttered basement store with tiny fitting rooms, you'll find staples for every woman's wardrobe, from classic white linen shirts to well-cut trousers and lady-like skirts. *Læderstræde 5.* ☎ *45 3313 1405. AE, MC, V. Metro: Kongens Nytorv. Map p 72.*

Design Shops

★★ Designer Zoo VESTERBRO This ultra-cool design temple sells the work of in-house furniture designers, ceramic artists, glass blowers, and jewelry makers all under one roof. Explore two floors of changing displays and seven workshops where you can see some of the products being made. *Vesterbrogade 137.* ☎ *45 3324 9493. www.dzoo.dk. AE, MC, V. Bus: 6A. Map p 72.*

★★★ Georg Jensen Damask STRØGET Here is a treasure trove of luxurious damask tablecloths, towels, kimonos, and bed linen in all shades from anthracite to the purest white. No relation of Georg Jensen the silversmith (p 81). *Ny Østergade 19.* ☎ *45 3312 2600 www.damask.dk. AE, DC, MC, V. Metro: Kongens Nytorv. Map p 72.*

★★★ GUBI Store STRØGET Set in a former warehouse for Illum, GUBI sells a wealth of Danish design featuring not just GUBI's own household products but handpicked pieces from around the

The design aesthetic of GUBI Store.

world. The building's interior is as beautiful as its wares, with towering ceilings and an old swivel staircase. *Møntergade 19. ☎ 45 5361 6368. www.gubi.dk. AE, MC, V. Metro: Kongens Nytorv. Map p 72.*

★★ **Hay House** LATIN QUARTER The ultimate in functional design is sold here, with minimalist furniture created by contemporary greats Jakob Wagner, Louise Campbell, and Hay's own design studio. Bright and funky carpets mix and match with quirky household accessories in edgy colors. *Østergade 61, 2. ☎ 45 4282 0820. www.hay.dk. MC, V. Metro: Kongens Nytorv. Map p 72.*

★★★ **Illums Bolighus** STRØGET Copenhagen's favorite interior design store sells contemporary and accessible Danish design in elegant surroundings. Lighting by the great Arne Jacobsen sits alongside products by Hay Studio and trendy white china and glassware from Normann Copenhagen (see below). *Amagertorv 10. ☎ 45 3314 1941. www.illumsbloighus.com. AE, DC, MC, V. Metro: Kongens Nytorv. Map p 72.*

★★ **Kartell** LATIN QUARTER An homage to minimalist design, this store carries chairs, stools, glassware by Philippe Starck, lampshades in garish colors, and transparent plastic tables. Still considered a design leader, but I think it's all looking a bit dated. *Kristen Bernikowsgade 6. ☎ 45 3332 1205. www.kartell.dk. www.kartell.com. AE, MC, V. Metro: Nørreport. Map p 72.*

★★★ **Normann Copenhagen** ØSTERBRO A relative newcomer to the vibrant Copenhagen design scene, this is a true lifestyle emporium selling everything from clothes by Acne and Noir to glassware by Marcel Wanders. Located in an ex-sound studio flooded with white light and display stands. *Østerbrogade 70. ☎ 45 3555 4459. www.normann-copenhagen.com. AE, MC, V. Bus 1A. Map p 72.*

Minimalist furniture at Hay House.

Illums Bolighus is one-stop shopping for interior design.

Flowers

★★ Bering Flowers LATIN QUARTER Here you'll find spectacular arrangements in pretty glass vases, as well as wedding flowers, roses in baskets, and exquisite table decorations. There are lots of unusual vases and candles for sale as well. Staff will deliver to some of the larger hotels. *Landemærket 12. ☎ 45 3315 2611. www.beringflowers.com. AE, MC, V. Metro: Nørreport. Map p 72.*

★★★ Blomsterskuret FREDERIKSBERG This tiny rustic flower shop overflows with starter plants, topiaries, and freshly-cut flowers. Floral designer Martin Reinicke's small black shed creates a charming nature haven in the middle of an urban street. *Værnedamsvej 3A. ☎ 45 33 21 6222. www.blomsterskuret.dk. MC. V. Metro: Frederiksberg. Map p 72.*

Gifts

★★ Girlie Hurly VESTERBRO Come here for a confection of feminine, pink household gifts; purple vases, crimson lamp stands, Moroccan glasses, patterned straw baskets, and pretty smocked tops. *Istedgade 99. ☎ 45 3324 2241. www.girliehurly.dk. MC. V. Bus: 10, 14. Map p 72.*

★ House of Amber NYHAVN With the high quality of the wares guaranteed by the adjacent Museum of Amber, this shop is full of dramatic amber jewelry set in gold and silver or studded with diamonds. Not the cheapest of souvenirs, but certainly the most beautiful. Check website for other locations. *Kongens Nytorv 2. ☎ 45 33 11 67 00. www.houseofamber.com. AE, DC, MC, V. Metro: Kongens Nytorv. Map p 72.*

Gourmet & Organic Food

★★★ Emmerys VESTERBRO For high quality and often organic breads, sandwich fillings, coffees, teas, and wines, head to one of the 20-plus branches of Emmerys, some of which have small cafes attached (see website for other locations.) A great stop-off for picnic fodder. *Ved Vesterport 3. ☎ 45 3322 7763. www.emmerys.dk. MC, V. Bus: 5A, 6A, 9A. Map p 72.*

Tiny Blomsterskuret flower shop, a rustic refuge in Frederiksberg.

Trendy Shopping Streets

Copenhagen's compact heart is neatly dissected by Strøget (see p 8), the longest pedestrianized shopping street in Europe, which connects the tourist hotspots of Nyhavn and Tivoli. Towards Rådhuspladsen the boutiques are predominantly mass-market chain stores, with shops becoming progressively smarter heading north towards **Kongens Nytorv,** where you'll find top-end labels Gucci, Chanel, Bottega Veneta, and Cartier as well as Birger Christensen (p 76), Georg Jensen (p 81), and the Royal Copenhagen flagship store (p 76). Nearby the streets of **Læderstræde** and **Kompagnistræde** are full of independent designers and basement shops crammed with silver and glassware. **Grønnengade** has a selection of upscale independent fashion stores, while galleries and museum-quality antique shops line decorous **Store Kongensgade** and **Bredgade.** Once-gritty **Istedgade** in Vesterbro is now home to funky clothing boutiques and gourmet food shops, while Nørrebro is the place for second-hand finds along **Birkegade** and **Elmegade.**

★★ **Heaven** STRØGET This charming little store in an 18th-century landmarked building sells gourmet delicacies from across Scandinavia and southern Europe, such as organic jams, mustards, chutneys, and impeccably sourced olive oils. Sip on a perfectly brewed coffee while chatting to passionate owners Henrik and Ingo. *Gråbrødretorv 7. ☎ 45 5367 9777. www.heaven-gastro.dk. AE, MC, V. Metro: Kongens Nytorv. Map p 72.*

★★★ **Nimb** TIVOLI Occupying the Moorish palace at Tivoli (p 10), Nimb is a gastronomic paradise with an organic dairy, chocolate factory, and deli featuring foods from Summerbird (p 76) and Løgismose (a famed Danish deli with a branch on Nordre Toldbod 16). *Bernstoffsgade 5. ☎ 45 8870 0000. www.nimb.dk. AE, MC, V. Bus: 2A, 5A, 9A, 250S. Map p 72.*

Jewelry

★★★ **Ole Lynggaard Copenhagen** STRØGET Over the past 50 years, the extraordinary goldsmith Ole Lynggaard, together with his family, has produced some of Europe's finest jewelry with pieces rooted in classic and elegant design. There is also a branch at Kastrup airport. *Ny Østergade 4. ☎ 45 3333 0345. www.olelynggaard.com. AE, MC, V. Metro: Kongens Nytorv. Map p 72.*

★★ **P Hertz** STRØGET Jeweler to the Danish Court, P Hertz has been selling traditional designs since 1834; it is very much the place where Copenhageners buy their engagement and wedding rings. Any design can be created in its workshop. *Købmagergade 34. ☎ 45 3312 2216. www.phertz.dk. MC, V. Metro: Nørreport. Map p 72.*

Malls

★★ kids **Field's** ØRESTAD Ten minutes out of town by train or metro, Copenhagen's mammoth shopping center has 140 shops, including benchmark stores Bilka OneStop, Elgiganten (electronics), and Magasin. On Level 2 you'll find cafes and restaurants as well as

Browsing the food stalls at Torvehallerne in Nørrebro.

mini-golf, a fitness center, and a large play area for toddlers. *Arne Jacobsens Allé 12.* ☎ *45 7020 8505. www.fields.dk. AE, DC, MC, V. Metro: Ørestad. Map p 72.*

★★ kids **Fisketorvet** VESTERBRO Sitting just over a footbridge from Dybbølsbro station on the Kalvebod Brygge waterfront, this spacious covered mall houses more than 120 big-brand stores, 15 cafes and restaurants, and a 10-screen movie theater. The shopping center takes its name from Copenhagen's old fish market, which was located here until 1999. *Kalvebod Brygge 59.* ☎ *45 3336 6400. www.fisketorvet.dk. AE, DC, MC, V. S-tog: Dybbølsbro. Map p 72.*

Markets

★★ **Frederiksberg Flea Market** FREDERIKSBERG Copenhagen's poshest flea market runs on Sundays, from April to October. Get down to this affluent district of town early for the chance to pick up a bargain or two—expect more designer clothing than antiques. Parking lot behind City Hall. ☎ *45 38 19 21 42, ext. 4016. www.frederiksberg.dk/loppetorv. No credit cards. Metro: Frederiksberg. Map p 72.*

★★★ **Torvehallerne** NØRREPORT The bustling stalls and stands of this gourmet covered market pull in over 60,000 shoppers every week, lured by smoked meats, gourmet chocolate, exotic spices, and artisanal fast food. Don't leave without sampling the traditional Italian pizzas of **Gorm's,** the much-hyped porridge of **GRØD, Ma Poule**'s mouthwatering duck baguette, or the healthy snacks and salads of **Smag.** *Frederiksborggade 21. www.torvehallernekbh.dk. Metro: Nørreport. Map p 72.*

Shoes

★★ **Hr Sko** LATIN QUARTER Tucked away in a charming little arcade, this has one of the widest ranges of men's shoes in Copenhagen, be it an expensive pair of brogues or Timberland boots. *Jorcks Passage, Vimmelskaftet 42B.* ☎ *45 3315 3222. www.hrsko.dk MC, V. Metro: Kongens Nytorv. Map p 72.*

★★★ **Scarpa** STRØGET Located down a side street that leads from Amagertorv to a beautiful backyard, this petite shop sells high-quality Danish-designed (but Italian-made) leather shoes in classic styles. *Amagertorv 14.* ☎ *45 3393 1501. www.scarpa.dk. MC, V. Metro: Kongens Nytorv. Map p 72.*

Silverware

★★★ **Georg Jensen** STRØGET At the world-famous silversmith's

Unleash your creativity at the LEGO Store.

beautiful flagship store, you'll find quality cutlery, gold and silver decorative arts, and immaculate handcrafted jewelry, as well as a few less expensive wares such as money-clips, business-card holders, and the iconic elephant bottle opener. *Amagertorv 4. ☎ 45 3311 4080. www.georgjensen.com. AE, DC, MC, V. Metro: Kongens Nytorv. Map p 72.*

Toys

★★ kids Build-a-Bear TIVOLI Kids get to design their favorite bear or bunny, stuff them, dress them up, and take them home. You get to pay handsomely for this, but it's worth it to see their enraptured faces. Cleverly placed by the main entrance to Tivoli to lure you in while standing in line for tickets. *Vesterbrogade 3. ☎ 45 33 13 80 30. www.buildabear.dk. AE, DC, MC, V. Bus: 2A, 6A, 12, 26. Map p 72.*

★★★ kids LEGO STRØGET The world's best-known toy manufacturer has a flagship store on Strøget offering both classic and newly released sets as well as some exclusive pieces you won't find anywhere else. There's a great interactive play area called the Living Room, a Pick-A-Brick Wall featuring any size and color you can think of, and loads of model displays. *Vimmelskaftet 37. ☎ 45 5215 9158. www.lego.com. AE, MC, V. Metro: Kongens Nytorv. Map p 72.*

Vintage

★★ Carmen Copenhagen LATIN QUARTER One of the city's oldest and best-loved second-hand shops features well-worn leather jackets, 70s dresses, sturdy coats, and the odd designer handbag. *Larsbjørnsstræde 5. ☎ 45 2683 3036. MC, V. Metro: Nørreport. Map p 72.*

Wine & Beer Merchant

★★ BarleyWine KONGENS NYTORV With fine wines, champagnes, and hand-made chocolates for sale, the major selling point here is the expertise of Jan Filipe, Copenhagen's premier beer sommelier. There are beers from Danish microbreweries, Belgian beers (Trappist and Weissbier), English stouts, and even a few US labels. *Admiralgade 21. ☎ 45 3391 9397. www.barleywine.dk. AE, MC, V. Metro: Kongens Nytorv. Map p 72.* ●

5 Copenhagen **Outdoors**

Copenhagen **Outdoors**

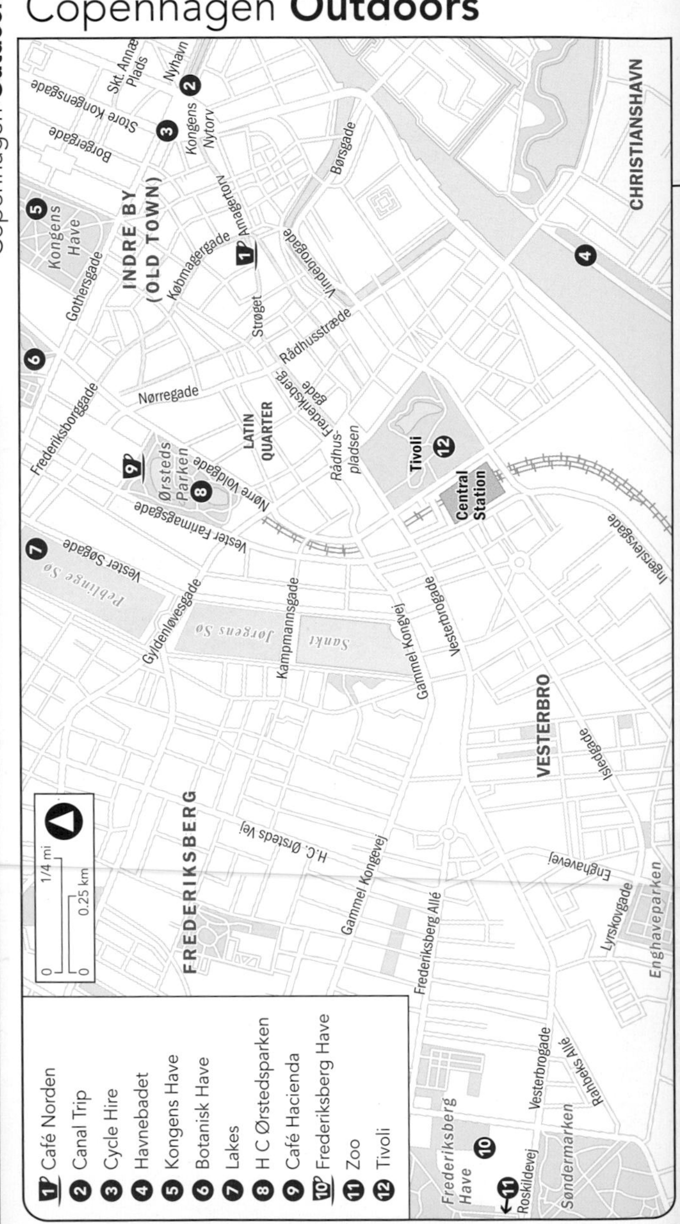

Previous page: Sunbathing in a park in Copenhagen.

Compact as it is, the city of Copenhagen isn't densely urban. In fact, it is a surprisingly green, outdoorsy city, with vast areas of parkland and water. Cyclists throng the streets; sunbathers, joggers, and walkers crowd the huge landscaped royal parks; cafes spill onto the streets and yachts pack the Øresund in summer. What follows is a series of outdoor experiences by bike to make for a satisfying day in the saddle. START: **Metro to Kongens Nytorv.**

1 ★★ **Café Norden.** Only early birds get a table outside this prime Strøget meeting place but it's worth the scramble for delicious smoked salmon salads and chocolate cake to follow. *Østergade 61. ☎ 45 3311 7791. www.cafenorden.dk. $$.*

2 ★ kids **Canal Trip.** Get an overview of the city by taking the hop-on, hop-off waterbus, which sails between Gammel Strand, the Little Mermaid (p 59), and Fisketorvet, with 10 stops on the way. You can hop on and off as many times as you like during the 48 hours the ticket is valid. There are multi-language guided tours available—check website for details. *www.canaltours.com.*

3 ★★★ kids **Cycle Hire.** Copenhagen has truly embraced this green trend with ample cycle lanes and easy access to bike hire. **Bycyklen** (The City Bike) provides rental bikes all over central Copenhagen and Frederiksberg with docking stations situated at most metro stations. The all-white electric smart bikes cost 25DKK an hour but users must sign up online beforehand. Pick up your bike in Kongens Nytorv. *Bike hire: Baisikeli, 80DKK–140DKK for 24 hr., www.cph-bike-rental.dk. City Bikes: Byccyklen, www.bycyklen.dk.*

The harbor pool at Havnebadet.

4 ★★ kids **Havnebadet.** If Copenhagen's uncertain summer temperatures are high, cycle down Niels Juels Gade and Christians Brygge and over Langerbro to Islands Brygge. Here spend the day with sun worshippers at a manmade harbor pool. Grab a deckchair, swim in the pristine waters, or join a game of volleyball. *Havnebadet: Islands Brygge. ☎ 45 3089 0469. www.teambade.kk.dk. Daily early June to late Aug 7am–7pm.*

5 ★★ kids **Kongens Have (King's Garden).** If the beach is not your thing, pedal straight up Gothersgade to Denmark's oldest royal park. The King's Garden surrounds Rosenborg Slot (castle, see p 21) and dates back to 1606; it's dotted with sculpture, including a well-loved figure of storyteller H C Andersen (p 44). Danish families come here in droves to relax, stroll with prams, meet up with friends, and enjoy the summer sunshine. The herbaceous borders, rose gardens, and herb beds are

Wintertime Fun

Frederiksberg Runddel, by the entrance to Frederiksberg Have, is flooded to form an ice rink in the winter months. Admission is free; skate rentals are available for 50DKK an hour. It's open late November to late February, Monday to Friday 11am to 9pm and weekends 10am to 9pm. There are also free outdoor ice rinks at **Genforeningspladsen** and **Toftegårds Plads**, where the grand Kongens Nytorv rink has moved while metro construction work takes place.

reminiscent of Luxembourg Gardens in Paris. Stop off if you wish to explore the castle. 🕓 *2 hr. if touring castle. Øster Voldgade 4A. ☎ 45 3392 6300. www.rosenborgslot.dk. Daily. Metro: Nørreport.*

❻ ★ Botanisk Have (Botanical Garden). Across Øster Volgade is another of Copenhagen's green havens; a botanical garden and part of the Natural History Museum of Denmark. Park your bike and stroll around the thyme- and mint-scented grounds, cultivated with around 15,000 species of plant. Stretch out by the ornamental lake or climb the stairs to the top of the rotund Palm House (open Apr–Sept 10am–3pm) reminiscent of the palm house in London's Kew Gardens. For those with a great interest in fungi and plant life, there is a botanical museum by the main entrance. 🕓 *1 hr. Øster Farimagsgade 2B. ☎ 45 3532 222. botanik.snm.ku.dk. Summer daily 8.30am–6pm; winter Tues–Sun 8.30am–4pm.*

❼ ★ Lakes. Ride on up Gothersgade for the three artificial lakes separating the city center from Østerbro and Nørrebro. Built in the 16th century as part of Christian IV's defense system guarding the western edge of the city, they were later used as reservoirs. In 1959 they were commandeered by joggers and walkers, and now provide a peaceful respite with a smattering of cafes around the banks. Snooze in summer sunshine on a bench overlooking Sortedams Sø, or watch the swans bob among the pedalos and boats for hire. 🕓 *1-hr walk. Sankt Jørgens Sø, Peblinge Sø, Sortedams Sø. Metro to Nørreport or Østerbro.*

Children romp in the Botanical Garden.

Get Out of Town

Once a royal hunting ground, **Dyrehaven** boasts a splendid 16th-century hunting lodge high on a hill overlooking the estate. Pack a picnic from **Ostehjørnet** and head off to spot deer roaming free in leafy cultivated woodland 10km north of Copenhagen. Trot around the park by horse-drawn carriage; you'll find them for hire just inside the red entrance gates. *Klampenborg.* ☎ ***45 3997 3900.*** *Train: S-Tog to Klampenborg or 20-minute drive along the coast road E152.*

Alternatively, slip anchor and head out into the Øresund early in the morning for a perfect day's sailing in sheltered waters. My favorite escape from Copenhagen is to head to the tiny Swedish island of Ven (spelt **Hven** in Danish). The 16th-century home of moustachioed astronomer Tycho Brahe, who lived here, has been opened as a museum. There are lots of yacht-charter companies around; you can take a day trip on the **M/S Jeppe**, sailing from Nyhavn harbor almost daily throughout the summer. *Havnegade 39.* ☎ ***45 3333 9355.*** *www.sparshipping.dk.*

8 ★ H C Ørstedsparken. A hop from the Lakes, this delightful park—originally part of the same defense system—is named after Danish scientist and inventor H C Ørsteds. Lanscaped in 1879, it offers rural vistas among the relaxed English-style parklands and pathways dotted with classical statues. Local children pack the playground at the north end of the lake. At night the park becomes a cruising haunt. ⏲ *40 min. Nørre Voldgade.* ☎ *45 3315 7875. Dawn–dusk daily. Metro: Nørreport.*

9 kids Café Hacienda. Great views over the lake in the Ørstedsparken. Get there early for a lunchtime seat on the terrace and a simple selection of smørrebrød; if you have worked up a thirst, sample a pint of dry Swedish cider. *Nørre Farimagsgade 6.* ☎ *45 3333 8533. $.*

10 ★★★ kids Frederiksberg Have (gardens). A 25-minute pedal down Vesterbrogade brings you to the elegant boulevard of Frederiksberg Allé. This leads to the sweeping park of Frederiksberg Have, which feels like a local secret. Designed in French neoclassical style, with English landscaping, pathways lead here and there past a Chinese pavilion (open Sun May 1–Sept 1, straight on from the main gates), ornamental lakes and fountains, and even a Greek temple. Dominating all the follies is a real palace—austere Frederiksberg Slot (castle, see p 52). *Frederiksberg Runddel 1a. www.ses.dk. Daily 6am–11pm in summer. Bus 6A, 8A, 26.*

11 ★★ kids Zoo. Since you're already in Fredericksberg Have, why not stop at the zoo? Cycle through the gardens and join often snaking entrance lines to enjoy the open-air animal enclosures; see hippos paddling around underwater and giraffes thoughtfully chewing hay. The big attractions are the Arctic Ring and the modern showpiece Norman Foster elephant house. ⏲ *2 hr. Roskildevej 32.* ☎ *45 7220 0200. www.zoo.dk. Admission*

Tivoli's Japanese Pagoda, agleam in the summer evening.

170DKK, 95DKK children 3–11. June 27–Aug 9 daily 10am–10pm; June 1–27 & Aug 10–31 10am-6pm (until 7pm weekends); Apr–May & Sept–Oct 10am–5pm (until 6pm weekends); Nov–Mar 10am–4pm (until 5pm weekends). Bus: 6A, 72.

⓬ ★★★ kids **Tivoli by Night.** Ride back to Tivoli and drop off your bikes to round off a long day with some night-time jollity. Two million fairy lights make Tivoli come to life at night; kids mob the 30-plus fairground rides—one for every age and nerve—plus the tacky arcades, hot dog stands, and aquarium. You could visit time and time again to sample more than 40 restaurants and cafes (see p 10) and roam the ornamental gardens twinkling with Japanese lanterns. Inaugurated in 1843, Tivoli's magical gardens cover six hectares and entertain 4.5 million visitors (mostly Danes) each year. *See p 10 for details.* ●

Cycling in the City

If you decide to hire a bycykel (city bike) for the day be aware that the maximum rental period is 12 hours, after which the bike will be considered missing and you could incur high penalty costs. Docking stations can be found as far north as Emdrup and south to Ørestad. Some family-oriented trips include a ride along the esplanade of Langelinie (see p 17) to visit the Little Mermaid (see p 59); fit families may enjoy the 5km cycle to Amager Beach for a paddle in the sea and a visit to Den Blå Planet (see p 37). You can always drop off the bike there and take the metro back from the beach, at no extra charge.

6 The Best Dining

Copenhagen Dining

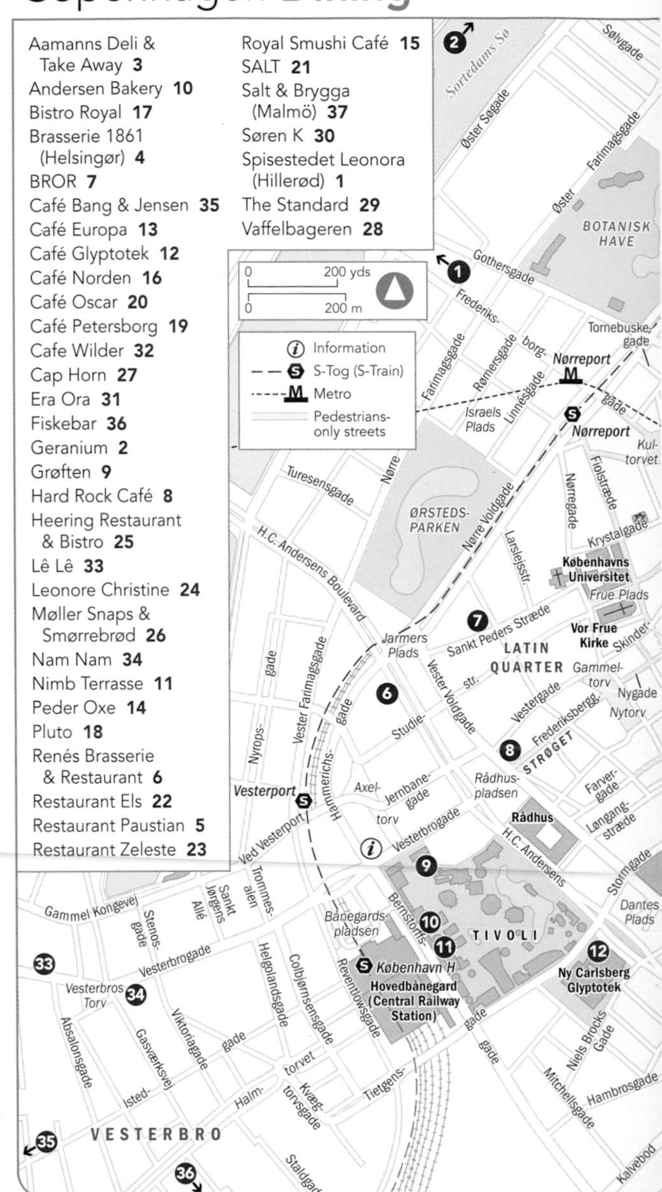

Previous page: Fresh fish from Fiskebar.

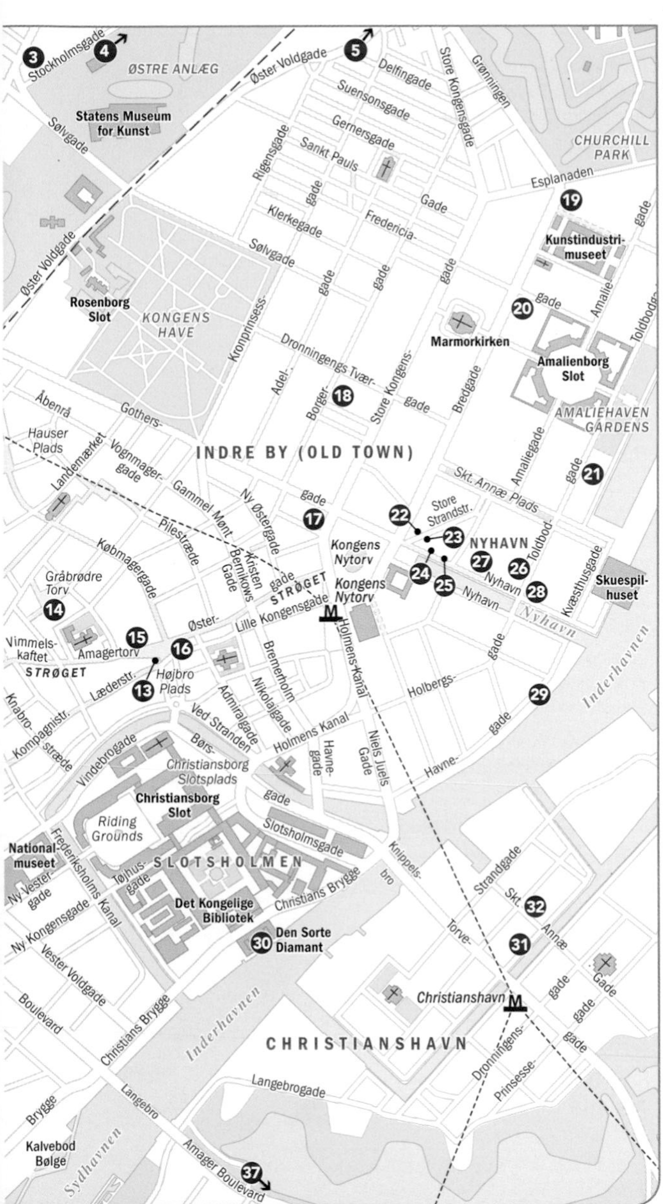
ØSTRE ANLÆG
Statens Museum for Kunst
Rosenborg Slot
KONGENS HAVE
CHURCHILL PARK
Kunstindustri-museet
Marmorkirken
Amalienborg Slot
AMALIEHAVEN GARDENS
INDRE BY (OLD TOWN)
NYHAVN
Skuespil-huset
Kongens Nytorv
STRØGET
Gråbrødre Torv
Amagertorv
Højbro Plads
Christiansborg Slotsplads
Christiansborg Slot
Riding Grounds
National-museet
SLOTSHOLMEN
Det Kongelige Bibliotek
Den Sorte Diamant
Christianshavn
CHRISTIANSHAVN
Inderhavnen
Sydhavnen
Kalvebod Bølge

Dining Best Bets

Best **Bite-Sized Smørrebrød**
★★★ The Royal Smushi Café $$ *Amagertorv 6 (p 100)*

Best **Pickled Herring**
★★★ Café Petersborg $$ *Bredgade 76 (p 95)*

Best **Snaps & Smørrebrød**
★★ Møller Snaps & Smørrebrød $$ *Toldbodgade 5 (p 98)*

Best **Fresh Seafood in Nyhavn**
★★ Cap Horn $$$ *Nyhavn 21 (p 95)*

Most **Romantic Nyhavn Dinner**
★★★ Leonore Christine $$$ *Nyhavn 9 (p 98)*

Best **Champagne Brunch**
★★ Café Norden $$ *Østergade 61 (p 95)*

Best **Dinner & Jazz Combo**
★★★ The Standard $$$$$ *Havnegade 44 (p 101)*

Best for **Courtyard Dining**
★★ Restaurant Zeleste $$$$ *Store Strandstræde 6 (p 100)*

Best **New York-Style Brasserie**
★★ Pluto $$$ *Borgergade 16 (p 99)*

Most **Spectacular Waitstaff**
★★★ Peder Oxe $$$ *Gråbrødretorv 11 (p 99)*

Best **Organic Cuisine**
★★★ Geranium $$$$$ *Per Henrik Lings Allé 4 (p 96)*

Best **Tivoli Dining**
★★★ Nimb Terrasse $$$$ *Bernstorffsgade 5 (p 99)*

Best **Trendy Vietnamese**
★★★ Lê Lê $$$ *Vesterbrogade 40 (p 97)*

Best **Place to People-Watch**
★★ Café Europa $$ *Amagertorv 1 (p 94)*

Most **Laid-Back Eatery**
★ Café Bang & Jensen $$ *Istedgade 130 (p 94)*

Most **Beautiful Cafe**
★★ Café Glyptotek $$$ *Dantes Plads 7 (p 94)*

Best for **Hungry Kids**
★ Hard Rock Café $$ *Rådhuspladsen 45–47 (p 97)*

Best **Tivoli Hot Dog**
★★ Andersen Bakery $ *Bernstorffsgade 5 (p 93)*

Best **Ice Cream**
★★ Vaffelbageren $ *Nyhavn 49 (p 102)*

Best **Sea Views in Helsingør**
★★★ Brasserie 1861 $$$$ *Nordre Strandvej 2, Helsingør (p 102)*

Lobster at Bistro Royal.

Copenhagen Dining A to Z

★★ Aamanns Deli & Take Away ØSTERBRO *SMØRREBRØD* Setting new standards for smørrebrød, Aamanns offers an innovative interpretation of the open-faced sandwich with dishes such as pear-braised pork jaw and cured veal topside with roasted celery puree. *Øster Farimagsgade 10. ☎ 45 3555 3344. www.aamanns.dk. Entrees 65DKK. AE, DC, MC, V. Mon–Fri 11am–8pm; Sat 11am–4:30pm; Sun noon–4:30pm. Bus: 14, 37. Map p 90.*

★★ Andersen Bakery TIVOLI *PATISSERIE* Sitting opposite central station in Tivoli's Nimb building, this sublime bakery founded by Japanese baker Shunsuke Takaki turns out authentic Danish pastries, cakes, and breads. Fill up on whole-wheat kanelsnegles (cinnamon snails), blue cheese, honey and walnut bread or the famed Andersen gourmet hot dog, wrapped in brioche and topped off with a rich remoulade sauce. *Bernstorffsgade 5. ☎ 45 3375 0735. www.andersen-danmark.dk. Pastries from 10DKK, hot dogs 50DKK. AE, DC, MC, V. Mon–Fri 7am–6pm; Sat–Sun 7am–5pm. Bus 2A, 5A, 9A, 250S. Map p 90.*

★★ kids Bistro Royal KONGENS NYTORV *BISTRO* For quick, unfussy, but quality food in the thick of Kongens Nytorv, you can't go wrong with Bistro Royal's burgers, steaks, salads, open-faced sandwiches and grilled fish. It's a popular lunchtime spot for refueling shoppers and large family outings; theatergoers often drop in before shows at The Royal Theatre. The dinner menu takes things up a notch with rib-eye steaks, turbot fillets, and whole fried lobster. *Kongens Nytorv 26. ☎ 45 3841 4164. www.madklubben.dk/bistro-royal. Entrees 100DKK–300DKK. AE, DC, MC, V. Mon–Fri 8am–midnight, Sat noon–midnight, Sun noon–11pm. Metro: Kongens Nytorv. Map p 90.*

★★★ BROR LATIN QUARTER *NORDIC* Opened by two former Noma sous-chefs, Bror ("brother"

Fresh hot cross buns at Andersen Bakery.

Café Glyptotek in the Winter Garden at NY Carlsberg Glyptotek.

in Danish) offers a relaxed and affordable take on New Nordic gastronomy with rustic furniture and simple yet innovative seasonal food. Besides the set menus, you can opt for creative bite-sized snacks like herring liver, cod cheeks, or bull's testicles. *Skt. Peders Stræde 24A.* ☎ *45 3217 5999. www.restaurantbror.dk. Set menus from 395DKK; snacks 50DKK. AE, DC, MC, V. Wed–Sun 5:30pm–midnight. Metro: Nørreport. Map p 90.*

★ kids **Café Bang & Jensen** VESTERBRO *BRUNCH* Boho and laid-back, this is *the* Vesterbro hotspot for a lazy Sunday brunch. Sit on the street and catch the sun or relax with a paper in the slightly scruffy back room over all-day breakfasts, enormous salads, and pasta dishes. *Istedgade 130* ☎ *45 3325 5318. www.bangogjensen.dk. Entrees 69DKK–96DKK. MC, V. Mon–Fri 7:30am–2am, Sat 10am–2am, Sun 10am–midnight. Bus 10, 14. Map p 90.*

★★ **Café Europa** STRØGET *PATISSERIE* Sip an award-winning espresso in stylish surroundings on the corner of Læderstræde and Amagertorv, the very heart of Copenhagen's pedestrianized shopping streets. You'll be in pole position to watch Copenhagen passing by while indulging in strawberry cheesecake or a carrot-and-orange gateau. *Amagertorv 1.* ☎ *45 3314 2889. www.europa1989.dk. Entrees 179DKK–199DKK. AE, MC, V. Mon–Sat 7:45am–11pm (Fri until midnight), Sun 9am–10pm. Metro: Kongens Nytorv. Map p 90.*

★★ **Café Glyptotek** RÅDHUSPLADSEN *DANISH* Hidden away in the palm-and-statue-filled Winter Garden at the NY Carlsberg Glyptotek (p 14), this smart cafe is the perfect pit-stop for organic teas, Florentines, and patisserie after visiting the sculpture galleries. Gourmet open sandwiches of prawns, herring, or pork are served at lunchtime. *Dantes Plads 7.* ☎ *45 3341 8128. www.glyptoteket.com. Entrees 68DKK–139DKK. MC, V. Lunch Tues–Sun. Bus: 1A, 2A, 9A, 12, 33, 37. Map p 90.*

★★ Café Norden STRØGET *CAFE SNACKS* A favorite for hungry shoppers after a spree along the Strøget, Café Norden is best known for its champagne brunch with fresh breads, homemade jams, smoothies, smoked salmon, and sweet cakes all washed down with a crisp glass of fizz. Burgers, soups, and salads are served later in the day. *Østergade 61. ☎ 45 3311 7791. www.cafenorden.dk. Brunch 200DKK. Entrees 130DKK–190DKK. AE, DC, MC, V. Daily 8:30am–midnight. Metro: Kongens Nytorv. Map p 90.*

★ Café Oscar FREDERIKSSTADEN *CAFE SNACKS* The chatter of smart ladies toting large shopping bags resonates in this intimate Bredgade venue for mid-morning hot chocolate and pastries. Burgers, fish cutlets, and heaped salads are available all afternoon, along with organic juices, coffees, and wines. *Bredgade 58. ☎ 45 3312 5010. www.cafeoscar.dk. Entrees 89DKK–198DKK. MC, V. Daily 10am–11pm. Metro: Kongens Nytorv. Map p 90.*

★★★ Café Petersborg FREDERIKSSTADEN *SMØRREBRØD* Open for business since 1746, Café Petersborg was once a favorite with Russian naval officers. The place is full of rickety charm and an equally charming waitstaff. Order schnitzel or tender steak for entrees, but don't miss out on the best herring in town, served marinated, pickled, and curried. *Bredgade 76. ☎ 45 3312 5016. www.cafe-petersborg.dk. Entrees 55DKK–190DKK. MC, V. Mon–Fri 11:45am–11pm, Sat 11:45am–4pm. Metro: Kongens Nytorv. Map p 90.*

★ Cafe Wilder CHRISTIANSHAVN *FRENCH/ITALIAN* Popular with locals, this raucous cafe in a restored Christianshavn canal house can be chaotic in the evenings with cramped tables, loud conversation, and flowing beer. In the calmer daytime, drop by for a lunch of fresh tomatoes and mozzarella on ciabatta or an early evening glass of wine, served under an extraordinary painting of a nude Anita Ekberg. *Wildersgade 56. ☎ 45 3254 7183. www.cafewilder.dk. Entrees 79DKK–209DKK. MC, V. Daily 9am–11pm (Fri–Sat until midnight; closes 10pm Sun). Metro: Christianshavn Torv. Map p 90.*

★★ Cap Horn NYHAVN *SEAFOOD* Housed in a 17th-century

Cap Horn, a longtime favorite on Nyhavn.

townhouse overlooking the canal, Cap Horn was an early leader of Copenhagen's organic revolution. Try the superb fresh langoustines and wild duck dressed with prunes and apple chutney. If it's crowded inside (it usually is), grab a table under the awnings. *Nyhavn 21. ☎ 45 3312 8504. www.caphorn.dk. Entrees 140DKK–200DKK. AE, MC, V. Mon–Fri 10am–midnight, Sat–Sun 9am–midnight. Metro: Kongens Nytorv. Map p 90.*

★★★ **Era Ora** CHRISTIANSHAVN *ITALIAN* The only Michelin-starred Italian restaurant in Scandinavia, Era-Ora deserves its ranking: The decor is elegant, the terrace overlooks Christianshavn Kanal, and the waiters are charming. The wine list features a range of enticing Italian wines; the light Italian dishes, such as *ferretti* pasta with mushrooms and veal tenderloin, are simply superb. *Reservations required.* The owners have another venue well worth checking out: Tuscan home cooking at **L'Altro** (Torvegade 62, ☎ 45 3254 5406). *Overgaden Neden Vandet 33B. ☎ 45 3254 0693. www.era-ora.dk. 4 courses 830DKK; 6 courses 1,350DKK. AE, DC, MC, V. Mon–Sat noon–3pm & 6:30pm–midnight. Metro: Christianshavn. Map p 90.*

★★★ **Fiskebar** KØDBYEN *SEAFOOD* Like many restaurants in Vesterbro's trendy Meatpacking District, Fiskebar ("fish bar") nods to its past with a stripped-down industrial-chic interior; today it's all about some of the best seafood you'll find in this city. Opt for a large fish entree or tuck into a few starters at the bar, such as the succulent oysters, creamy seared scallops, or delicate raw mackerel. Look for Fiskebar's equally impressive sister restaurant, **Musling,** across from Torvehallerne (p 81). *Flæsketorvet 100. ☎ 45 3215 5656. www.fiskebaren.dk. Entrees 155DKK–255DKK. AE, DC, MC, V. Mon–Fri 5:30pm–midnight (Fri until 2am), Sat 11:30am–2am, Sun 11:30am–midnight. S-Tog: Dybbølsbro. Map p 90.*

Geranium's head chef, Rasmus Kofoed.

★★★ **Geranium** ØSTERBRO *GOURMET ORGANIC* Owned by culinary darling Rasmus Kofoed, who was voted the world's best chef in 2011 (while at Bocuse d'Or), Geranium holds a coveted three Michelin stars; locals tend to prefer it to its showier rival Noma (which closed in late 2016). *Reservations essential.* The mainly organic menu features the finest crab, lemon sole, or tender venison. The restaurant sits on the 8th floor of Parken football stadium offering knockout views of leafy Østerbro. *Per Henrik Lings Allé 4. ☎ 45 6996 0020. www.geranium.dk. Tasting menu 1,400 DKK & 1,800DKK. AE, DC, MC, V. Wed–Sat noon–3:30pm & 6:30pm–midnight. Bus: 1A, 14. Map p 90.*

★★ **Grøften** TIVOLI *DANISH* One of Tivoli's oldest and most venerable restaurants, established in 1874, Grøften ("the ditch") is decked out with red-checked tablecloths and fairy lights. Smørrebrød classics are served alongside hearty Danish staples such as rolled pork sausage and fried fillet of plaice. It gets a little busy; book ahead. *Vesterbrogade 3. ☎ 45 3375 0675. www.groeften.dk. Entrees 145DKK–385DKK. AE, DC, MC, V. Closed Oct–Mar. Daily 11am–11pm (Fri–Sat until midnight). Bus 2A, 6A, 12, 26, 250S. Map p 90.*

★ kids Hard Rock Café RÅDHUSPLADSEN *BURGER BAR* The perfect antidote for kids who have run themselves ragged in Tivoli. Service is brisk and friendly, and the burgers and steaks are just what you'd expect from this international chain. Sensible prices make this a sure hit with families. *Rådhuspladsen 45–47. ☎ 45 3312 4333. www.hardrock.com. Entrees 155KK–260DKK. AE, DC, MC, V. Mon–Fri noon–11pm, Sat–Sun 10am–11pm. Bus 2A, 10, 12, 26, 33, 250S. Map p 90.*

★★★ Heering Restaurant & Bistro NYHAVN *SEAFOOD* Here's one of my favorite Nyhavn spots for a leisurely lunch of marinated herring and *smørrebrød,* piled high with salmon, garlicky mayo, and dill. On sunny days, grab a table under the awning by the street-side bar and order a chilled dark lager. Inside, the cheery dining room has the bare brick walls and uneven floors of a typical 17th-century Nyhavn canal house. *Nyhavn 15. ☎ 45 3314 5614. restaurantheering.dk. Entrees 185DKK–245DKK. AE, MC, V. Daily 9am–midnight. Metro: Kongens Nytorv. Map p 90.*

★★★ Lê Lê VESTERBRO *VIETNAMESE* You can't book tables for this ever-popular Vesterbro restaurant, so join the crowd at the cavernous bar, all happily awaiting top-notch Vietnamese fusion food. Savor dim sum starters, followed by delicate pancakes stuffed with chili chicken, sweet and sour pork, or delicious rice noodles flavored with coriander and lemon grass. Service is friendly despite the warehouse-size proportions of the venue.

Vietnamese food at Le Le.

Vesterbrogade 40. ☎ 45 3331 3125. www.lele.dk. Sharing menus 355DKK–535KK. MC, V. Mon–Thurs 5–11:30pm, Fri–Sat 5pm–1am. Bus 6A, 9A, 26, 31. Map p 90.

★★★ Leonore Christine NYHAVN *SEAFOOD* In Copenhagen's oldest building (standing since 1681), this charming Nyhavn restaurant has gently sloping floors, and walls dotted with portraits of Danish kings and queens. By evening candlelight, it's a very romantic spot. Lunchtime best buys include pickled herrings served with capers and a rich pork pâté smothered with bacon and mushrooms. *Nyhavn 9. ☎ 45 3313 5040. www.leonore-christine.dk. Entrees 148DKK–208DKK. AE, DC, MC, V. Daily 9am–11pm. Metro: Kongens Nytorv. Map p 90.*

★★ Møller Snaps & Smørrebrød NYHAVN *SMØRREBRØD* There are plenty of places to get lunchtime schnapps and sandwiches around Nyhavn, but Andreas Møller's place stands out, with his unique take on the classic fried herring, fish fillet. and chicken salad smørrebrød. Chefs come out from the kitchen to tell you all about their dishes, ingredients, and which of their 60 homemade schnapps to pair them with. *Toldbodgade 5. ☎ 45 3150 5075. www.snapsogsmoerrebroed.dk. Entrees 98DKK–128DKK. AE, DC, MC, V. Mon–Sat 11am–4pm. Metro: Kongens Nytorv. Map p 90.*

★★★ Nam Nam VESTERBRO *SINGAPORE* In this cool and casual Singaporean restaurant, a striking interior blends Asian color and style with Scandinavian detailing. Snack on Asian crudités and seafood spring rolls before feasting on hoisin-marinated spareribs, slow-cooked chicken curry, or tender pork shank braised in caramelized sugar, rice wine, and soy. Take-out is also available. *Vesterbrogade 39. ☎ 45 4191 9898. www.restaurantnamnam.dk. Entrees 110DKK–185DKK. AE, DC, MC, V.*

Outdoor dining at Nimb Terrasse.

Industrial-chic brasserie Pluto.

Tues–Wed 5pm–midnight, Thurs–Sat 5pm–late. Bus: 6A, 9A, 26, 31. Map p 90.

★★★ **Nimb Terrasse** TIVOLI *GOURMET* Part of the vast culinary Nimb empire, this French-inspired Scandinavian bistro sits under a leafy canopy of trees in the heart of Tivoli. The menu's simple but immaculate dishes center on local harvests and seasons, using many of Nimb's own herbs and vegetables. Come summer, an outdoor barbecue is fired up on the terrace, grilling catch of the day, beef steaks. and fresh Danish langoustine. *Bernstorffsgade 5. ☎ 45 3375 0750. www.terrasse.nimb.dk. Meals 250DKK–425DKK. AE, DC, MC, V. Mon–Fri noon–2:30pm & 5:30–11pm. Closed Oct–Mar. Bus: 2A, 5A, 9A, 250S. Map p 90.*

★★★ kids **Peder Oxe** LATIN QUARTER *DANISH* Book in advance for a blow-out dinner at one of Copenhagen's oldest (and noisiest) restaurants, with what may be the most beautiful waitstaff in the city. In a series of lively dining rooms with wooden floors and tables squeezed in at odd angles, dishes range from organic steak to melt-in-the-mouth sole, accompanied by fresh salads from the buffet. Set it off with Chablis and round off with a selection of tasty Danish cheeses. *Gråbrødretorv 11. ☎ 45 3311 0077. www.pederoxe.dk. Entrees 145DKK–235DKK. AE, DC, MC, V. Daily 10am–11:30pm. Metro: Kongens Nytorv. Map p 90.*

★★ **Pluto** KONGENS NYTORV *BRASSERIE* With its concrete pillars and long industrial metal bar, Pluto feels more like a downtown New York hangout than a Danish restaurant. The French-leaning menu features everything from snacks and charcuterie to foie gras, hanger steak, and desserts. This is quality food at palatable prices, plus the bar slams out some mean cocktails. *Borgergade 16. ☎ 45 3316 0016. www.restaurantpluto.dk. Entrees 95DKK–195DKK. 12 courses 450DKK. AE, DC, MC, V. Mon–Thurs*

5:30pm–midnight, Fri–Sat 5:30pm–2am. Metro: Kongens Nytorv. Map p 90.

★ **Renés Brasserie & Restaurant** TIVOLI *BRASSERIE* A well-priced option only a step away from Tivoli (p 10), this French-style brasserie has a zinc-topped bar and a menu of burgers, grills, and fish dishes. Try the lunch plate—herring, fillet of plaice, shrimps, and fried beef tartar—it certainly chased away my hunger pangs. *Axel Torv 6. ☎ 45 3314 8501. www.renesrestaurant.dk. Entrees 169DKK–249DKK. MC, V. Daily 11am–midnight. Bus: 5A, 6A, 9A, 12, 14, 31, 34. Map p 90.*

★ **Restaurant Els** NYHAVN *DANISH CONTINENTAL* This atmospheric candle-lit dining room with Art Nouveau murals has slipped a bit since its 19th-century heyday, but it's still worth coming here for the Hans Christian Andersen-era ambiance. The lunch menu offers a variety of sandwiches and salads; dinner moves toward steaks and roast chicken. *Store Strandstræde 3. ☎ 45 3314 1341. www.restaurant-els.dk. Entrees 179DKK–295DKK. AE, DC, MC, V. Daily 11am–11pm. Metro: Kongens Nytorv. Map p 90.*

★★★ **Restaurant Paustian** ØSTERBRO *DANISH* Housed in one of the few Jørn Utzon-designed modernist buildings in Denmark, harborfront Restaurant Paustian earned its fame through the molecular gastronomy of celebrity Danish chef Bo Bech. Today his talented young replacement, Chris Ladegaard Jensen, serves up simple but vibrant Danish lunches of salmon, beef, or veal tartar, salads, and smørrebrød. *Kalkbrænderiløbskaj 2. ☎ 45 3918 5501. www.restaurantpaustian.dk. 2 courses 180DKK; 3 courses 235DKK. AE, DC, MC, V. Mon–Sat 10am–4pm. Train: S-Tog to Nordhavn. Map p 90.*

SALT Restaurant in the Copenhagen Admiral hotel.

Restaurant Zeleste NYHAVN *DANISH/FRENCH* With a vine-strewn courtyard at the back and a bow-fronted dining room inside, Zeleste just may be the most visually appealing restaurant in town. Luckily the standard of food matches the decor; Danish dishes with French overtones include grilled lobster and venison cooked in blueberries and wine. Seasonal specials change nightly. *Store Strandstræde 6. ☎ 45 3316 0606. www.zeleste.dk. Entrees 135DKK–195DKK. AE, DC, MC, V. Mon–Thurs 11am-10pm, Fri 11am–11pm, Sat 10am–11pm, Sun 10am–10pm. Metro: Kongens Nytorv. Map p 90.*

★★★ **The Royal Smushi Café** STRØGET *SMØRREBRØD* This cafe gives new meaning to the word "kitsch": Think pink walls, a metallic sheen on the glitzy leaf-patterned ceiling, and spoof Old Masters on the walls. There's an array of coffees and teas and the lunch-time menu includes *smushi*, a happy mash-up of *smørrebrød* and sushi—curried herring, burgers, and tasty fish fillets all served in miniature. Other options include soups, salads, and tangy lemon desserts. *Amagertorv 6.* ☎ *45 3312 1122. www.royalsmushicafe.dk. Entrees 48DKK–145DKK. AE, MC, V. Mon–Sat 10am–7pm, Sun 10am–6pm. Metro: Kongens Nytorv. Map p 90.*

★★ **SALT** NYHAVN *DANISH MODERN EUROPEAN* The nautical theme of the Copenhagen Admiral Hotel (see p 129) continues in the dining room, where Chef Rasmus Møller Nielsen garners applause for his confident European-style dishes with a Danish twist. The menu changes seasonally and might feature poached crab with mushrooms and spinach, or oxtail and sweetbreads. There's a direct shuttle from here to the Operaen (see p 119) across the Øresund. *Toldbodgade 24.* ☎ *45 3374 1414. www.saltrestaurant.dk. Entrees 100DKK–295DKK. AE, DC, MC, V. Daily noon–10:30pm. Metro: Kongens Nytorv. Map p 90.*

Gourmet Nordic cuisine at The Standard.

★★★ **The Standard** NYHAVN NORDIC This critically-acclaimed food and jazz emporium from Claus Meyer of Noma fame offers three dining spaces, two bars, and a jazz club. The first-floor Michelin-starred Studio is the standout option, serving gourmet Nordic fare from Torsten Vilgaard (also a Noma alum). Think pan-seared cauliflower with truffle garden sorrel, or wild duck with beets, blackberries, and thyme. *Havnegade 44.* ☎ *45 7214 8808. www.thestandardcph.dk. 5-course dinner with wine pairing 1,800DKK; 7 courses 2,150DKK. AE, DC, MC, V. Lunch Thurs–Sat noon–3pm; dinner Tues–Sat 7pm–midnight. Metro: Kongens Nytorv. Map p 90.*

★★★ **Søren K** CHRISTIANSHAVN MODERN EUROPEAN Named for Copenhagen's gloomiest philosopher, Søren Kierkegaard, this sleekly modern spot is an expensive night out but worth the price for the views over the Øresund from the Royal Library's *Sorte Diamond* (Black Diamond, see p 29). Under head chef Jens Søndergaard, its light modern European fare introduces flashes of nouvelle cuisine. The menu boasts lots of vegetarian options, healthy grilled fish dishes, and thinly sliced carpaccio. In summer sit outside on the waterview terrace. *Søren Kierkegaards Plads 1.* ☎ *45 3347 4949. www.soerenk.dk. 4-course menu 795DKK. Mon–Sat noon–4pm & 5:30–10pm. DC, MC, V. Metro: Kongens Nytorv. Map p 90.*

Vaffelbageren, the source for Copenhagen's best ice cream.

★★ **Vaffelbageren** NYAHVN *ICE CREAM* The best ice cream in central Copenhagen, where homemade cones are piled with toffee, coffee, or strawberry flavors, plus several kinds of icy slush from a gurgling machine by the doorway. Eat in or sit on the deck outside the Kongelige Teater Skuespilhus (Danish Royal Playhouse, p 121) and watch the world go by. *Nyhavn 49.* ☎ *45 3314 0698. www.vaffelbageren.dk. Ice cream scoops & waffles 30DKK–40DKK. AE, DC, MC, V. Daily 10am–midnight. Metro: Kongens Nytorv. Map p 90.*

Helsingør

★★★ **Brasserie 1861** HELSINGØR *FRENCH* This exceptional French-inspired hotel restaurant has a regularly changing menu featuring lobster, prawns, grilled meat, and steak dishes plus a vegetarian option. If you're here on a clear evening, grab a table facing the Øresund to watch the sun slip into the sea. *Hotel Marienlyst, Nordre Strandvej 2, Helsingør.* ☎ *45 4928 0158. www.marienlyst.dk. Entrees 188DKK–258DKK. AE, DC, MC, V. Sun–Thurs noon–3pm & 6–9:45pm, Fri–Sat 5:30–9:45pm. Train: Helsingør. Map p 90.*

Hillerød

★★ **kids** **Spisestedet Leonora** HILLERØD *DANISH SNACKS* Tucked in the shadows of Frederiksborg Slot (see p 142), this buzzing cafe has airy dining rooms and a large cobbled terrace overlooking meadows. Plates of fish fillets, roast meats and pickles, salads, and open sandwiches are guaranteed to buck up feet weary from traipsing around the castle. *Frederiksborg Slot, Hillerød.* ☎ *45 4826 7516. www.leonora.dk. Entrees 50DKK–145DKK. MC, V. Daily 10am–5pm (closes at 3:30pm in winter). Train: Hillerød. Map p 90.*

Malmö

★★ **Salt & Brygga** MALMÖ, SWEDEN *INTERNATIONAL* With fantastic views overlooking the Øresund bridge and harbor, this stylish organic restaurant mixes Swedish staples with Mediterranean classics. There's a strict eco ethos with all local ingredients and an allergy-free interior. Expect wholesome seaside dishes such as moules frites, lobster soup, and baked cod. *Sundspromenaden 7, Malmö.* ☎ *46 40 611 59 40. saltobrygga.se. Entrees 140DKK–205DKK. AE, DC, MC, V. Lunch Mon–Fri 11:30am–2:30pm, Sat noon–5pm; dinner Mon–Sat 5–11pm. Train: Malmö. Map p 90.* ●

7 The Best Nightlife

Copenhagen Nightlife

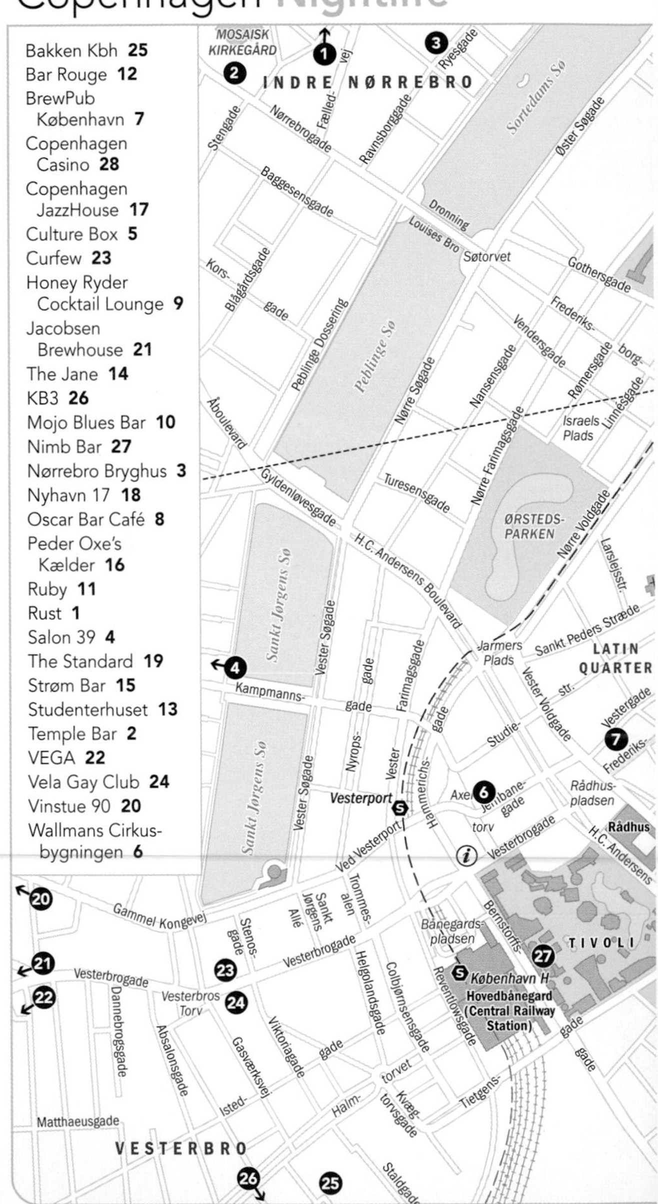

Previous page: Show at Wallmans.

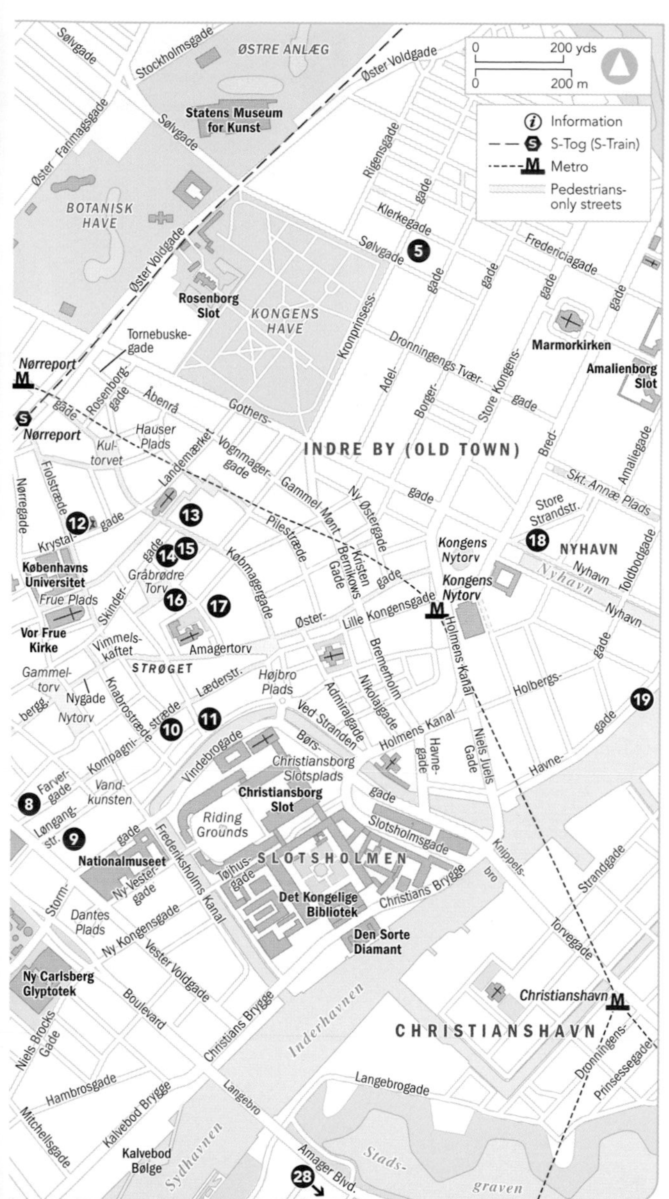
0 200 yds
0 200 m
Information
S-Tog (S-Train)
Metro
Pedestrians-only streets
ØSTRE ANLÆG
Statens Museum for Kunst
BOTANISK HAVE
Rosenborg Slot
KONGENS HAVE
INDRE BY (OLD TOWN)
Marmorkirken
Amalienborg Slot
NYHAVN
Nyhavn
Nørreport
Hauser Plads
Kultorvet
Københavns Universitet
Frue Plads
Vor Frue Kirke
Gråbrødre Torv
Amagertorv
STRØGET
Gammeltorv
Nytorv
Højbro Plads
Kongens Nytorv
Christiansborg Slotsplads
Christiansborg Slot
Riding Grounds
SLOTSHOLMEN
Nationalmuseet
Det Kongelige Bibliotek
Den Sorte Diamant
Dantes Plads
Ny Carlsberg Glyptotek
Christianshavn
CHRISTIANSHAVN
Inderhavnen
Kalvebod Bølge
Sydhavnen
Stadsgraven
Sølvgade
Stockholmsgade
Øster Voldgade
Øster Farimagsgade
Rigensgade
Klerkegade
Fredericiagade
Kronprinsessegade
Dronningens Tværgade
Adelgade
Borgergade
Store Kongensgade
Bredgade
Amaliegade
Tornebuskegade
Rosenborggade
Åbenrå
Gothersgade
Vognmagergade
Landemærket
Fiolstræde
Nørregade
Krystalgade
Skindergade
Gammel Mønt
Pilestræde
Ny Østergade
Kristen Bernikows Gade
Købmagergade
Østergade
Lille Kongensgade
Skt. Annæ Plads
Store Strandstr.
Toldbodgade
Holmens Kanal
Bremerholm
Nikolajgade
Admiralgade
Ved Stranden
Børsgade
Vimmelskaftet
Læderstr.
Knabrostræde
Kompagnistræde
Nygade
Vindebrogade
Havnegade
Niels Juels Gade
Holbergsgade
Farvergade
Vandkunsten
Løngangstr.
Frederiksholms Kanal
Ny Vestergade
Tøjhusgade
Slotsholmsgade
Christians Brygge
Knippelsbro
Strandgade
Torvegade
Stormgade
Ny Kongensgade
Vester Voldgade
Boulevard
Niels Brocks Gade
Hambrosgade
Mitchellsgade
Kalvebod Brygge
Langebro
Langebrogade
Amager Blvd.
Dronningensgade
Prinsessegade
5
8
9
10
11
12
13
14
15
16
17
18
19
28

Nightlife Best Bets

Smartest Nightclub in Town
★★★ The Jane, *Gråbrødretorv 8* *(p 110)*

Most Elusive Bar
★★★ Ruby, *Nybrogade 10 (p 109)*

Best for Hygge (Danish Hospitality)
★★ Nyhavn 17, *Nyhavn 17 (p 107)*

Best for Dinner & Jazz
★★★ The Standard, *Havnegade 44 (p 112)*

Best for Alternative Music
★★ Rust, *Guldbergsgade 8 (p 112)*

Best for Las Vegas Style
★★★ The Stage, *Jernbanegade 8 (p 111)*

Weirdest Cocktail Mix
★★ Honey Ryder Cocktail Lounge, *Løngangstræde 27 (p 109)*

Cheapest Pint
★ Studenterhuset, *Købmagergade 52 (p 107)*

Best Mircobrewery Beers
★★★ Nørrebro Bryghus, *Ryesgade 3 (p 107)*

Ruby, an elegant cocktail bar hidden away in the heart of the city.

Best for Late-Night Dancing
★★★ Bakken Kbh, *Flæsketorvet 19–21 (p 110)*

Biggest Dance Club
★★★ VEGA, *Enghavevej 40 (p 111)*

Copenhagen Nightlife A to Z

Bars & Pubs

★★★ BrewPub København RÅDHUSPLADSEN Firmly on the tourist track, this microbrewery has a changing menu of seven house beers daily, as well as European guest ales. Grab a table in the courtyard to sample a dark Belgian stout or German wheat beer over traditional English steak pie. *Vestergade 29. ☎ 45 3332 0060. www.brewpub.dk. Bus: 2A, 12, 10, 26, 33. Map p 104.*

★ Jacobsen Brewhouse VALBY Pay a visit to the Carlsberg Brewery (p 50) and claim your two pints of Tuborg, Carlsberg, or Jacobsen lager (included in the entrance price). This stylish venue with a curved copper bar made from old brewing vats also serves a selection of rare brews that can only be bought here. *Gamle Carlsberg Vej 11. ☎ 45 3327 1282. www.visitcarlsberg.com. Train: Enghave. Map p 104.*

Pulling a draft beer at BrewPub København.

★★★ Nørrebro Bryghus NØRREBRO This well-established brewery was at the forefront of Copenhagen's early microbrewing scene and is still one of the best in town. It typically serves 10 different types of beer, including a zesty lemon ale, a fruity American brown ale, and a malty Bombay pale ale, along with classic pub grub. *Ryesgade 3. ☎ 45 3530 0530. www.noerrebrobryghus.dk. Metro: Nørreport. Map p 104.*

★★ Nyhavn 17 NYHAVN With a serious list of whiskies and a copious selection of draught beers (Trappist, stout, dark lagers), this pub sticks to its nautical Nyhavn roots. Inside is cluttered with old boat propellers; merry crowds spill out onto the street for a convivial late-night atmosphere. Live music most nights. *Nyhavn 17. ☎ 45 3312 5419 www.nyhavn17.dk. Metro: Kongens Nytorv. Map p 104.*

★★ Peder Oxe's Kælder LATIN QUARTER Underneath Peder Oxe restaurant (p 99), this bar opens onto a cobbled medieval square in summer, a perfect spot for balmy evenings. Inside these old monastery cellars, space is tight and things can get noisy as the evening unwinds. *Gråbrødretorv 11. ☎ 45 3311 0077. www.pederoxe.dk. Metro: Kongens Nytorv. Map p 104.*

★ Studenterhuset LATIN QUARTER Just the place for rubbing shoulders with the next generation of Jacobsens and Kierkegaards, this pub is situated opposite the university halls of residence, and it's as cheap and homey as you'd expect from a student dive. There are party nights with DJs playing hip-hop and techno, as well as Sunday Swing, afternoon jazz, and blues sessions. *Købmagergade 52. ☎ 45 3532 3861. www.studenterhuset.com. Metro: Nørreport. Map p 104.*

★★ **Temple Bar** NØRREBRO A relaxed atmosphere and sagging sofas attract a young clientele for an early evening beer or cocktail, a chat, and a round of foosball. There's an entertaining weekly open stage on Tuesday at 9pm for up-and-coming songwriters and performers from jugglers to acrobats. *Nørrebrogade 48. ☎ 45 3537 4414. Metro: Nørreport. Map p 104.*

★★ **Vinstue 90** FREDERIKSBERG Don't be in a hurry when you visit this traditional Vesterbro-bordering bodega, home of "slow beer." Here, pouring uncarbonated Carlsberg takes up to 15 minutes per pint; the result is a smooth drink with a frothy head that stays until the glass is empty. *Gammel Kongevej 90. ☎ 45 3331 8490. www.vinstue90.dk. Bus: 9A, 31, 71. Map p 104.*

Casino

★ **Copenhagen Casino** AMAGER Try your luck at poker, black jack, punto banco, and roulette at this casino, part of the Radisson Blu Scandinavia complex (see p 133). Dress codes apply; don't forget photo ID even if you're just playing the slots. *Amager Boulevard 70. ☎ 45 3396 5965. uk.casinocopenhagen.dk. Admission 85DKK. Metro: Islands Brygge, Amagerbro; Bus: 5A, 77. Map p 104.*

Cocktail Bars

★ **Bar Rouge** LATIN QUARTER During the week, this ultra-cool bar serves coffees and goblets of Chablis to well-heeled ladies. At the weekend the music steps up a gear, generating the hottest address in town. DJs play ambient music while an affluent crowd of

The vintage-styled bar at Curfew.

An expert mixologist at work at Nimb Bar.

thirty-somethings knock back expensive cocktails. *Krystalgade 22.* ☎ *45 3345 9100. www.sktpetri.com. Metro: Nørreport. Map p 104.*

★★★ **Curfew** VESTERBRO A short walk from Central Station, Curfew is the intimate vintage-styled cocktail bar of award-winning bartender Humberto Marques. The menu offers plenty of seasonal drinks, classic concoctions, and modern interpretations, many made with Humberto's own liqueurs, bitters, and syrups. *Stenosgade 1.* ☎ *45 2929 9276. www.curfew.dk. S-Tog: Hovedbanegården (Central Station). Map p 104.*

★★ **Honey Ryder Cocktail Lounge** RÅDHUSPLADSEN This buzzing bar furnished with simple Danish designs is in trendy Hotel Twentyseven (p 130). Mixologists take their job very seriously here, creating cocktails with ingenious names like the Lip-Gloss Martini. At the weekend, the young-ish hotel clientele mixes effortlessly with chic locals. *Løngangstræde 27.* ☎ *45 7027 5627. www.firsthotels.com. Bus: 1A, 2A, 9A, 12, 26, 33, 37. Map p 104.*

★★ **Nimb Bar** TIVOLI Another top-notch hangout in the Nimb empire (p 132), this bar has a huge fireplace that's perfect for lounging beside on rainy spring afternoons. Take afternoon tea (served with champagne, of course) with the Copenhagen moneyed set, or sink into a cozy armchair for an after-dinner digestif (see Nimb Terrasse, p 99). *Hotel Nimb, Bernstorffsgade 5.* ☎ *45 8870 0030. www.bar.nimb.dk. Bus: 2A, 5A, 9A, 250S. Map p 104.*

★★★ **Ruby** KONGENS NYTORV So hip it's almost impossible to find, this elegant cocktail bar is hidden behind what looks like a private doorway on the landward side of Nybrogard. Sample the excellent ruby daiquiris, flavored with rhubarb, or try an Apple Smash, vodka infused with apple, lime, mint, and a kick of champagne. A sophisticated start to any evening. *Nybrogade 10.* ☎ *45 3395 1203. www.rby.dk. Metro: Kongens Nytorv. Map p 104.*

Dress Code

Going out in Copenhagen is largely a casual affair; jeans and sneakers suffice in most bars, cafés, and pubs. However, if you intend to enter clubbing territory, dress to impress to get past the velvet ropes. Designer bars with door policies and cocktail menus also expect a modicum of effort on the sartorial front.

Designer cocktail at Strøm Bar.

★★★ **Salon 39** FREDERIKSBERG In a rapidly gentrifying part of town, this elegant bar with discreet lighting and an unusual cocktail list has proved a big hit. There's a short supper menu and occasional jazz too. *Vodroffsvej 39. ☎ 45 3920 8039. www.salon39.dk. Metro: Forum. Map p 104.*

★★ **Strøm Bar** LATIN QUARTER A sophisticated 1930s-themed cocktail bar offers flawlessly attired waiters mixing top-notch cocktails in art deco surroundings. Drinkers congregate around the bar or sit in dimly lit booths. *Niels Hemmingsensgade 32. ☎ 45 8118 9421. www.strombar.dk. Metro: Kongens Nytorv. Map p 104.*

Dance Clubs

★★★ **Bakken Kbh** KØDBYEN This low-key Meatpacking District club throws a great party at the weekend when crowds overflow onto a colorfully lit patio. DJs and bands crank up the action in an adjoining former slaughtering hall. The club stays open weekends until the wee hours. *Flæsketorvet 19-21. www.bakkenkbh.dk. S-Tog: Dybbølsbro. Map p 104.*

★★ **Culture Box** NØRREBRO A haven for electronic music, this three-part venue presents a solid line-up of international and local artists from the underground scene. White Box is the pre-club bar, Red Box is the intimate lower floor, and Black Box is the main party room. *Kronprinsessegade 54. ☎ 45 3332 5050. www.culture-box.com. Metro: Nørreport/ Østerport. Bus 26. Map p 104.*

★★★ **The Jane** LATIN QUARTER Plush leather chesterfields, open fireplaces, and antique bookcases make this one of the smartest nightclubs in town. After midnight, head downstairs to the late-night club or seek out secret doors revealing more hidden bars. *Gråbrødretorv 8. www.thejane.dk. Metro: Nørreport. Map p 104.*

★★ **KB3** KØDBYEN Another worthy addition to the Meatpacking District, giant KB3 has room for 800 revelers across its massive dance floor, lounge areas, outdoor smoking area, and 40-foot-long bar. *Kødboderne 3. ☎ 45 3323 4597.*

Where to Go

To pick up on the hippest bars, events and openings, check out the ***Copenhagen Post,*** a weekly English-language newspaper with a detailed entertainment section; find it online at www.cphpost.dk. Gay and lesbian visitors can check www.out-and-about.dk or download the free GAY CPH app for news, guides, and events. The Copenhagen Visitor Service can also provide up-to-date information: Vesterbrogade 4, ☎ **45 70 222 442,** www.visitcopenhagen.com.

The patio buzzes at Bakken.

www.kb3.dk. S-Tog: Dybbølsbro. Map p 104.

★★ **VEGA** VESTERBRO In the heart of once-gritty Vesterbro, VEGA is in a landmarked 1950s building. The mix of concerts and weekend club nights with top guest DJs makes this venue immensely popular; expect lines to get in. *Enghavevej 40. ☎ 45 3325 7011. www.vega.dk. Train: Enghave. Map p 104.*

Dinner Show

★★ **The Stage** TIVOLI Vegas comes to Copenhagen in a glitzy series of themed dinner shows, with live music, singing, stunts, and acrobatics. The circular venue, once a circus ring, has four dance floors for an after-dinner boogie. *Jernbanegade 8. ☎ 45 3316 3700. www.wallmans.dk. Tickets 529DKK–1,399DKK, includes dinner. Bus 5A, 6A, 14. Map p 104.*

Gay Copenhagen

★★ **Oscar Bar Café** RÅDHUSPLADSEN Copenhagen's best-known gay cafe serves draught beers, coffees, and a straightforward menu with omelets, nachos, salads, sandwiches, and steaks. Come down for the Friday night party, when DJs play R'n'B and soul. *Rådhuspladsen 77. ☎ 45 3312 0999. www.oscarbarcafe.dk. Bus: 2A, 12, 26, 33. Map p 104.*

★ **Vela Gay Club** VESTERBRO This small, cramped lesbian nightclub has a vaguely Oriental theme. The tiny bar is always packed but the party really gets going after midnight at the weekend, helped along by a cracking cocktail menu.

A concert crowd at VEGA.

Getting together at the Oscar Bar Café.

Viktoriagade 2–4. ☎ 45 3331 3419. www.velagayclub.dk. Bus: 6A, 9A, 26, 31. Map p 104.

Live Music

★ Copenhagen JazzHouse LATIN QUARTER Come here for jazz concerts every night but Monday, from both emerging stars and established legends; they're followed by a dance club in the basement after midnight on Friday and Saturday. Buy tickets through the website to get discounts. *Niels Hemmingsens Gade 10. ☎ 45 3315 4700. www.jazzhouse.dk. Metro: Nørreport. Map p 104.*

★★ Mojo Blues Bar RÅDHUSPLADSEN This hugely popular blues club has live sessions nightly; walls are plastered with black-and-white images of venerable blues players. Get here before 9:30pm to ensure a seat; book for Friday and Saturday nights, when there's a cover charge. *Løngangstræde 21c. ☎ 45 3311 6453. www.mojo.dk. Bus: 1A, 2A, 9A, 12, 26, 33. Map p 104.*

★★ Rust NØRREBRO Mostly indie or hip-hop bands looking for a break play regular gigs at Rust. Friday and Saturday club nights sprawl over three floors until 5am, showcasing some of Denmark's finest DJs and an impressive roster of international names and producers. *Guldbergsgade 8. ☎ 45 3524 5200. www.rust.dk. Metro: Nørreport. Map p 104.*

★★★ The Standard NYHAVN The high-profile brainchild of Noma co-founder Claus Meyer and musician Niels Lan Doky, this dinner and jazz club is housed in a waterside art deco building, serving up international music acts alongside quality cuisine. *Havnegade 44. ☎ 45 7214 8808. www.thestandardcph.dk. Metro: Kongens Nytorv. Map p 104.*

Copenhagen JazzHouse draws headliners such as Sun Ra Arkestra and Marshall Allen.

8 The Best Arts & Entertainment

Copenhagen Arts & Entertainment

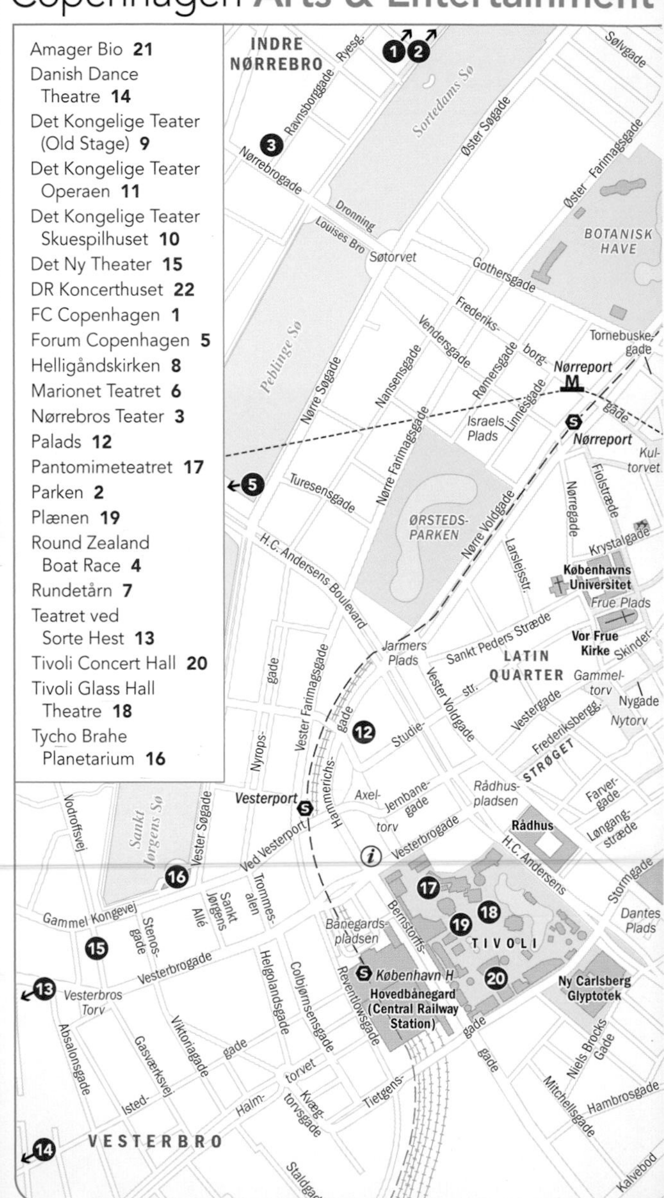

Previous page: Outdoor theatre in Tivoli.

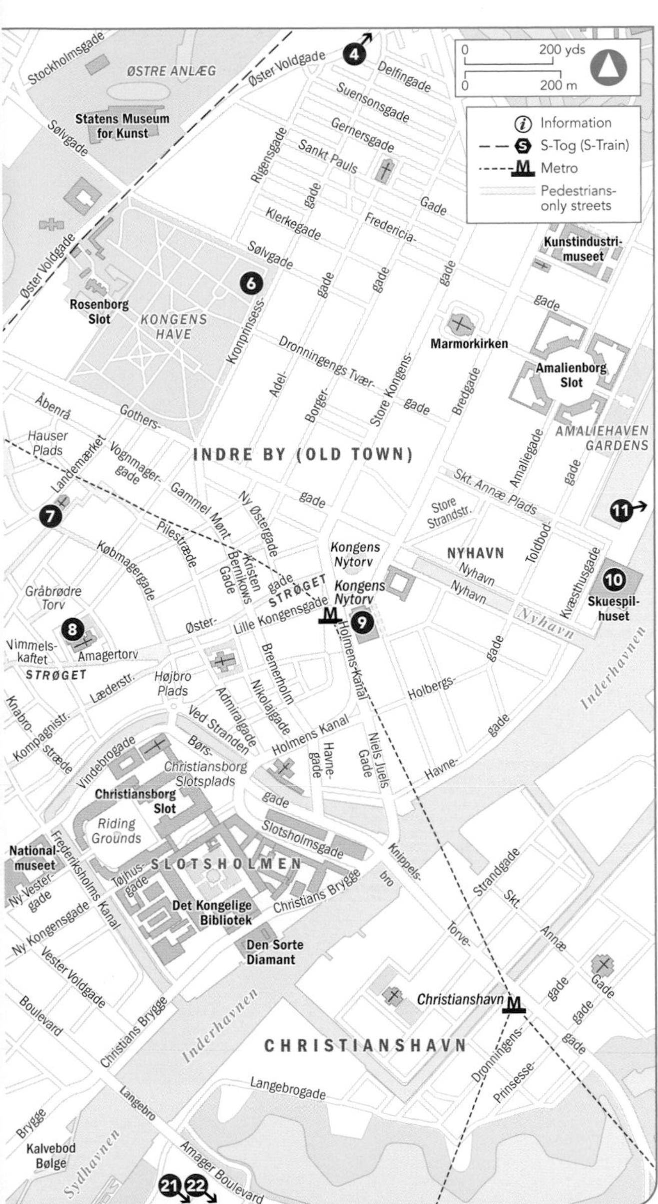
0 200 yds
0 200 m
Information
S-Tog (S-Train)
Metro
Pedestrians-only streets
Stockholmsgade
ØSTRE ANLÆG
Øster Voldgade
Delfingade
Suensonsgade
Gernersgade
Sankt Pauls Gade
Statens Museum for Kunst
Sølvgade
Rigensgade
Klerkegade
Fredericia-gade
Kunstindustri-museet
Rosenborg Slot
KONGENS HAVE
Kronprinsess-gade
Dronningens Tvær-gade
Marmorkirken
Amalienborg Slot
AMALIEHAVEN GARDENS
Adel-gade
Borger-gade
Store Kongens-gade
Bredgade
Åbenrå
Gothers-gade
Hauser Plads
Landemærket
Vognmager-gade
INDRE BY (OLD TOWN)
Gammel Mønt
Ny Østergade
Skt. Annæ Plads
Store Strandstr.
Amaliegade
Toldbod-gade
Pilestræde
Købmagergade
Kristen Bernikows Gade
Kongens Nytorv
NYHAVN
Nyhavn
Kvæsthusgade
Skuespil-huset
Gråbrødre Torv
STRØGET
Lille Kongensgade
Holmens Kanal
Vimmels-kaftet
Amagertorv
Øster-gade
Læderstr.
Højbro Plads
Bremerholm
Nikolajgade
Admiralgade
Ved Stranden
Holbergs-gade
Inderhavnen
Knabro-stræde
Kompagnistr.
Vindebrogade
Børs-gade
Christiansborg Slotsplads
Havne-gade
Niels Juels Gade
Christiansborg Slot
Riding Grounds
Slotsholmsgade
National-museet
Frederiksholms Kanal
Tøjhus-gade
SLOTSHOLMEN
Christians Brygge
Knippels-bro
Strandgade
Ny Vester-gade
Det Kongelige Bibliotek
Ny Kongensgade
Torve-gade
Skt. Annæ Gade
Den Sorte Diamant
Vester Voldgade
Christianshavn
Boulevard
CHRISTIANSHAVN
Dronningens-gade
Prinsesse-gade
Langebrogade
Langebro
Brygge
Kalvebod Bølge
Sydhavnen
Amager Boulevard

Arts & Entertainment **Best Bets**

Best **Seat in the Arts Scene**
★★★ Det Kongelige Teater Skuespilhus, *Sankt Annæ Plads 36 (p 121)*

Best **Acoustics**
★★★ Operaen, *Ekvipagemestervej 10 (p 119)*

Best **Live Music Venue**
★★ Plænen (Open-air Stage Tivoli), *Vesterbrogade 3 (p 120)*

Best for **Dance Performances**
★★★ Danish Dance Theatre, *Pasteursvej 20 (p 119)*

Best **Spot for Formal Dressing**
★★★ Det Kongelige Teater Old Stage, *Kongens Nytorv 2 (p 121)*

Best **Venue for Musicals**
★★ Det Ny Theater, *Gammel Kongevej 29 (p 117)*

Biggest **Moviehouse**
★★ Palads, *Axeltorv 9 (p 119)*

Strangest **Venue for Concerts**
★★ Rundetårn, *Købmagergade 52a (p 118)*

Biggest **Rock Festival**
★★★ Roskilde Festival, *Roskilde (p 122)*

Best **Venue to See *Hamlet***
★★★ Kronborg Castle, *Helsingør (p 122)*

Amager Bio, one of the city's biggest music venues.

Copenhagen Arts & Entertainment A to Z

Children's' Entertainment

★ kids Marionet Teatret KONGENS HAVE Families can watch free kiddies' shows daily in summer at the Marionet. Subject matter is quite eccentric. You'll find the puppet theater in the northeast corner of Kongens Have in a small pavilion. *Kronprinsessgade 2. ☎ 45 3312 1229. www.marionetteatret.dk. Tickets free. June 1–Sept 7 2pm & 3pm. Metro: Nørreport. Map p 114.*

★★★ kids Pantomimeteatret Tivoli TIVOLI Decked out in the style of a garish Chinese pavilion, this theater just inside the main Tivoli entrance features mime, dance, and pantomimes for a young audience. *Vesterbrogade 3. ☎ 45 3312 1012. billetnet.dk. Ticket prices vary. Bus 2A, 6A, 12, 26. Map p 114.*

Concert Halls

★★ Amager Bio AMAGERBRO One of the city's biggest music venues, Amager Bio stages up to 125 concerts a year; its eclectic line-ups encompass everything from classical and opera to bluesy rock, heavy metal, and electronica. Housed in a former cinema, the 1600-capacity hall has great acoustics. *Øresundsvej 6. ☎ 45 3286 0880. www.amagerbio.dk. Ticket prices vary. Metro: Amagerbro. Map p 114.*

★★ kids Det Ny Theater VESTERBRO Built in 1908, the majestic Danish home of international musicals is highly ornate, inside and out. *Gammel Kongevej 29. ☎ 45 3325 5075. www.detnyteater.dk. Ticket prices vary. Bus: 6A, 9A, 26, 31. Map p 114.*

★★ DR Koncerthuset ØRESTADEN Part of the trend-setting Ørestaden development (see p 31), this critically-acclaimed venue for world-class concerts was designed by French architect Jean Nouvel. It boasts an audience capacity of 1,600, a stage that accommodates 200, and four recording studios. *Emil Holms Kanal 20. ☎ 45 3520 6262. www.dr.dk/koncerthuset. Ticket prices vary. Metro: Vestamager. Map p 114.*

★★ Helligåndskirken STRØGET In summer, catch weekly organ recitals in this grand old red-brick church; in winter, you can hear a series of the classics (Brahms, Fauré) and Gregorian chant recitals. *Niels Hemmingsens Gade 5. ☎ 45 3315 4144. www.helligaandskirken.dk. Tickets free–140DKK. Metro: Kongens Nytorv. Map p 114.*

The grand Det Ny Teater has found new life as a home for musicals.

Tivoli Concert Hall hosts classical and some pop music.

★★ Nørrebros Teater NØRREBRO Known for encouraging up-and-coming talent, this theater puts on mainstream musicals, dance performances and comedy. The current director is homegrown dramatist Mette Wolf. *Ravnsborggade 3. ☎ 45 70 272 272. www.nbt.dk. Ticket prices vary. Metro: Nørreport. Map p 114.*

★★ Rundetårn (Round Tower) LATIN QUARTER Concerts held here year-round range from guitar soloists playing Rodrigo to Scarlatti clavichord concerts or samba jazz sessions. They are held in the Library Hall, which also hosts contemporary art exhibitions. ***Købmagergade 52a.*** *☎ 45 3373 0373. www.rundetaarn.dk. Tickets 70DKK–150DKK. Metro: Nørreport. Map p 114.*

★★ Tivoli Concert Hall TIVOLI Tivoli's main concert hall, built in 1956, is home to the Tivoli Symphony Orchestra. Nightly performances range from the New York Ballet to chamber ensembles to rock legends. *Tivoli Ticket Office,*

What's On

For the latest concert, theater, film, and event listings, pick up the weekly the ***Copenhagen Post,*** which has an excellent entertainment guide. Free copies can be found at various hotels, bars and cafes. ***Where2go Copenhagen,*** published quarterly, covers everything from design to shopping; international editions in English are found in most hotels. The Copenhagen Visitor Service is also very helpful: Vesterbrogade 4. ☎ 45 70 222 442. www.visitcopenhagen.com.

Vesterbrogade 3. ☎ 45 3312 1012. billetnet.dk. Ticket prices vary. Bus: 2A, 6A, 12, 26, 250S. Map p 114.

★ kids Tivoli Glass Hall Theatre TIVOLI Old-fashioned variety shows of varying standards, but good family fun, are housed in a lovely wrought-iron and glass pavilion. *Tivoli Ticket Office, Vesterbrogade 3. ☎ 45 3312 1012. billetnet.dk. Ticket prices vary. Bus: 2A, 6A, 12, 26, 250S. Map p 114.*

Dance

★★★ Danish Dance Theatre VESTERBRO Denmark's leading contemporary dance outfit has gone from strength to strength under the auspices of English dancemeister Tim Rushton. He presents a program of wildly imaginative modern dance; even if you are not usually a fan, give this company a chance. *Dansehallerne, Pasteursvej 20. ☎ 45 3388 8000. www.danskdanseteater.dk. Ticket prices vary. Metro: Nørreport. Map p 114.*

The colorful Palads Teatret cinema

IMAX and 3-D films accompany exhibits at the Tycho Brahe Planetarium.

Film

★★ Palads TIVOLI You can't fail to spot this brightly painted cinema complex near Tivoli. It is Copenhagen's biggest, with 17 screens. International blockbusters are shown in their native language with Danish subtitles. *Axeltorv 9. ☎ 45 7013 1211. www.nfbio.dk/palads. Tickets 70DKK–105DKK. Bus: 5A, 6A, 9A, 12, 14, 31, 34. Map p 114.*

★★★ kids Tycho Brahe Planetarium VESTERBRO Ten-minute ever-changing 3-D films exploring the mysteries of space are shown continually just off the foyer; you'll need to book ahead for the hour-long shows on the IMAX screen. *Gammel Kongevej 10. ☎ 45 3312 1224. www.tycho.dk. Tickets 144DKK, including 1 IMAX film or 1 3D movie. Bus: 9A, 31. Map p 114.*

Opera

★★★ Det Kongelige Teater Operaen (Opera House)
DOKØEN Henning Larson's masterly opera house is reputed to have

Rock concert at The Forum.

perfect acoustics. It has become the Danish turf of international opera stars and runs major-league productions of classics like *La Traviata* and *Der Rosenkavalier* in addition to experimental chamber works and symphony concerts. Smaller-scale productions take place in the Takkelloft, a so-called "black box" theater. *Ekvipagemestervej 10.* ☎ *45 3369 6933. www.kglteater.dk. Ticket prices vary. Boat: Harbor boat service from Nyhavn. Map p 114.*

Rock Venues

★★ Forum Copenhagen FREDERIKSBERG The Forum is a purpose-built venue with capacity for 10,000 standing in the stadium. Concerts, trade fairs, and fashion shows are held here. *Thomsens Plads 1.* ☎ *45 3247 2000. www.forumcopenhagen.dk. Ticket prices vary. Metro: Forum. Map p 114.*

★★ Parken ØSTERBRO Denmark's national stadium has played host to many rock stalwarts (Rolling Stones, Springsteen, Elton John) and is also the home of FC Copenhagen (see p 121). Crowd capacity is 40,000. *Øster Alle 50.* ☎ *45 3543 3131. www.parken.dk. Ticket prices vary. Train: Østerport. Map p 114.*

★★ Plænen (Open-air Stage Tivoli) TIVOLI Regular Friday Rock concerts are held over the summer at the open-air stage smack in the middle of Tivoli (p 10). Take wet-weather gear if it's

During July's Jazz Festival, music takes to the water on a floating stage.

The Royal Theater's elegant Old Stage now hosts ballets and concerts.

raining—there's no shelter. *Tivoli Ticket Office, Vesterbrogade 3. ☎ 45 3312 1012. www.billetnet.dk. Ticket prices vary. Bus: 2A, 12, 26, 250S. Map p 114.*

Sporting Events

★★ FC Copenhagen ØSTERBRO Copenhagen's soccer team plays from Parken, the stadium also used for mainstream rock concerts (p 120). The most successful club in Danish football, they have a considerable passionate following. *Øster Alle 50. ☎ 45 3543 7400. www.fck.dk. Ticket prices vary. Train: Østerport. Map p 114.*

★★ Round Zealand Boat Race HELSINGØR This classic annual boat race starts and ends in Helsingør, with hundreds of sailing ships covering a course of over 200 nautical miles around the island of Zealand—which means plenty of coastline vantage points for spectators to watch the action. This three-day event takes place at the end of June; there are also smaller regattas on the Øresund to watch all summer long. *Helsingør Sejlklub (Sjælland Rundt), Strandpromenaden 6. ☎ 45 2654 8494. www.sjaellandrundt.dk. Train Helsingør St. Map p 114.*

Theater

★★★ Det Kongelige Teater (Old Stage) KONGENS NYTORV Under the same aegis as the **Skuespilhuset** (see below) and **Operaen** (p 119), the granddaddy of Danish theater now hosts ballet and Sunday afternoon concerts. Performances in this fresco-ceilinged theater, built in 1748, are glamorous affairs, drawing a well-attired audience. *Kongens Nytorv 9. ☎ 45 3369 6933. www.kglteater.dk. Ticket prices vary. Metro: Kongens Nytorv. Map p 114.*

★★★ Det Kongelige Teater Skuespilhuset (Royal Danish Playhouse) NYHAVN A sister theater to the **Operaen** (p 119) across the Øresund, the handsome contemporary Playhouse is

Copenhagen Summertime

Scandinavia's hippest city goes into festival overdrive in summer. **Copenhagen Distortion** (www.cphdistortion.dk) kicks off with the biggest clubbing session of the year in June, with the **Jazz Festival** (www.festival.jazz.dk) close on its heels in July. **Copenhagen Summer Dance** (www.danskdanseteater.dk) rolls into town in August, while the **CPH:PIX** film festival keeps things lively in September (www.cphpix.dk). Out of town, July's weeklong **Roskilde Festival** (www.roskilde-festival.dk) is one of the biggest in Europe; attracting mainstream acts. Hamlet and other characters pay homage to Shakespeare (www.hamletsommer.dk) in the courtyard of Kronborg Castle in **Helsingør** during July and August. For further information about Copenhagen festivals, see p 158.

Denmark's national center of dramatic art. Designed by Danish firm Lundgård & Tranberg (see p 30), the building incorporates three stages, a tinted glass waterfront foyer, restaurant, and a wide wooden boardwalk. The Playhouse's year-round season includes both homegrown and foreign plays; most performances are in Danish. *Sankt Annæ Plads 36. ☎ 45 3369 6933. www.kglteater.dk. Ticket prices vary. Metro: Kongens Nytorv. Map p 114.*

★★ Teatret ved Sorte Hest (Black Horse Theater)

VESTERBRO This compact theater, tucked away in an old coach house, has won attention for introducing new stars to the Copenhagen arts firmament. Currently there are five avant-garde productions per year, mainly in Danish. *Vesterbrogade 150. ☎ 45 3331 0606. www.teatretvedsortehest.dk. Ticket prices vary. Bus: 6A Map p 114.* ●

9 The Best **Lodging**

Copenhagen **Lodging**

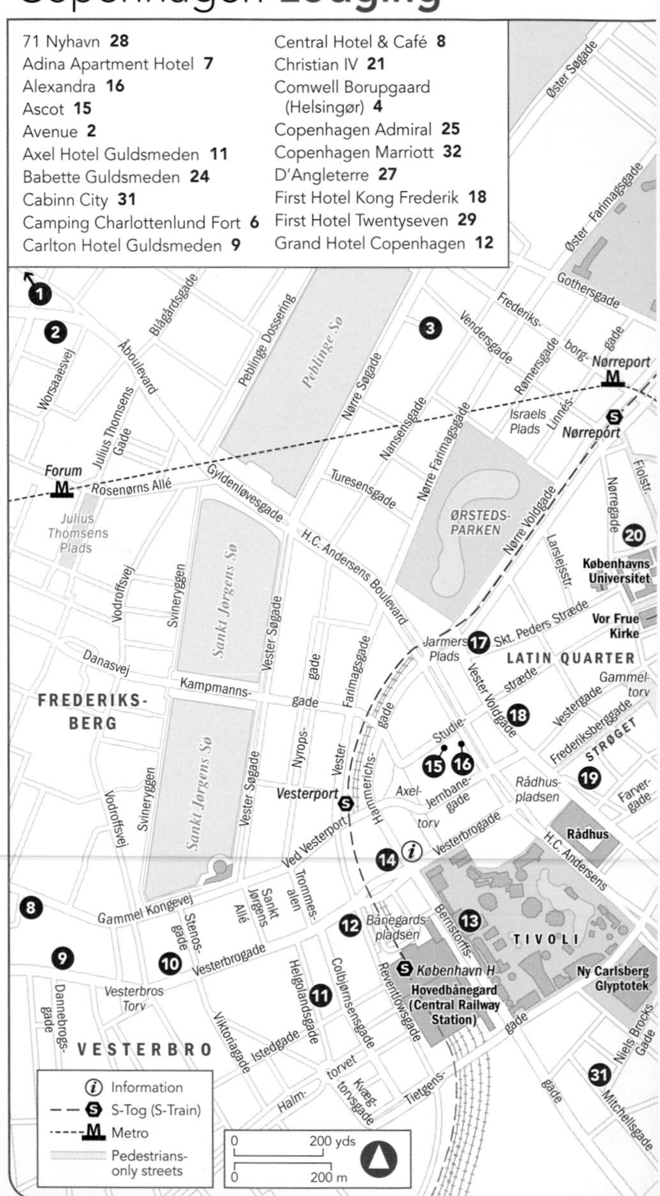

Previous page: Guest room at Nimb.

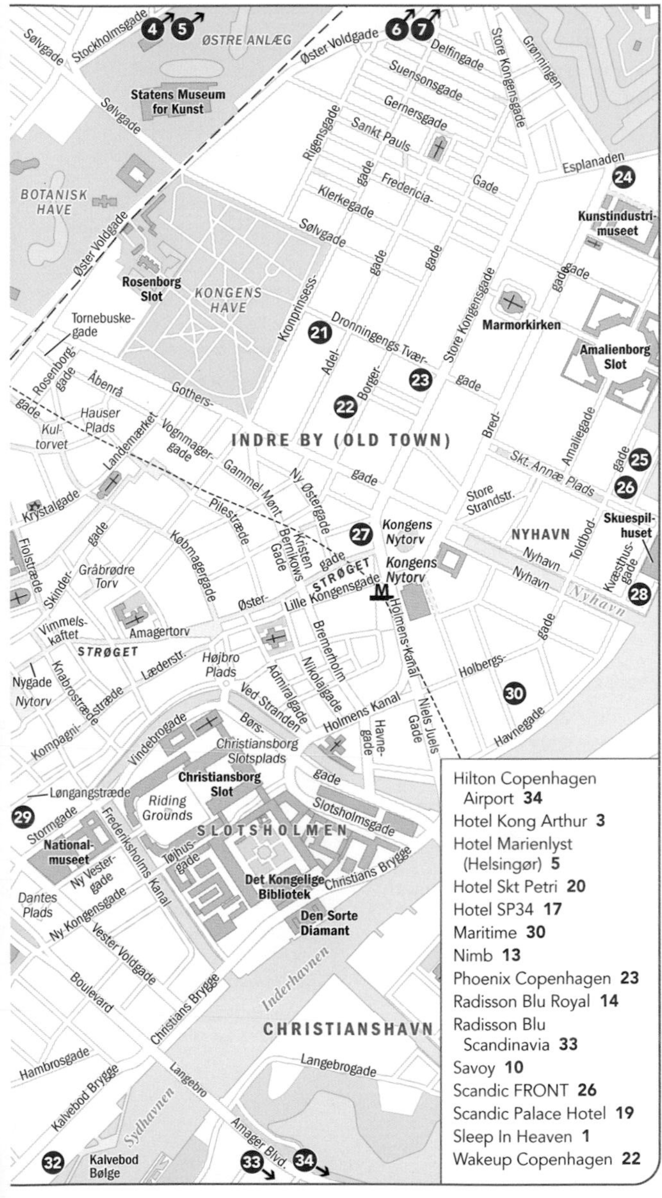
ØSTRE ANLÆG
Statens Museum for Kunst
BOTANISK HAVE
Rosenborg Slot
KONGENS HAVE
Kunstindustrimuseet
Marmorkirken
Amalienborg Slot
INDRE BY (OLD TOWN)
Kongens Nytorv
NYHAVN
Skuespilhuset
STRØGET
Gråbrødre Torv
Amagertorv
Højbro Plads
Christiansborg Slotsplads
Christiansborg Slot
Riding Grounds
SLOTSHOLMEN
Nationalmuseet
Det Kongelige Bibliotek
Den Sorte Diamant
Dantes Plads
Inderhavnen
CHRISTIANSHAVN
Sydhavnen
Kalvebod Bølge
Sølvgade
Stockholmsgade
Øster Voldgade
Delfingade
Suensonsgade
Gernersgade
Sankt Pauls Gade
Fredericiagade
Klerkegade
Rigensgade
Store Kongensgade
Grønningen
Esplanaden
Kronprinsessegade
Dronningens Tværgade
Adelgade
Borgergade
Bredgade
Amaliegade
Skt. Annæ Plads
Store Strandstr.
Toldbodgade
Kvæsthusgade
Nyhavn
Holbergsgade
Havnegade
Niels Juels Gade
Holmens Kanal
Havnegade
Holmens Kanal
Lille Kongensgade
Østergade
Bremerholm
Nikolajgade
Admiralgade
Ved Stranden
Børsgade
Slotsholmsgade
Christians Brygge
Tøjhusgade
Frederiksholms Kanal
Ny Vestergade
Ny Kongensgade
Vester Voldgade
Boulevard
Hambrosgade
Kalvebod Brygge
Langebro
Amager Blvd.
Langebrogade
Tornebuskegade
Rosenborggade
Åbenrå
Gothersgade
Hauser Plads
Kultorvet
Landemærket
Vognmagergade
Gammel Mønt
Ny Østergade
Kristen Berrikows Gade
Pilestræde
Købmagergade
Krystalgade
Fiolstræde
Skindergade
Vimmelskaftet
Lædersrtr.
Nygade
Nytorv
Knabrostræde
Kompagnistræde
Vindebrogade
Løngangstræde
Stormgade
M
Hilton Copenhagen Airport 34
Hotel Kong Arthur 3
Hotel Marienlyst (Helsingør) 5
Hotel Skt Petri 20
Hotel SP34 17
Maritime 30
Nimb 13
Phoenix Copenhagen 23
Radisson Blu Royal 14
Radisson Blu Scandinavia 33
Savoy 10
Scandic FRONT 26
Scandic Palace Hotel 19
Sleep In Heaven 1
Wakeup Copenhagen 22

Lodging Best Bets

Most **Palatial Hotel**
★★★ Hotel D'Angleterre $$$$$ *Kongens Nytorv 34 (p 130)*

Best **Water Views**
★★ Copenhagen Admiral Hotel $$$$ *Toldbodgade 24 (p 129)*

Best for **Fireside Romance**
★★★ Avenue Hotel $$$ *Åboulevard 29 (p 128)*

Best **Family Hotel**
★★ Christian IV $$ *Dronningens Tværgade 45 (p 129)*

Best for **Business Travelers**
★★★ Radisson Blu Scandinavia $$$$ *Amager Boulevard 70 (p 133)*

Best **Boutique Hotel & Spa**
★★★ Axel Hotel Guldsmeden $$$ *Helgolandsgade 7–11 (p 127)*

Best **Boutique on a Budget**
★★★ Wakeup Copenhagen $ *Borgergade 9 (p 134)*

Best for **Fashionistas**
★★★ First Hotel Twentyseven $$$$ *Løngangstræde 27 (p 130)*

Best for **Wealthy Stylistas**
★★ Hotel Skt Petri $$$$$ *Krystalgade 22 (p 131)*

Best **Danish Design Showcase**
★★ Hotel Alexandra $$$ *H C Andersens Boulevard 8 (p 127)*

Best **Copenhagen Landmark**
★★ Radisson Blu Royal $$$$$ *Hammerichsgade 1 (p 132)*

Only **Hotel Along Nyhavn**
★★ 71 Nyhavn Hotel $$$$ *Nyhavn 71 (p 127)*

Best **Carbon Neutral Hotel**
★★ Hotel Kong Arthur $$ *Nørre Søgade 11 (p 131)*

Best **Self-Catering**
★★★ Adina Apartment Hotel $$$ *Amerika Plads 7 (p 127)*

Best **Budget Hotel**
★★ Savoy Hotel $$ *Vesterbrogade 34 (p 133)*

Best **Hostel**
★★★ Sleep in Heaven $ *Struenseegade 7 (p 134)*

Best **Old-World English Charm**
★★★ First Hotel Kong Frederik $$$$ *Vester Voldgade 25 (p 131)*

Best **Tivoli Views**
★★★ Hotel Nimb $$$$ *Bernstorffsgade 5 (p 132)*

The Central Hotel & Café boasts being the world's smallest hotel, with just one room.

Copenhagen **Lodging A to Z**

★★ 71 Nyhavn NYHAVN The only hotel along party-loving Nyhavn, 71 is a soothing mixture of contemporary style and original features in two superbly renovated gabled warehouses. Rooms are decorated in neutral colors; some have harbor or canal views. If you don't feel like going out, the hotel restaurant Pakhushælderen serves up a mean Danish/French fusion menu. *Nyhavn 71. ☎ 45 3343 6200. www.71nyhavnhotel.com. 130 units. Doubles 1,099DKK–4,500DKK w/ breakfast. AE, DC, MC, V. Metro: Kongens Nytorv. Map p 124.*

★★★ kids Adina Apartment Hotel NORDHAVN A 15-minute walk along pretty Langelinie north of the city center, the cool Adina is based at the glossy development near the ferry terminal. This is one of Copenhagen's best self-catering hotels, with stylish modern apartments and top-notch facilities including a pool, gym, and restaurant. Ask for a seventh-floor room for great views over the city. *Amerika plads 7. ☎ 45 3969 1000. www.adina.dk. 128 units. From 850DKK. AE, MC, V. Train: S-Tog to Østerport. Map p 124.*

★★ Alexandra RÅDHUSPLADSEN The lobby at the Alexandra is decked out with stylish Danish furniture and art, while 13 plush "design" rooms feature chairs by such illustrious Danish furniture designers as Finn Juhl and Arne Jacobsen. Light sleepers should opt for standard rooms at the back of the hotel, however—the "design" rooms overlook noisy Rådhuspladsen. One floor is equipped with anti-allergy bedding, giving the place a coveted Green Key award for environmental considerations. *H C Andersens Boulevard 8. ☎ 45 3374 4444. www.hotel-alexandra.dk. 61 units. Doubles 1,075DKK–2,075DKK w/breakfast. AE, MC, V. Bus: 10, 33. Map p 124.*

★ Ascot TIVOLI You'll be greeted at the door of the Ascot by staff wearing full Danish national costume; upstairs, the rooms are spotless and reasonably sized for Copenhagen. The hotel's array of connected restaurants includes the Reef N' Beef, serving an unusual menu of bush foods such as Australian kangaroo and vegemite steak; there are also tapas and Italian eateries in the hotel. Tivoli is only a short walk away. *Studiestræde 61. ☎ 45 3312 6000. www.ascot-hotel.dk. 194 units. Doubles 1,790DKK–3,190DKK w/breakfast. AE, MC, V. Bus: 5A, 6A, 14, 33. Map p 124.*

★★★ Axel Hotel Guldsmeden VESTERBRO At this stylish, Balinese-influenced hotel (part of the excellent Guldsmeden group), rooms have four-poster beds and tiny but perfectly constructed tiled bathrooms with showers and luxury toiletries. Most food and drink is organic, the chunky crockery is

The Alexandra Hotel near Tivoli and Rådhuspladsen.

FairTrade, and there is a beautifully designed spa tucked in the basement. *Helgolandsgade 11.* ☎ *45 3331 3266. www.hotelguldsmeden.com. 125 units. Doubles 995DKK–2,995DKK. AE, DC, MC, V. Bus: 6A, 10, 14, 26. Map p 124.*

★★★ kids **Avenue** FREDERIKSBERG Indisputably my favorite Copenhagen hotel for its relaxed atmosphere, The Avenue welcomes guests with roaring open fires, flickering candles, a well-stocked bar, board games, and a library—it's a real home-from-home. Rooms are spacious and soothingly decorated in a pale palette, with pristine white-tiled bathrooms. A limited but tasty menu of classics such as tapas and Caesar salads are served throughout the day in the bar. There's also a sunny terrace at the back, parking (28 spots), and free Wi-Fi. *Åboulevard 29.* ☎ *45 3537 3111. www.avenuehotel.dk. 68 units. Doubles from 1,095DKK w/breakfast. AE, DC, MC, V. Metro: Forum. Map p 124.*

★★★ **Babette Guldsmeden** FREDERIKSSTADEN Another of the exceptional Guldsmeden boutique hotels, the Babette has a gorgeous Balinese-meets-Scandinavian décor and rooms with four-poster beds and free-standing baths. The Babette's main selling point is its proximity to many of Copenhagen's major sights; the Little Mermaid (p 59), Designmuseum Danmark (p 27), Amalienborg Palace (p 40) and the exclusive shops of Bredgade. Nip round the corner for *smørrebrød* at Café Petersborg (see p 95). *Bredgade 78.* ☎ *45 3314 1500. www.guldsmedenhotels.com. 98 units. Doubles 995DKK–2,395DKK. AE, MC, V. Metro: Kongens Nytorv. Map p 124.*

★★★ **Cabinn City** TIVOLI It's certainly not a luxury destination, but what you *do* get in this purpose-built, low-cost concept hotel is a serviceable modern room with private bathroom and free internet access. Breakfast and parking are optional extras. If you're happy with the basics and don't expect to be pampered, this is a good bet in a generally very pricey city. *Mitchellsgade 14.* ☎ *45 3346 1616. www.cabinn.com. 352 units. From 495DKK. MC, V. Bus: 1A, 5A, 250S. Map p 124.*

★★ kids **Camping Charlottenlund Fort** CHARLOTTENLUND Situated by a long, sandy beach on the Øresund, a mere 6km from the center of Copenhagen, this campsite is ideal for families who want the great outdoors combined with city sightseeing. Tents, caravans, and mobile homes are all welcome. Facilities include communal restrooms, laundry, hot-dog stands, and

Four-poster bed at the Hotel Babette Guldsmeden.

an on-site fast-food restaurant. Kids love the pedalos, bouncy castle, and safe swimming in the virtually tideless sea. Open March to October. *Strandvejen 144B, Charlottenlund. ☎ 45 44 22 00 65. www.campingcopenhagen.dk. 98 units. From 35DKK. 6km north of Copenhagen. MC, V. Bus no. 1A runs to Copenhagen center every 10–20 min. Map p 124.*

★★ Carlton Hotel Guldsmeden

VESTERBRO If you're seeking a bargain but don't want to sacrifice on style, try the Carlton, the Vesterbro outpost of the chic Guldsmeden chain. Rooms are decorated in French Colonial style with teak four-poster beds, gilt mirrors, and Persian rugs. The breakfast menu is largely organic. Parking at the back. *Vesterbrogade 66 ☎ 45 3322 1500. www.hotelguldsmeden.com. 74 units. Doubles 995DKK–2,295DKK. AE, DC, MC, V. Bus: 6A, 26. Map p 124.*

★★ Central Hotel & Café

VESTERBRO Billed as "the world's smallest hotel" this cute five-seat coffee shop also has just one room upstairs in a former shoemaker's garret. The room is barely bigger than its bed but what it lacks in size it makes up for with charm, resembling a classic ocean-liner cabin with built-in wood furniture. *Tullinsgade 1. ☎ 45 2615 0186. www.centralhotelogcafe.dk. 1,800DKK w/ breakfast. AE, MC, V. Map p 124.*

★★ kids Christian IV

FREDERIKSSTADEN A small, family-run hotel in a quiet backwater, this is an ideal base for families with children who can run off energy in the nearby Kongens Have park (see p 85). The rooms are starkly decorated in grays and blues, with contrasting scarlet wall hangings and curtains; there is a generous buffet breakfast and the cheery staff will advise on nearby eating options. *Dronningens Tværgade 45. ☎ 45 3332 1044. www.hotelchristianiv.dk. 42 units. Doubles 795DKK–1,995DKK w/breakfast. MC, V. Metro: Kongens Nytorv. Map p 124.*

★★ Copenhagen Admiral

NYHAVN A venerable old boy on the Copenhagen hotel scene, the Admiral stretches along the waterfront in a warehouse dating from 1787. The interior is crammed with original pine beams, and a nautical theme runs through the ground floor; guest rooms are decorated with teak. Those at the front of the hotel have a bird's-eye view of the Opera House (p 119). The hotel's restaurant, SALT (p 101) is a gastronomic treat in a brick-vaulted dining room. *Toldbodgade 24–28. ☎ 45 7022 2442. www.admiralhotel.dk. 366 units. Rooms 745DKK–2,895DKK. AE, DC, MC, V. Metro: Kongens Nytorv. Map p 124.*

★★ Copenhagen Marriott

TIVOLI This luxurious chain hotel has a wonderful position overlooking the waters of Sydhavnen. Plenty of business travelers come here to use the extensive meeting facilities, but vacationers will be happy enough with the gleaming health club, city views from the sunny Terraneo Terrace, and spacious, elegantly furnished guest rooms. *Kalvebod Brygge 5. ☎ 45 8833 9900.*

The Copenhagen Admiral hotel has a prime waterfront location.

Minimalist cool at First Hotel Twentyseven.

www.marriott.com/hotels/travel/cphdk-copenhagen-marriott-hotel. 402 units. Doubles 2,095DKK–3,699DKK. AE, DC, MC, V. Bus: 5A, 34, 66. Map p 124.

★★★ D'Angleterre KONGENS NYTORV Dominating Copenhagen's buzzing main square, this palatial hotel is synonymous with luxury and sophistication. Opened in 1855, it is presently under the auspices of NP Hotels, who have restored the grand high-ceilinged public areas. Well-appointed rooms are carefully furnished with traditional Danish pieces in chic neutral tones; suites come in four levels of opulence, with prices to match. There's a glamorous Michelin-star restaurant, a champagne bar, and a large basement spa called Amazing Space. *Kongens Nytorv 34. ☎ 45 3312 0095. www.dangleterre.com. 90 units. Rooms 4,500DKK–47,500DKK. AE, DC, MC, V. Metro: Kongens Nytorv. Map p 124.*

★★ First Hotel Kong Frederik RÅDHUSPLADSEN In an ancient building tucked away from the din of Rådhuspladsen, Kong Frederik retains the air of an old-fashioned English country hotel. There are creaking corridors, hunting prints, chintz-upholstered bedroom furniture, wood-paneled walls, and a flower-filled courtyard. Its charming Italian restaurant serves freshly made pizzas, antipasti or al dente pasta dishes alongside a decent range of wines. *Vester Voldgade 25. ☎ 45 3312 5902. www.firsthotels.com/Destinations/Copenhagen. 110 units. From 736DKK. AE, DC, MC, V. Bus: 5A, 6A, 14, 10, 33. Map p 124.*

★★★ First Hotel Twentyseven RÅDHUSPLADSEN A bastion of cool, Twentyseven is well placed near the major museums. Staff members are unbelievably hip and helpful, and the rooms (ask for one at the back if you want to sleep past 5:30am) are designed in smart reds and white, complete with inky-black bathrooms. A large breakfast buffet is served daily in the Wine Room, and the enclosed courtyard is a great spot for candle-lit evenings of wine, cocktails, and music. The popular Honey Ryder Cocktail Lounge (p 109) has mixologists whipping up all manner of creative concoctions. *Løngangstræde 27. ☎ 45 7027 5627. www.firsthotels.com/Our-hotels/Hotels-in-Denmark/Copenhagen. 200 units. From 662DKK w/breakfast. MC, V. Bus: 1A, 2A, 9A, 26, 37. Map p 124.*

★★ Grand Hotel Copenhagen VESTERBRO Set in a pastel-painted mansion dating back to 1890, the Grand is a bit generic inside, but location is all: it's close to the Copenhagen Visitor Service, Tivoli, and the train station, with easy access to the airport. The rooms come in six sizes from small double to suite; don't be tempted by the tiny savings price-wise on the small doubles because spacewise they are tiny too. There's a decent Italian restaurant, Frascati, often full of business travelers. *Vesterbrogade 9.* ☎ *45 3327 6900. www.grandhotelcopenhagen.com. 161 units. From 500DKK per person sharing w/breakfast. AE, DC, MC, V. Bus: 6A, 26. Map p 124.*

★ Hilton Copenhagen Airport KASTRUP Bland and functional the rooms may be, but this Hilton is connected to the airport's Terminal 3 and so is the perfect pit-stop for travelers on overnight trips. It's a 20-minute metro journey right to all the main sights of the city, so you can dine out in central Copenhagen and get back to the hotel in time for a last drink in the swish Axis Bar & Lounge. Too tired to move? There's also a pool and spa. *Ellehammersvej 20.* ☎ *45 3250 1501. www.hilton.co.uk/copenhagen. 378 units. Doubles 1,395DKK–4,195DKK. AE, DC, MC, V. Metro: Kastrup. Map p 124.*

★★ Hotel Kong Arthur NØRREPORT In a handsome 18th-century building, this hotel has been transformed into a CO_2-neutral environment. Bedrooms are jauntily decked out with striped bedspreads in pastel hues and carefully chosen artwork. In the summer, you can enjoy a beer or breakfast on the little terrace. Free access to a soothing spa and the location in trendy, cafe-filled Nørreport add to the attraction of this convivial hotel. *Nørre Søgade 11.* ☎ *45 3311 1212. www.kongarthur.dk. 155 units. Doubles 1,540DKK–2,880DKK w/breakfast. AE, MC, V. Metro: Nørreport. Map p 124.*

★★★ kids Hotel Skt Petri LATIN QUARTER A renovated warehouse with star quality, this vibrant design hotel makes a good claim to providing Copenhagen's hippest accommodation. The guestrooms are perfectly appointed, as befits a five-star establishment, but it's the enormous lobby that grabs attention; a huge black reception desk, walls scattered with artwork, and contemporary furniture. Dine in at the smart but casual modern restaurant Central Kitchen or hang out in bakery-cum-bar BRØL, which serves freshly baked bread, pastries, and craft beers. There's also a sun terrace and plunge pool. *Krystalgade 22.* ☎ *45 3345 9100. www.sktpetri.com. 268 units. Doubles 1,431DKK–3,031DKK w/breakfast. AE, DC, MC, V. Metro: Nørreport. Map p 124.*

★★ Hotel SP34 LATIN QUARTER A boutique hideway befitting its bohemian district, Hotel SP34 has applied smart, muted colors and typical Scandi design aesthetics to its three high-ceilinged townhouses a stone's throw from the city hall

Bohemian hip at Hotel SP34 in the university area.

An executive suite at the Nimb hotel.

square and Strøget. An all-organic breakfast is served in one of three restaurants, there's a daily afternoon wine hour at the bar, and for movie buffs the hotel has its own private 25-seat cinema. *Sankt Peders Stræde 34. ☎ 45 3313 3000. www.brochner-hotels.dk. 118 units. Doubles from 1,200DKK w/breakfast. AE, MC, V. Bus: 2A, 5A, 6A, 14. Map p 124.*

★ Maritime KONGENS NYTORV Quietly located in a residential street a step away from Nyhavn, this unassuming place has brightly decorated if slightly spartan rooms and old-fashioned bathrooms, all with showers. It's reasonable value for the center of Copenhagen if you don't mind the simple accommodations. *Peder Skrams Gade 19. ☎ 45 3313 4882. www.hotel-maritime.dk. 64 units. Doubles 895DKK–1,900DKK. MC, V. Metro: Kongens Nytorv. Map p 124.*

★★★ Nimb TIVOLI The boutique hotel arm of the vast Nimb entertainment empire won't fail to impress; most of its 17 individually designed suites come with antique furniture and open fires, and are particularly popular with fashion-conscious travelers. The food at gourmet restaurant Nimb Terrasse (p 99) is praised for its seasonal cuisine, while Nimb Brasserie offers less formal dining. Combine all that with great views over Tivoli and this place is a sure-fire winner, albeit an expensive one. The hotel is currently expanding as part of the Tivoli Corner development and will add 20 more suites, as well as a stunning roof terrace with pool, restaurant, and bar, by the end of 2017. *Bernstorffsgade 5. ☎ 45 8870 0000. www.nimb.dk. 17 units. Rooms 3,000DKK–25,000DKK. AE, DC, MC, V. Bus: 2A, 5A, 9A, 250S. Map p 124.*

★ Phoenix Copenhagen FREDERIKSSTADEN The glamorous big sister of The Grand (p 130) boasts a fine 17th-century home in gentrified Bredgade. Redolent of a mini-Versailles inside, the rooms and public spaces may be a little too gilded for some tastes, and the suites are positively over the top, but the overall impression is one of refined gentility from a bygone age. There's a sleek restaurant and an English-inspired brasserie and café. *Bredgade 37. ☎ 45 3395 9500. www.phoenixcopenhagen.dk. 213 units. From 590DKK per person sharing w/breakfast. AE, DC, MC, V. Metro: Kongens Nytorv. Map p 124.*

★ Radisson Blu Royal TIVOLI Copenhagen's iconic and original skyscraper hotel, designed from top to toe by Arne Jacobsen (see p 78), is visible all over the city. There are Egg chairs in the foyer, a devilishly beautiful twisted spiral staircase, and elements of his work throughout guest rooms, all updated with modern amenities such as free Wi-Fi. Suite 606 contains original Jacobsen pieces. (Jacobsen, however, reportedly hated many of his creations for the hotel and refused to use the cutlery.) Book dinner at the Alberto K restaurant—the views across the city are spectacular. *Hammerichsgade 1. ☎ 45 3342 6000. www.radissonblu.com/en/royalhotel-copenhagen. 260 units. Doubles 1,745DKK–3,045DKK w/breakfast. AE, DC, MC, V. Bus: 5A, 6A, 9A, 12, 14, 31. Map p 124.*

★★ Radisson Blu Scandinavia AMAGER Close to the train station and 15 minutes from the airport, Copenhagen's soon-to-be expanded premier business hotel has facilities for small meetings on up to conferences of 1,750 delegates. Junior suites and business-class rooms enjoy great views towards Nyhavn. Most appealing are the urban-themed standard bedrooms with chunky glass walls behind the beds and good-sized bathrooms. Three restaurants, two bars, a casino, and a fitness center complete the slick package. *Amager Boulevard 70. ☎ 45 3815 6500. www.radissonblu.com/en/scandinaviahotel-copenhagen. 544 units. Doubles 1,645DKK–3,045DKK w/breakfast. AE, DC, MC, V. Metro: Amagerbro; Islands Brygge. Bus: 5A, 77. Map p 124.*

★★ Savoy VESTERBRO Despite the ritzy name, this Savoy is a bargain hotel in a handy location not too far from the train station. Rooms are plainly furnished along clean Scandinavian lines, all with windows overlooking a peaceful internal courtyard. Choose a top-floor room for sloping ceilings and views over city rooftops. *Vesterbrogade 34. ☎ 45 3326 7500. www.savoyhotel.dk. 66 units. Doubles 900DKK–2,500DKK w/breakfast. MC, V. Bus: 6A, 9A, 26, 31. Map p 124.*

★★★ Scandic FRONT NYHAVN Part of the reliable Scandic hotels chain, this is one of the best-value stays in town. Black lacquered furniture, plum bed throws, plasma screen TVs, and quality white linen combine with classy bathrooms in pale shades. Ask for a room overlooking the Øresund and Operaen (p 119). Downstairs there's a small gym, and breakfast is served in the bar, which doubles as a diner serving classic grilled dishes. *Sankt Annæ Plads 21. ☎ 45 3313 3400. www.scandichotels.com/Hotels/Denmark/Copenhagen. 132 units. Doubles 1,116DKK–2,995DKK. AE, DC, MC, V. Metro: Kongens Nytorv. Map p 124.*

★ Scandic Palace Hotel RÅDHUSPLADSEN The grand old lady of Rådhuspladsen, built in 1910, is sharp and contemporary in style inside, although some rooms are tiny. Still, it's at the heart of Copenhagen's busiest square and right opposite Tivoli; this too has its drawbacks—traffic by day and reveling Danes by night. *Rådhuspladsen 57. ☎ 45 3314 4050. www.scandichotels.com/Hotels/Denmark/Copenhagen. 166 units. Doubles 1,481DKK–3,895DKK w/breakfast.*

Iconic mid-century furnishings at the Radisson Blu Royal.

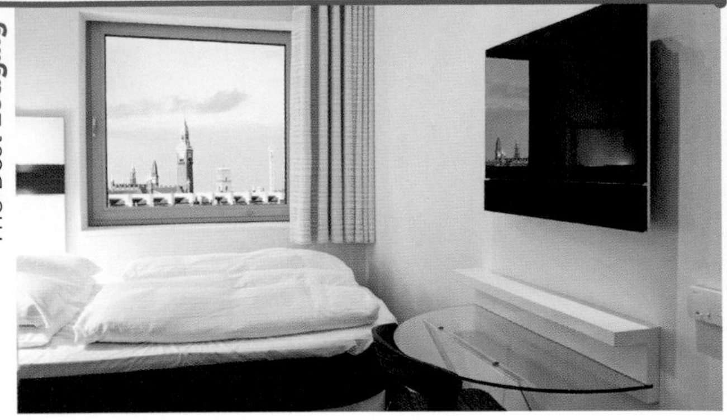

Mod design at a budget price at Wakeup Copenhagen.

AE, DC, MC, V. Bus: 5A, 6A, 10, 14, 33. Map p 124.

★★ Sleep in Heaven NØRREBRO This buzzy hostel offers dorms with some scarily high three-story bunks. Open 24 hours, it's mostly the spotless preserve of backpackers. *Struenseegade 7. ☎ 45 3535 4648. www.sleepinheaven.com 80 units. Dormitory beds 170DKK. MC, V. Bus: 12, 66. Map p 124.*

★★★ Wakeup Copenhagen KONGENS NYTORV Don't let the two-star label fool you: this centrally-located and minimalist Kim Utzon-designed hotel offers a quality boutique experience at surprisingly budget prices. Funky décor and sleek furnishings inhabit a mod brick building studded with windows. A similar-looking sister property is near Kalvebod Brygge. *Borgergade 9. ☎ 45 4480 0090. www.wakeupcopenhagen.dk. 498 units. 500DKK–1,000DKK. AE, MC, V. Metro: Kongens Nytorv. Map p 124.*

Helsingør

★★ Comwell Borupgaard HELSINGØR Surrounded by immaculate gardens, this manor-house spa hotel south of Helsingør is ideal for a night of R&R and is only a 10-minute stroll to the coast. Inside this whitewashed mansion, standard rooms are bright and modern; go for the upgraded rooms to get beautiful woodland views. Prices are reasonable and the large luxury spa is a treatl after a long day's sightseeing. *Nørrevej 80, Snekkersten. ☎ 45 4838 0333. www.comwellborupgaard.dk. 149 units. Doubles 1,498DKK–2,198DKK w/breakfast. MC, V. Train: Snekkersten. 50km north of Copenhagen. Map p 124.*

★★★ kids Hotel Marienlyst HELSINGØR With marvelous views across the Øresund to Sweden, this splendid seaside hotel has an atmosphere reminiscent of times past. Families make good use of the indoor pool, slides, and splash pools or swim off the strip of sandy beach. A recent renovation has spruced up the superior-class rooms; several offer fantastic ocean views. There are two restaurants and a casino full of smartly dressed thirty-somethings. *Nordre Strandvej 2, Helsingør. ☎ 45 4921 4000. www.marienlyst.dk. 222 units. Doubles 1,096DKK–1,475DKK w/breakfast. AE, DC, MC, V. Train: Helsingør. 50km north of Copenhagen. Map p 124.* ●

10 The Best Day Trips & Excursions

Arken, Museum of Modern Art

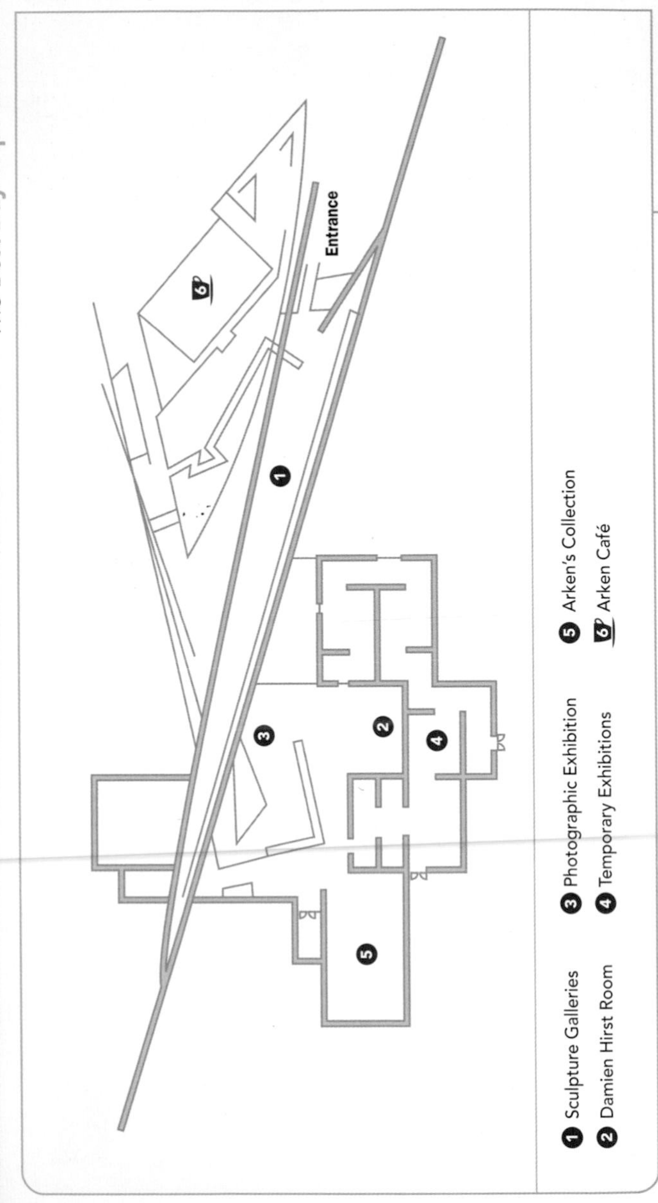

Previous page: Arken.

Southwest of Copenhagen, the Arken museum is housed in an extraordinary building by Danish architect Søren Robert Lund; when viewed from the right spot, it resembles a ship looming out of the sea. Take a half-day trip (2 to 3 hours) to see this collection of ground-breaking contemporary art in superlative surroundings. Combine it with a visit to the beach at Ishøj Strand for a fun, family day out. START: **Follow the E20 17km from the center of Copenhagen and take exit 26 to Ishøj Strand. By rail, take S-trains A or E from Hovedbanegården (Central Station) to Ishøj. From there, bus 128 runs straight to the museum.**

1 ★★ Sculpture Galleries. Arken reopened in 2008 following the addition of a new, light-flooded sculpture gallery, with installations on show from the permanent collection. Look for Olafur Eliasson's *Light Ventilator Mobile,* illuminating with a searchlight and circulating air with four fans. Close by is Jeppe Hein's *Mirror Spiral Labyrinth,* which leads confused visitors around in circles.

2 ★★★ Damien Hirst Room. The biggest collection of Hirst's work in Scandinavia is for me the museum's biggest draw. See spot paintings and a sinister silk print of his infamous gem-encrusted skull, *For the Love of God,* scattered with sparkling diamond dust. More celebratory is *The Four Elements*, four colored blocks appropriately subtitled *Who's Afraid of Red, Yellow, Green and Blue*?

3 ★★★ Photographic Exhibition. There are some very moving images in the permanent collection, especially Richard Billingham's evocative series of family shots. A favorite of mine is the massive *Bringing it All Back Home* by Claus Carstensen & Superflex; figures pose in scrubland wearing animal masks.

4 ★★★ Temporary Exhibitions. This gallery has featured some stunners in the past, such as works by the Skagen painters (Danish Impressionists, see p 25) and a surrealist exhibition with works by Dalí and Miró.

5 ★ Arken's Collection. Revolving exhibitions show off selections from the gallery's 300 pieces of contemporary Danish art after 1990. Look for Ai Weiwei's *The Circle of Animals/ Zodiac Heads* and Anselm Reyle's *Untitled*, evoking a kitsch Caribbean sunset.

6 ★★ kids Arken Café has views of Køge Bay. If the weather is fine, head to the beach afterwards for a swim and picnic lunch.

Practical Matters: Arken

Admission to Arken is 95DKK, 75DKK students and seniors, children under 17 free; you can use your Copenhagen Card (see p 163). There are English-speaking guided tours on Wednesday and Sunday; book in advance online. *Skovvej 100, 2635 Ishøj. ☎ 45 4354 0222. www.arken.dk. Open Tues–Sun 10am–5pm (Wed until 9pm). Closed Mon.*

Viking Ship Museum, Roskilde

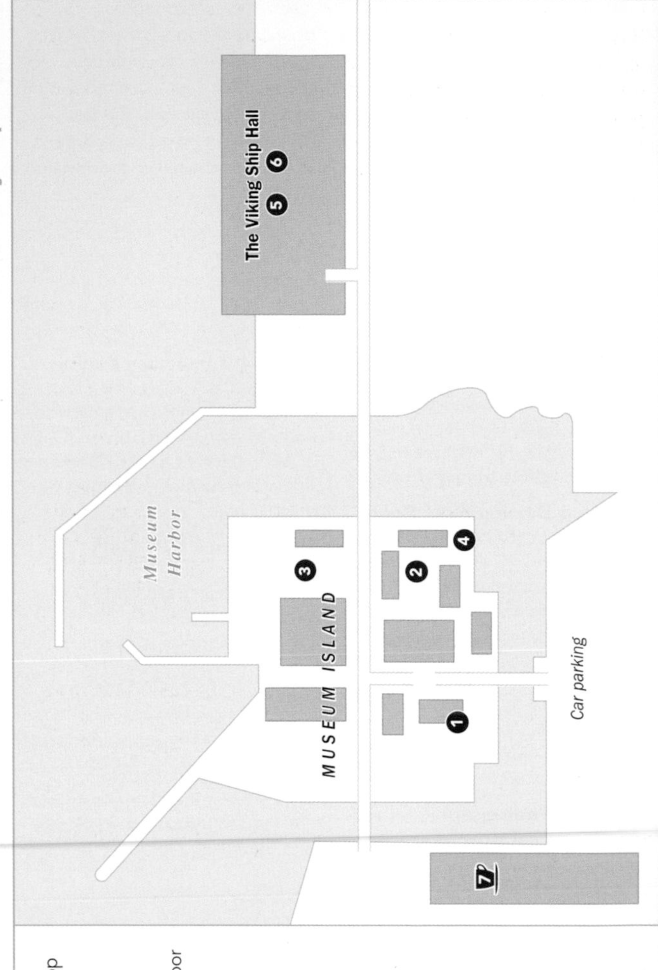

1 Archaeological Workshop

2 Viking Meeting Place

3 Boat Yard

4 Boat Trips from the Harbor

5 Viking Ship Hall

6 Skuldelev Ships

7 Restaurant Snekken

An easy journey west from Copenhagen, Roskilde is perfect for a family day out at the Viking Ship Museum, a complex partly set on an island of reclaimed land at the edge of the fjord at Roskilde. An attractive old town full of historic buildings, with a traffic-free center, Roskilde's other claim to fame is the majestic Gothic cathedral, traditional burial place of the Danish Royal Family (see p 141). START: **To travel the 30km to Roskilde by car, follow the E21 from the center of Copenhagen and take exit 11. The museum is signposted through the center of town. By rail, take the Intercity train from Hovedbanegården (Central Station) to Roskilde; they depart every 20 minutes and the journey takes half an hour. From there, bus 203 runs to the museum, or it's 20 minutes on foot.**

❶ ★ **Archaeological Workshop.** Step into Museum Island's workshop to see the painstaking reconstruction work involved in restoring a 12th-century cargo ship called *Roskilde 6*, found just west of the museum in the fjord. Nine medieval wrecks were found around the bay when Museum Island was constructed in the 1990s.

❷ ★ kids **Viking Meeting Place (Tunet).** A courtyard offers a hive of traditional Viking activity with workshops for kids; they can try coin minting, wood planing, and painting, or watch the blacksmith (sadly not wearing his Viking helmet) heat his fire with bellows. Coopers and rope-makers are also hard at work, and there are archery demonstrations here in the summer.

❸ ★★ kids **Boat Yard.** The craftsmen at this working boatyard make reconstructions of Viking and medieval designs by traditional methods; some of the boats are sailed from the adjacent harbor but many are sold overseas to provide income for the museum. There's a mine of pictorial information in Danish and English around the yard, explaining each step of the boat-building process, from selecting the wood to making the nails.

❹ ★★★ kids **Boat Trips from the Harbor.** A 50-minute trip around Roskilde Fjord on a reconstructed square-sailed longboat

Ancient longboat at the Viking Ship Museum.

The great gold altarpiece at Roskilde Cathedral.

gives you the chance to get that real Viking experience—but be warned: if there is no wind you'll have to row! It's fun even if the weather is doing its worst. Kids can dress in Viking clothes and have their pictures taken on the reconstructed cargo boats nearby. In summer there are occasional evening boat trips to admire the late-setting sun. 🕓 *50 min.*

❺ ★ **Viking Ship Hall.** Across the wooden harbor bridge from Museum Island, the wonderfully designed and light-filled Viking Ship Hall has massive glass walls overlooking the fjord. This houses the museum's permanent exhibition and five reconstructed Viking longboats. One exhibition hall is dedicated to the voyages of *The Sea Stallion*, a replica longboat that sails between the museum and Glendalough in County Wicklow, Ireland. In another room, a short film is shown in English, telling the Viking tale and summarizing the work of the museum. There's also a series of posters depicting the progress of an 11th-century raid on Roskilde from the sea.

❻ ★★★ kids **Skuldelev Ships.** The absolute highlights of the museum, these five Viking wrecks

Practical Matters: Viking Ship Museum

Admission to the Viking Ship Museum is 120DKK (105DKK students and seniors, free kids under 17) May to September; a 25% discount is available with Copenhagen Cards (see p 163). *Vindeboder 12, 4000 Roskilde.* ☎ *45 4630 0200. English-speaking guided tours,* ☎ *45 4630 0253. www.vikingeskibsmuseet.dk. Boat trips 100DKK. Open daily 10am–5pm.*

Domkirke—Royal Burial Place

You'll find Roskilde's splendid brick cathedral a few hundred meters up a steep hill from the **Viking Ship Museum.** There has been a church on the site since the 9th century, but this tall, austere Gothic incarnation was commissioned by Bishop Absalon, the founder of Copenhagen, in the 1200s. It contains the tombs of most Danish royals since the Lutheran Reformation in 1536 to the present day. Opulent chapels off the main aisle house the elaborate sarcophagi of many Frederiks, Christians, and their queens. The remains of Harald Bluetooth, the 10th-century first Christian king of Denmark, are buried in a pillar on the left of the sanctuary. Look for the wonderfully named "tomb of the ghost horse" behind the sanctuary. The great gold altarpiece, depicting Christ's trials in Holy Week, was crafted in Ghent in the 1560s. The latest royal incumbents of the cathedral are the parents of the present queen, who are buried in a new tomb in the gardens. *Domkirkepladsen 3, 4000 Roskilde. ☎ 45 4635 1624. www.roskildedomkirke.dk. Admission 60DKK, 40DKK students & seniors. Apr–Sept Mon–Sat 9am–6pm, Sun 1–6pm; Oct–Mar Mon–Sat 10am–4pm, Sun 1–4pm. Guided tours in English take about 1 hr.; for details, contact* ***Roskilde Tourist Information Bureau,*** *Stændertorvet 1, 4000 Roskilde (☎* ***45 4631 6565;*** *info@visitroskilde.dk; www.visitroskilde.com).*

were scuttled in the 11th century near Skuldelev, north of Roskilde, to provide a defense barrier against rival Viking raids. They lay there until they were excavated in 1962 in thousands of pieces. After a long period of reconstruction the ships are now semi-intact, lurking in eerie splendor against the backdrop of the fjord. Made of oak, the fastest was *Skuldelev 2*, an ocean-going warship 30 meters long and capable of speeds of up to 20 knots. She was built near Dublin somewhere around 1042. Of the others, two were trading vessels and one an in-shore fishing boat.

7 ★★ **Restaurant Snekken.** A better option than the museum cafe (which serves pricey salads and lager), Snekken is by the entrance to the Viking Ship Museum. It has views across the fjord, fresh sushi during the day, and a quality brasserie menu in the evening. Booking is advisable, especially during school holidays. *Vindeboder 16, 4000 Roskilde. ☎ 45 4635 9816. www.snekken.dk. $$.*

Frederiksborg Slot, Hillerød

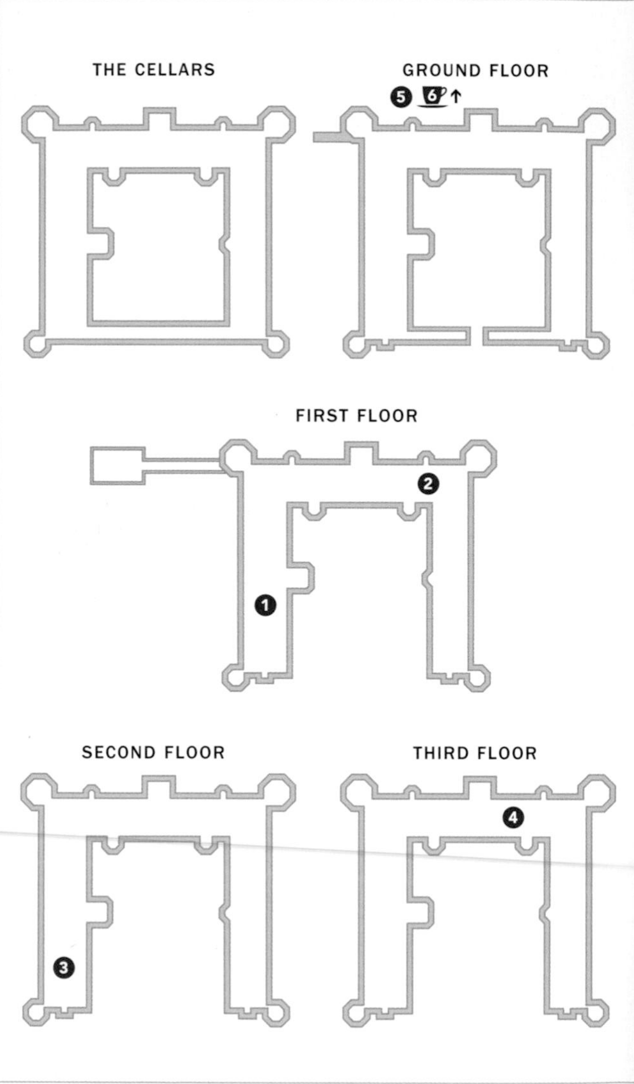

1 Coronation Chapel
2 Decorative Arts
3 Historical Paintings
4 Modern Collection
5 Baroque Gardens
6 Spisestedet Leonora

Gloriously romantic Frederiksborg Castle is perched on a lake in Hillerød, an otherwise unassuming little town northwest of Copenhagen. Built in the early 17th century in the reign of Christian IV, the copper roofs of this fairy-tale confection glisten in the sun. It's set on three tiny islands, overlooking picture-perfect formal gardens, and entered through a cobbled courtyard with an extravagant central fountain. The rambling Dutch Renaissance palace contains Denmark's **Museum of National History,** founded by brewing magnate JC Jacobsen in 1878, as well as an awesomely opulent chapel, magnificent public rooms, and a collection of modern portraits. START: **By car from Copenhagen, take the E47 north and turn off at junction 9, signposted Hillerød; the journey is 38km. The castle is not well signposted but it's easy to spot when driving through the town. By rail, take S-train A from Hovedbanegården (Central Station) to Hillerød; they depart every 10 minutes and the journey takes 40 minutes. From there, it's a 20-minute walk (follow the little blue signposts) or a 10-minute bus ride on routes 301 or 302 to the castle.**

❶ ★★★ Coronation Chapel. Once in the castle, head for the vaulted **Knights Room**, reconstructed following the fire of 1859, which destroyed sections of the original castle. From here, take the stairs up to the second-floor **chapel**, which escaped fire damage, and check out the eye-catching gilded ceiling. Royal portraits adorn the walls and an ornate, world-famous organ by German master craftsman Esaias Campenius (1560–1617) installed in 1610 dominates the far end of the chapel. Add to this the jewel-like stained-glass windows and you have a riot of color fit for the coronation of monarchs between 1671 and 1840. On leaving the chapel, make sure you see the baroque **Audience Chamber**, where a hatch in the floor reveals the throne used to lift the king into the room. It's down a corridor with a carved marble ceiling and entered through marble curtains held back by cherubs.

Frederiksburg Slot's ornate chapel, traditional site for coronoations.

The fountain courtyard of Frederiskborg Slot.

❷ ★ Decorative Arts. Wander through the magnificent state rooms of the castle and you'll spy Delft pottery, spindly rococo furniture, and Flemish tapestries hanging on the walls. Wherever you go, you'll see heavily decorated ceilings and elaborately patterned marbled floors. The ceiling of Room 31 depicts the night sky in bright blues and golds, while Room 36 is laid out for a ghostly dinner party, complete with scarlet walls and cardboard cutouts of bewigged gentlemen. They are watched over by a series of oil paintings of past kings and queens. The impressive Great Hall (Room 38) has an intricate marble floor and ceiling decorated with cherubim, gilding, and mythical paintings; the room is laid out as it was in the time of Christian IV, chief architect of Copenhagen. Room 39 houses the elaborate Celestial Globe (1657), ornamented with figures representing the 12 signs of the zodiac. Parts of the original Flora Danica dinner service (see p 145) are on display along with an eclectic collection of Danish-designed furniture of varying ages and styles.

❸ ★ Historical Paintings. An impressive set of massive historical paintings showing seminal

Practical Matters: Frederiksborg Castle

Admission to Frederiksborg Castle is 75DKK, 60DKK students and seniors; 20DKK children 6–15; 150DKK family ticket; Copenhagen Cards (see p 163) are welcome. Labeling in English is scant. There are English guided tours; book in advance at the phone number below. *3400 Hillerød.* ☎ *45 4826 0439. www.frederiksborg slot.dk. Apr–Oct 10am–5pm; Nov–Mar 11am–3pm.*

moments in Danish culture are scattered throughout the castle. Look at the walls of the Great Hall for mammoth-sized oils. A small selection of prints and drawings from a collection of over 40,000 is also on display, many of them depicting the castle.

4 ★ Modern Collection. This collection contains many portraits of often-obscure Danes, but there are some important exceptions. One image of Queen Margrethe shows her elegantly attired, but oddly placed on a stool in the middle of a field. Another, very different take on the Queen is the surprisingly conventional portrait in profile by Andy Warhol. Look for the self-portrait by Skagen painter Peter Severin Kroyer (see p 25), black-and-white images of Danish resistance heroes, and an arresting image of an elderly Karen Blixen (see p 21) dressed as a Pierrot. On the same floor is a photography gallery featuring a selection of portraits and changing exhibitions.

5 ★★ Baroque Gardens. Revived in the 1990s according to original drawings, these delightful formal gardens stretch into the distance across the castle's moat. Four sections of box hedge are shaped into royal monograms; from there steps lead through new planting and lush lawns to a romantic expanse of ancient trees and Frederik II's folly Bath House Castle, occasionally used by the Royal Family for hunting lunches.

6 ★★ kids Spisestedet Leonora. A family-oriented establishment serving up salads, roasts, fish dishes, and smørrebrød is the only restaurant in the palace complex. There's a great terrace for sunny days. See details on p 102. *Frederiksborg Slot, Hillerød. ☎ 45 4826 7516. www.leonora.dk. $$.*

Flora Danica

Royal Copenhagen's most exquisite porcelain design came into being in 1790 when Christian VII's brother commissioned the company to produce a china service that would impress Empress Catherine II of Russia, who was being wooed as a potential royal bride. She died in 1796 before the service was finished, and so it remained among the treasures of the Royal Household. Craftsman Johann Christoph Bayer copied the delicate flower designs from the 51-volume botanical work *Flora Danica* over a period of 12 years. No two pieces are alike.

Of the original 1,802-piece Flora Danica service, 1,530 have survived. Some are here in Frederiksborg, others in Rosenborg Slot (see p 21). Queen Margrethe uses the service on state occasions and the pattern remains in production today, still hand-painted from the prints in the *Flora Danica*. The service is sold in the Royal Copenhagen shop in Strøget, Copenhagen (p 76).

Kronborg Slot, Helsingør

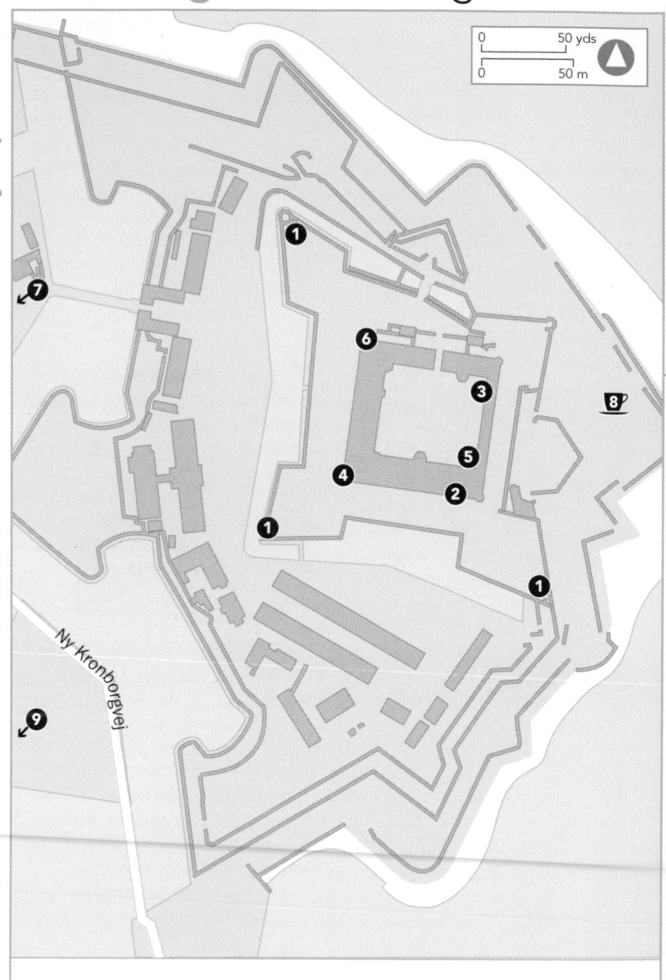

1 Ramparts
2 Chapel
3 Royal Chambers
4 Telegraph Tower
5 Ballroom & Little Hall
6 Casemates
7 M/S Maritime Museum of Denmark
8 Picnic
9 Helsingør

On a windswept headland on the northeast tip of North Zealand, majestic Kronborg Slot (Castle) guards the entrance to the Øresund and looks out towards Sweden. The UNESCO World Heritage Site you see today was built in 1585 for Frederik II to ward off attack from the sea, although a small castle had existed here since the 1420s, built by Erik of Pomerania. Famous as the fictional setting for William Shakespeare's *Hamlet,* Kronborg is open to visitors throughout the year. Highlights are the Royal Chambers, the galleried chapel, the Knight's Ballroom, and underground casemates with a statue of Holger the Dane. Leave time to explore the town of Helsingør after visiting the castle. **START: Driving from Copenhagen, take the E47 north to Helsingør; the journey is 46km and takes an hour. The Øresundståg train from Hovedbanegården (Central Station) to Helsingør leaves every 20 minutes and takes 45 minutes. It's a 10-minute walk to the castle.**

1 ★★ kids Ramparts. The imposing ramparts and fortified bastions of the castle were built by Christian V in 1690. Follow the informative history trail as it explains how Helsingør became rich under the rule of Erik of Pomerania through taxes levied on trading ships sailing up the Øresund. From the ramparts, cannons point seaward, where you'll see the massive bulk of northern Europe's biggest castle across sparkling seas: Helsinborg, in Sweden, is tantalizingly close, only 4km away. The most romantic time to walk around these ramparts is at dusk in summer as the sun goes down.

Approaching Kronborg Castle

2 ★★★ Chapel. A lucky survivor of a 1629 fire that saw much destruction at Kronborg, the chapel is opposite the main entrance off the vast cobbled courtyard. The decoration here serves as a reminder of how the castle once looked; ceilings and walls are wood paneled and gilded, and the pulpit and private box in which the Royal Family attended Mass are ornately carved and brightly painted. Easily the most impressive part of the castle.

3 ★ Royal Chambers. Found on the second floor, these rooms are sparsely furnished and barewalled but have a certain austere splendor, if only for their size.

4 ★★ kids Telegraph Tower. Climb the spiral staircase to reach this flat-roofed former guidepost tower and gun turret for views up and down the coast. From here, signals were sent to Copenhagen in times of war; today, streams of ferries pass by on their way to Sweden.

❺ ★ **Ballroom & Little Hall.** At 62 x 12m, the largest hall in northern Europe was finished in 1585. The restoration hints at its former grandeur, with a magnificent marble floor and massive oil paintings adorning the walls. Tapestries in the Little Hall depict royal portraits, part of a series commissioned by Frederik II in 1580.

❻ ★★ **Casemates.** Dank, dark, and unsettling, these rambling dungeons have housed a thousand soldiers and their supplies for weeks in times of siege. Today they are enlivened by eerie contemporary art installations and a giant illuminated sculpture of Holger Danske, the mythical protector of Denmark. Legend goes that he sleeps in the casemates and will only awake to save his country when it is in mortal danger.

❼ ★★ kids **M/S Maritime Museum of Denmark.** Sitting in front of the castle and shaped like a giant ship, the Maritime Museum houses Denmark's largest collection of naval artifacts. It reflects the importance of the sea to this island state; an array of ephemera is presented in a seemingly endless series of subterranean rooms. Unless you are fanatical about all things nautical, cherry pick your way through the prime displays and experiences, which include coming face to face with a torpedo, inking a sailor's tattoo, testing your navigational skills, and seeing if you've got what it takes to run your own trade company. This museum was built around an old dry dock in the castle grounds—designed by the renowned Danish architects BIG—where uneven floors and wonky angles give the impression of being aboard a ship. The museum shop sells a booty of nautical-themed books, clothes, and toys. *Ny*

Kronborg's immense raftered banquet hall.

Practical Matters: Kronborg Castle

Ticket prices Kronborg Castle are 90DKK for adults, 80DKK students and seniors, 45DKK kids 4–17, and 80DKK per person in groups of 10 and above. If you visit the **M/S Maritime Museum of Denmark** the same day, you can get a 20% discount on castle entry by showing Maritime Museum tickets. Copenhagen Cards (see p 163) can be used for entrance to both the castle and Maritime Museum. English-language guided tours start from the shop at 12:30pm and 2:30pm. A castle visit takes approximately 3 hours; you'll need another 3 or 4 hours to explore the rest of the town and its museums. *Kronborg 2c, 3000 Helsingør.* ☎ *45 4921 3078. www.kronborg.dk. Open June–Aug 10am–5:30pm; rest of year daily 11am–4pm (closed Mon Nov–Mar).*

Kronborgvej 1. ☎ *45 4921 0685. www.mfs.dk. Admission 110DKK, 90DKK student & seniors, under 18 free. Free with Copenhagen Card. July–Aug daily 10am–5pm, Sept–June Tues–Sun 11am–5pm.*

8 ★★ kids **Picnic.** Buy picnic supplies and fresh fruit from the daily market in front of the Tourist Information Bureau in Havnepladsen and enjoy lunch in the castle grounds overlooking the sea. If you are in Helsingør at suppertime, head to La Dolce Vita for authentic Italian pasta dishes. *Kongensgade 6, Helsingør.* ☎ *45 4921 1880. www.la-dolcevita.dk.*

9 ★★★ **Helsingør.** This small, cheerful town has a cluster of half-timbered houses in a medieval quarter brimming over with tourists, plus lots of bars, cafes, and restaurants overflowing onto cobbled streets. Two sandy beaches around the marina at Nordhavn have shallow water and are safe for all the family; if the weather is poor, there is an indoor water park at the Hotel Marienlyst (see p 124). The **Bymuseum** of local history is in a medieval convent at Karmeliterhuset, Sankt Anna Gade 36, ☎ 45 4928 1800, www.helsingormuseer.dk (admission 30DKK, 20DKK seniors, free kids under 18; open Tues–Sat noon–2pm, Sun noon–4pm). **Danmarks Tekniske Museum** (National Museum of Science and Technology) is devoted to the groundbreaking technology of the late 19th and early 20th centuries with exhibits such as gramophones, steam engines, motorcars, and radios. Also on display is an airplane of the "Danish Edison," inventor J.C. Ellehammer, who in the minds of Danes was the first to fly in Europe in 1906. It's at Fabriksvej 25, ☎ 45 4922 2611 (admission 70DKK adults, 60DKK students, children under 18 free; open Tues–Sun 10am–5pm). The **Tourist Office** is at Havnepladsen 3, ☎ 45 4921 1333. www.visithelsingor.dk. It's open Mon–Fri 10am–4pm.

Malmö, Sweden

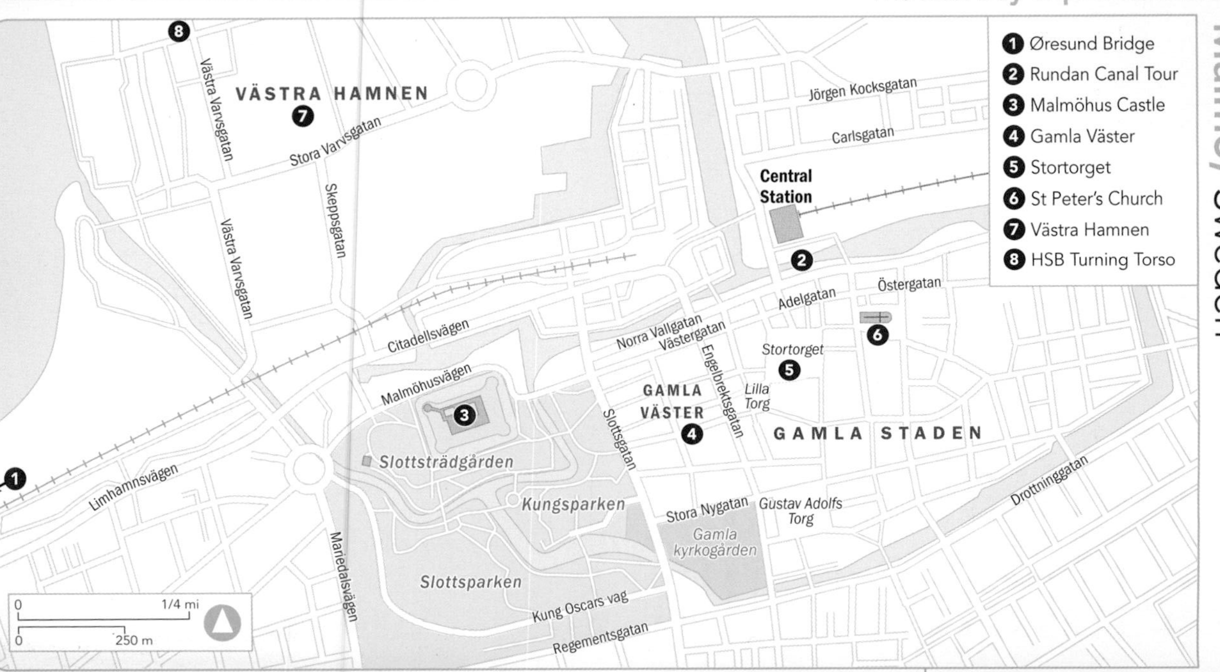

More than 18,000 commuters make their way across the Øresund Bridge daily from Malmö to Copenhagen; you can do it the other way around by taking the train to Sweden for the day. Malmö is a pleasant suburban city with an atmospheric old town packed with castles, churches, museums, and cafes juxtaposed with a burgeoning docklands area, its very own skyscraper, and sandy beaches. There's plenty to do and see within walking distance. **START: The Øresundståg train from Copenhagen airport to Malmö departs every 20 minutes and the journey takes 20 minutes. The Gråhundbus line 999 leaves Rådhuspladsen once an hour (not Sundays) and the journey takes 70 minutes. If you travel by car, the toll on the Øresund Bridge is 335DKK each way—it's sensible to take the train or the bus.**

1 ★★★ kids Øresund Bridge. Connecting Denmark with Sweden, the photogenic Øresund Bridge stretches across the water by bridge and tunnel and is both a rail and road bridge. Trains decant right into Malmö city center and the tourist office is in the station. The Malmö City Tunnel, a 17km rail network, connects the station to the bridge. *40 min. from Copenhagen, 10 min. to cross bridge.*

2 ★★ kids Rundan Canal Tour. Get your bearings with a boat trip along the canals that encircle Malmö's old town. Embarkation is at the boathouse outside the station and commentary is in English. The route skirts the Western Docks, where new buildings have shot up at an astounding rate, before passing through the grounds of **Malmöhus Castle** and chugging under a sequence of low bridges. If you order in advance, the boat can put together a picnic for your 50-minute trip. *50 min.* ☎ *46 40 611 7488.*

3 ★★ Malmöhus Castle. Turn right out of the station and walk for

The modern Øresund Bridge connect Denmark and Sweden.

Malmo's Storteget square is the heart of the historic town.

five minutes until you reach Malmö's 16th-century castle, built by the Danish monarch Christian III when the city belonged to Denmark. As at Kronborg Castle (p 146), Erik of Pomerania built the original citadel in 1434. Part of the castle is now a museum with well-preserved Renaissance interiors; the modern section houses an art museum and aquarium. ⏱ *1½ hr. Malmöhusvägen. ☎ 46 040 34 4437. www.malmo.se. Admission 40SEK; 20SEK students; under 20s free. Daily 10am–5pm.*

❹ ★★ **Gamla Väster.** Across Slottsgatan, like a miniature Prague (or Buda in Budapest), the narrow cobbled streets and piazzas of Malmö's pedestrianized medieval core are lined with brightly painted houses; a bohemian air prevails in the buzzing bars and cafes. Contemporary art galleries and expensive boutiques add to the mix. The little square of **Lilla Torget** is a charming place to lunch; on sunny days tables spread out across the cobbles under colored umbrellas. ⏱ *30 min.*

Practical Matters: Malmö

Malmö Tourist Information Centre is at Central Station, S-211 20 Malmö, Sweden (☎ 46 4034 1200). www.malmo.se. The Malmö City Card is a book of vouchers with hundreds of offers from shops, restaurants, and attractions, including half-price admission to museums, discounted sightseeing boat tours, free street parking, and 10% off taxi journeys. The card costs 100SEK from the tourist office and can also be downloaded as an app. For transport, you can buy a 24-hour (65SEK) or 72-hour (165SEK) ticket from the tourist office.

Øresund Bridge: The Facts

The bridge was opened on July 1, 2000, by Queen Margrethe (see p 151) after five years of construction; its main span is 490m and the highest pillar stands at 204m. At 7.8km in length it has four road lanes and two rail tracks, which run underneath the road. Soaring halfway across the Øresund from the Swedish coastline to Peberholm, a man-made island 4km long, the road-and-rail bridge tunnels under the sea and resurfaces on Danish soil 4.5km later. Designers created the tunnel on the Danish side, as the bridge is close to Copenhagen airport, and the high spans were considered too dangerous to incoming aircraft.

❺ ★★ **Stortorget.** Lying almost next to Lilla Torget, this square is at the heart of medieval Malmö. Surrounded by Gothic and Dutch Renaissance civic buildings, it is dominated by the massive facade of the **Rådhuset** (city hall), built in 1546 and reworked in Dutch Renaissance style in the 1860s. Close by, a copper King Karl X Gustav peers snootily from his vast equestrian perch; it was he who retrieved Malmö from its Danish conquerors in 1658. 🕓 *15 min.*

❻ ★★ **St. Peter's Church.** A step away from Stortorget, this cavernous church is Malmö's oldest building, dating from the early 14th century and constructed in what is known locally as Baltic Brick Gothic. Severe and suitably pinnacled on the outside, inside it is vividly white. The massive stone pulpit and the great gilt altar are fancifully elaborate in Renaissance style. My favorite corner of the church is the Kramarkapellet, a little chapel, with faded frescoes of dancing demons on the walls. 🕓 *45 min. Göran Olsgatan.* ☎ *46 4027 9043. Free admission. Mon–Fri 8am–6pm; Sat 9am–6pm; Sun 10am–6pm.*

❼ ★★ **Västra Hamnen (Western Harbor).** Across the harbor, Sweden's answer to London's Docklands development has radically changed the face of waterside Malmö. Industrial degeneration has been rapidly replaced by smart apartment blocks, jazzy office buildings, trendy bars and cafes, amid a tangible sense of affluence and purpose. Things get lively by night, when a smartly dressed crowd bar-hops along the quays. 🕓 *1 hr.*

❽ ★★★ **HSB Turning Torso.** This twisting, turning creation by Spanish architect Santiago Calatrava (designer of the dazzling Alamillo Bridge in Seville, Spain) stands out over the Western Docks. You'll spot it easily; as Sweden's tallest building, the tower stands 190 meters, built in nine 5-story segments that turn 90 degrees from top to bottom. Most floors house luxury apartments and there is no public access to the building, but you can take the virtual tour at the event center next door. It looks spectacular, especially when floodlit at night. 🕓 30 min. *Västra Varvsgatan 34.* ☎ *46 4017 4500. Turning Torso Event Centre Västra Varvsgatan 44.* ☎ *46 4017 4539. www.turningtorso.com.*

Louisiana Museum of Modern Art

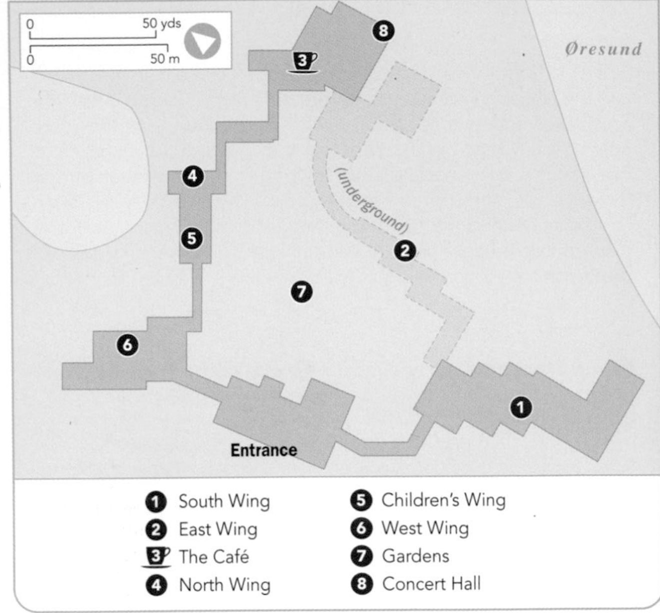

A delight for art hounds of all ages, Louisiana is an extraordinary museum-cum-gallery straddling hilltop grounds between Copenhagen and Helsingør, with views sweeping across the Øresund. Designed as an adjunct to an aristocratic mansion built in 1855, the new galleries snake across the park, flowing from wing to wing. Since opening in 1958, the museum's gradual expansion has been overseen by Danish architects Jørgen Bo and Vilhelm Wohlert. The whole outing from Copenhagen takes about 4 hours. **START: It's a 35km drive from Copenhagen; take the E47 north and leave at junction 4, signposted Humlebæk, or drive along the coast road (152); Louisiana is signposted on the right. The Øresundståg train from Hovedbanegården (Central Station) to Humlebæk departs every 20 minutes and the journey takes 35 minutes. From there, it's a good 15-minute walk to the museum.**

❶ ★★★ kids **South Wing.** On entering the gallery through the main doors of the old house, turn right to discover minimalist spaces exhibiting vast artworks from the rotating permanent collection. A few steps in and you might see a Rietveld *Red/Blue Chair* from 1918, the spectacular *Spider Couple* by Louise Bourgeois (1911–2010), or an

Practical Matters: Louisiana Museum

Admission to the Louisiana Museum costs 115DKK (100DKK students and seniors, children up to 18 go free). Copenhagen Cards (see p 163) are accepted. Opening hours are Tuesday to Friday 11am–10pm, Saturday and Sunday 11am–6pm; the museum is also open some Mondays during school vacations. Guided tours are available in English Tuesday–Thursday 11:15am–9pm, Friday 11:15am–7pm, and Saturday 11:15am–2pm; book in advance on the website. *Gammel Strandvej 13, 3050 Humlebæk.* ☎ *45 4919 0719. www.louisiana.dk.*

electrifying *Ctesiphon II*, painted by Frank Stella (1936–) in 1967. The curious *Half Circle* by Spanish installation artist Juan Moñoz (1953–2001) attracts lots of attention from kids, who adore the gurning faces on the half-sized figures portrayed in a gray-clad circle. A gallery at the top of the South Wing looks right over the Øresund and delights kids with a diving board pointing seaward.

❷ ★★ **East Wing.** A sun-filled passage leads on to the East Wing, passing indigenous American artifacts and leading to temporary exhibitions, which have included a Max Ernst retrospective and an exhibition of drawings by Philip Guston. Visit the website (www.louisiana.dk) for details of current and future shows.

3 ★★ kids **The Cafe.** With panoramic views across the sea and a summer terrace, the museum cafe serves pastries and a buffet throughout the day followed by Danish-influenced dishes at night. ***Closes at 8:30pm. $$.***

❹ ★★ **North Wing.** Featuring further works from the museum's own collection, the North Wing's highlights include drawings by Hockney and Picasso plus the lumpy *Lava Chair* by American sculptor Scott Burton (1939–89). Seminal Danish artist Asger Jorn (1914–73), a major figure with the CoBrA Group, has a room devoted to his garishly distorted images. Spindly sculptures on display in the Giacometti Gallery look as though they are about to walk away.

❺ ★★★ kids **Children's Wing.** Opening up the world of art for kids, this three-story block offers courses, group activities at the weekend, and the chance to experiment with paint and clay. There are family guided tours of important pieces in the museum. The computer room and story-telling room keep children absorbed.

❻ ★★ **West Wing.** Added in 1971, this wing displays changing artworks from the permanent collection. You might get to see American Pop Art from Andy Warhol or Roy Lichtenstein, or somber examples of German Expressionism by Georg Baselitz as well as mad sculptures by Jean Tinguely.

7 ★★ kids **Gardens.** Wander around rolling parkland and get up close to sculptures from Danish sculptor Henry Heerup and English sculptor Henry Moore. The Lake Garden showcases five different summerhouses by international architects. It's ideal for a summer's day, when children can let off steam in the open grounds.

8 ★★ **Concert Hall.** A yearly program of classical and jazz concerts is held here; see the website for details.

The **Savvy Traveler**

Before You Go

Government Tourist Offices

In the US: 655 Third Avenue, Ste. 1810, New York, NY 10017 (☎ 212/885 9700, www.visitdenmark.com), or PO Box 4649, Grand Central Station, New York, NY 10063. **In the UK:** 55 Sloane St, London SW1X 9SY (☎ 020 7259 5959, www.visitdenmark.com). **In Australia:** Level 4, 81 York Street Sydney, NSW 2000 (☎ 2/9262 5832, www.visitdenmark.com).

The Best Time to Go

It's always the right time to go to Copenhagen. The **spring** months are cool but often sunny; **May** through **September** are the warmest months, with long and balmy nights, but have the most rainfall and the most visitors. A visit in the **winter** will find a quieter city but the chance to ice skate in city parks (p 86) and huddle under blankets by the heaters in sidewalk cafes. Tivoli at Christmas is a rare treat for children, with visits from Santa and a festive market. Hotel prices may also be slightly lower in the winter months, with the exception of the weeks around Christmas and New Year.

Festivals & Special Events

SPRING. The **Wednesday Concerts** (www.onsdagskoncerter.dk), held Wednesdays throughout spring and autumn, are mainly classical. Free performances are given by students of the Royal Danish Academy of Music at the university, in the Theatre Museum, and in churches across Copenhagen. The **Copenhagen Carnival** (May, karneval-kbh.dk) takes place in Fælledparken and fills ity streets with crowds of colorful bands, dancers, and revelers.

SUMMER. Copenhagen Distortion (June, www.cphdistortion.dk) is the best clubbing event of the year; a massive five-day party with lots of improvisation, special club nights, and late-night frolics. July is the month when things really heat up in Copenhagen. The Copenhagen Jazz Festival (early July, www.festival.jazz.dk) kicks things off when international jazz musicians hit town to perform in a series of around 450 (mostly free) concerts in squares, parks, cafes, bars, and late-night clubs. Dizzy Gillespie, Sonny Rollins, Herbie Hancock, and Oscar Peterson have all played in years past. The most famous festival in Denmark is the huge Roskilde Festival (late June/ early July, www.roskilde-festival.dk), now up there with the biggest rock events in the world. Held in the countryside outside Roskilde, it draws over 130,000 music fans annually to see big-name and indie artists, and to enjoy the hundreds of stalls, theater, acrobatics, bars, cafes, and dance tents. Later in July, Santa Clauses from all over the world tip up at Bakken Amusement Park for the annual World Santa Claus Congress (www.worldsantaclauscongress.com), with lots of fun and games for kids. During the last week of July and first week of August, classical concerts are held every afternoon in Charlottenborg during the Copenhagen Summer Festival (www.copenhagensummerfestival.dk). Cultural **Harbor** (August, www.kulturhavn.dk) is a yearly jamboree around the harbor, with four days of cultural and leisure events, all for free.

Up north in Helsingør, the outdoor courtyard of Kronborg Castle (p 146, www.hamletsommer.dk) features a summer-long celebration of the works of Shakespeare and other playwrights. Back in Copenhagen, the first Saturday in August sees a huge concert (www.kglteater.dk) in the Fælledparken (p 69) starring the **Royal Opera** soloists and orchestra. During **Copenhagen Summerdance** (August, www.dansk danseteater.dk), Tim Rushton and the Danish Dance Theatre (p 119) perform outdoor shows in the courtyard of the Copenhagen City Police HQ. This is followed by the **Copenhagen International Ballet** festival (third week August, www.copenhageninternationalballet.com) of classical and modern dance, showcasing contemporary choreographers. Founder Alexander Kølpin works with dancers from all over the world. Gourmets convene in Tivoli and selected restaurants around town for the annual Nordic Food Festival, **Copenhagen Cooking** (August–September, www.copenhagencooking.com).

FALL. Golden Days in Copenhagen (September, www.goldendays.dk) aims to augment historical awareness through music, theater, ballet, and literature. **CPH PIX,** Denmark's leading film festival (September, www.cphpix.dk), focuses on new and bold talent, both Danish and international, with a comprehensive program of film screenings, Q&As, and star-studded events. **Mix Copenhagen** (October, www.mixcopenhagen.dk), formerly the Copenhagen Gay & Lesbian Film Festival, is the oldest film festival in town. For the past 17 years, the festival has become a fixture in the gay and lesbian subculture of Copenhagen, but is becoming increasingly mainstream. The following month, **CPH:DOX** (November, www.cphdox.dk) presents new and innovative documentaries, directors' Q&A sessions, and lectures along with music and club events.

WINTER. The **Copenhagen Irish Festival** arrives in the city in November with main concerts held in the old union hall at the Arbejdermuseet (p 67,) alongside smaller sessions at venues around town (see www.irishfestival.dk for full line-up). **Santa Claus's arrival at Tivoli** occurs in December amid much sparkle, following the opening of **Christmas in Tivoli** (November-December, www.tivoli.dk), with Christmas lights designed by Tiffany's head designer. At the start of the new year, countrywide jazz festival **Vinterjazz** (Jan–Feb, www.vinterjazz.dk) holds events in Copenhagen's Operaen (p 119). New fashion trends are showcased at the **International Fashion Fair** in February (www.ciff.dk), coinciding with the winter edition of **Copenhagen Fashion Week** (www.copenhagenfashionweek.com).

The Weather

Denmark has a moderate maritime climate with reasonably mild weather; but expect gray skies and some cold snaps, frost, and occasional snow during December and January. Even so, temperatures rarely fall below -1°C (30°F) due to Copenhagen's proximity to the sea's warming influence. In summer the mercury can get up as high as 25°C (77°F), with average highs around 20-22°C (68-72°F). Rainfall in Copenhagen is heaviest during the summer months, with up to 74mm (2.9 inches) in August. Due to its northern latitude, days are short in winter with about five hours of daylight in December and January. This of course is compensated for in the summer, with up to 18 hours of daylight, making May through October the most pleasant time to visit the city. The sea is warm enough to swim in by July, and if you wrap up well, the clear skies and frosts of a sunny winter's day can be a real treat.

COPENHAGEN'S AVERAGE AVERAGE RAINFALL

Avg. Rainfall	JAN	FEB	MAR	APR	MAY	JUNE
mm	43	25	36	41	41	53
inches	1.7	1.0	1.4	1.6	1.6	2.1

Avg. Rainfall	JULY	AUG	SEPT	OCT	NOV	DEC
mm	66	74	51	53	53	51
inches	2.6	2.9	2.0	2.1	2.1	2.0

COPENHAGEN'S AVERAGE AVERAGE TEMPERATURE

Avg. Rainfall	JAN	FEB	MAR	APR	MAY	JUNE
°F	32	32	35	44	53	60
°C	0	0	2	7	12	16

Avg. Temp	JULY	AUG	SEPT	OCT	NOV	DEC
°F	64	63	57	49	42	37
°C	18	17	14	9	6	3

Cell (Mobile) Phones

Most UK and European phones can send and receive calls/SMS on international roaming in Copenhagen. Most GSM (Global System for Mobiles) tri-band cell phones from the US will also work. Call your wireless operator and ask for "international roaming" to be activated or make sure the facility is triggered when you purchase your cell phone. But be warned—roaming charges can be high for texting and making calls. Cell phone reception is generally good in Copenhagen.

Rent **Nokia** or **Motorola** GSM mobiles in Copenhagen for around 200DKK per week; try the kiosks at Kastrup Airport. If you are staying for any length of time, it may be cheaper to buy a pay-as-you-go mobile phone package or SIM card rather than renting a handset. Try **Telia** (telia.dk), **TDC** (tdc.dk), or **Telenor** (www.telenor.dk). You can order a Danish SIM card online from **Lebara** (www.lebara.dk) if you have a Danish contact address. North Americans can rent a GSM phone before leaving home from **InTouch USA** (☎ 800/872-7626; www.intouchusa.us) or **RoadPost** (☎ 888/290-1616 or 416/253-4539; www.roadpost.com).

Car Rentals

Driving in Copenhagen isn't really necessary; the city is compact and the public-transport system works punctually (as well as being free if you purchase a Copenhagen Card—see p 163). Even outside the city, it is possible to get to all the tourist attractions (such as Hillerød, Helsingør, and Roskilde) by train. However, a car permits greater freedom when exploring the countryside, so you may want to consider renting one for a few days. The world's major car-rental companies, including **Avis** (www.avis.com), **Budget** (www.budget.com), **Enterprise** (www.enterprise.com), **Europcar** and **Hertz** (www.hertz.com) all have offices in Copenhagen as well as at Kastrup Airport and Hovedbanegården (Central Station). There are significant savings if you book online. **Sixt** (www.sixt.co.uk) and **Thrifty** (www.thrifty.co.uk) often have good deals if you book well in advance.

Useful Websites

All the websites listed below have English content.

- **www.cphpost.dk**: Online version of The Copenhagen Post, the weekly English-language newspaper, with up-to-the minute local news and events listings.
- **www.copenhagenet.dk**: A succinct history of Copenhagen plus a look at some of its main attractions and an events calendar.
- **www.goscandinavia.com**: Official site of the Scandinavian tourist authorities; good for maps, sightseeing information, and ferry schedules before you go.
- **www.hotels-in-denmark.dk**: A one-stop hotel booking service, with details of accommodation throughout Denmark.
- **www.rejseplanen.dk**: Find your way around Copenhagen's public transport system with ease.
- **www.visitdenmark.com**: Official site of the Danish Tourist Board; good for maps of areas outside Copenhagen and itineraries.
- **www.visitcopenhagen.com**: The superb official site of Wonderful Copenhagen. Very helpful on all aspects of a visit from nightlife to renting bikes and buying discount passes. Information constantly updated.

Getting **There**

By Plane

All travelers, whether coming from the US, Australia, or Europe, land at Copenhagen's **Kastrup Airport** (☎ 45 3231 3231, 12km from the city center). From there, there are several ways to get into town. **Air-rail trains** (www.dsb.dk) link the airport with Hovedbanegården (Central Station) in 12 minutes. Fares are 36DKK and the train terminal is under the arrivals hall, an escalator ride from the gates. Trains depart every 10 minutes during the day and 1-3 times an hour at night. **Bus** 5A (www.moviatrafik.dk) departs regularly from outside the arrivals hall to the city center; fares are 36DKK and the trip takes 30-35 minutes. The **Metro** M2 line (yellow, www.m.dk) leaves every 4–6 minutes from the airport and is an easy 15-minute journey into Kongens Nytorv; tickets cost 36DKK and the service runs continually 24 hours a day, seven days a week. **Licensed taxis** wait outside the arrivals hall; fares into Copenhagen are between 250-300DKK. A cab ride takes 25 minutes or more, depending on time of day.

By Car

European travelers choosing to drive to Copenhagen through **Germany** can catch a ferry to Gedser from Rostock, and follow the E55 highway straight into the southern outskirts of the city. Coming from **Sweden** across the Øresund Bridge brings drivers into the city past the airport on the E20.

By Bus

Buses from surrounding areas in Zealand pull in at the Rådhuspladsen terminal (☎ 45 3613 1415), as do services that run from Malmö in Sweden across the Øresund Bridge (see p 151). Rådhuspladsen is a two-minute stroll from the main railway station.

By Train

Run by **DSB** (www.dsb.dk), trains arrive at Hovedbanegården (Central Station, ☎ 45 7013 1415), right in the heart of the city. From here, local **S-Tog** trains depart to various destinations throughout greater Copenhagen, others to Funen, Odense, and Aarhus. Taxis wait outside the main entrance to the station, and buses run from Rådhuspladsen, an easy few minutes' walk from the station. As the city is so compact, it may be possible to walk to your destination from the station; pick up a map from the information desk by track 5. **Note:** until the new city circle Metro system opens (2018) neither of the current two lines connect to the main railway station Hovedbanegården. If you want to pick up the Metro, it is best to get off your train at Nørreport station.

Getting **Around**

By Boat

The **Movia** harbor bus services 991, 992, 993 (www.moviatrafik.dk) are a fun way to travel and useful when out sightseeing. They connect Den Sorte Diamond (Black Diamond, p 29) with stops at Knippelsbro for Christianshavn, Nyhavn, and Holmen Nord for the Operaen (p 119). Boats run every 10 minutes and the trip from one end to the other takes 20 minutes.

By Bike

Do as the locals do and whiz safely around town by bike, using the cycle lanes and backstreets. Bycyklen, all-white electric smart bikes, are available all over town at charging stations for 25DKK an hour; for details see p 85.

By Bus

Tickets bought for any of the public-transport systems can be used on Metro, bus, and train. A basic ticket on the yellow Movia buses costs 24DKK and allows an hour's journey and unlimited transfers within your zone. Alternatively, a 24-hour ticket for 130DKK or a 7-day Flexcard for 675DKK allows unlimited travel in all zones. An interesting route for visitors is service no. 26, which runs past Christiansborg (p 39), Kongens Nytorv, Amalienborg (p 40), and up to Langelinie (p 17). A-buses are the primary buses in central Copenhagen and run at all hours while S-buses run from 6am to 1am daily. Night buses (denoted by an N after the route number) run out to the suburbs from Rådhuspladsen between 1am and 5am.

By Car

As already mentioned in this section, there is little need for a car in Copenhagen unless you are planning to explore further in Zealand. Parking, which is divided into three zones (red, green and blue), is typically expensive and spaces elusive. Expect to pay upwards of 30DKK per hour in the city center; blue parking meters usually take credit cards but make sure you have coins to feed the meter just in case. Some hotels have private parking but nearly all charge for the facility.

By Metro

The **Metro** (☎ 45 70 15 16 15, www.m.dk) is driverless, modern, and reliable, running every 2-4 minutes during rush hours and every 7-15 minutes at night. Kongens Nytorv, Nørreport (which connects with local S-Tog trains), and Christianshavn are the most useful for tourists of the 22 stops along the two lines. Two new city circle (Cityringen) lines, due for completion in 2018, will intersect the M1 and M2 lines at Kongens Nytorv and Frederiksberg stations.

The most sensible way to journey is to purchase a **Copenhagen Card,** which allows free travel (see p 8). Otherwise, tickets can be bought from machines in all Metro stations. A single-trip 2-zone ticket is 24DKK, and an all-zone ticket is 108DKK; two zones will cover most travel within the city center. Tickets for zones 1–3 are valid for an hour, tickets for all other zones for two, and are valid on all Metro trains, buses and S-Tog (local trains). Two children under 12 can travel free with each adult. **Note:** until Cityringen opens neither Metro line goes to the main train station Hovedbanegården; to get to the main railway station, take the Metro to Nørreport and switch to an S-Tog train.

By Taxi

Taxis congregate around tourist attractions, notably Tivoli, Kongens Nytorv, Nyhavn, and Rådhuspladsen, as well as outside the airport and Central Station. In other places, cabs can be hailed if their light is showing the word "fri." Most taxi drivers speak English. The meter should be started when you get in; fares are fixed at a price per km. Round up the tip to the nearest kroner or add 10DKK if paying by credit card. Drivers will produce a receipt on demand. **Rickshaw taxis** also circle the city, especially around Nyhvan; be prepared to haggle over the price!

On Foot

Strolling in Copenhagen's pedestrianized heart is a pleasure, as is exploring the gardens, parks, and canalside paths. However, on major roads, pay close attention to the lights at marked pedestrian crossings, and don't attempt to jaywalk under any circumstances (it is illegal). Car drivers simply do not slow down; they even seem to enjoy hooting and flashing their lights as they zoom past your toes.

Fast **Facts**

APARTMENT RENTALS Among the options are **Adina Apartment Hotel** (☎ 45 3969 1000, www.adina.dk, see p 127), and high-end **Charlottehaven Serviced Apartments** (☎ 45 3527 1500. www.charlottehaven.com), catering for couples or business travelers. Apartments and penthouses are outfitted with fully functioning offices and the best-possible-taste kitchens and bathrooms. The spa is a bonus too. Copenhagen is also well served by **Airbnb** (www.airbnb.com) rooms, apartments, and houses as well as some stylish canal houseboats, particularly in Christianshavn.

ATMS/CASHPOINTS Most banks offer 24-hour ATMs. Maestro, Cirrus, and Visa cards are readily accepted at all ATMs. Change currency either at banks or at exchanges around the tourist areas of Rådhuspladsen and Strøget. Central Station's money exchange is open 8am–9pm daily. Automatic exchange machines are available at Jyske Bank, Vesterbrogade 5; Den Danske Bank, Vesterbrogade 9; and Nordea Bank, Vesterbrogade 8.

BUSINESS HOURS Banks are open Monday through Friday from 10am to 4pm (Thurs until 6pm).

CREDIT CARDS Call credit-card companies when you discover your wallet has been lost or stolen and file a report at the nearest police precinct. Your credit-card company or insurer will require a police report number or record. **Visa's** US emergency number is ☎ 800/847-2911, or ☎ 0800 89 1725 in the UK (www.visa.com). **American Express** (www.amex.com) cardholders and traveler's check holders should call ☎ 800/221-7282 in the US, or ☎ 800/587-6023 in the UK. **MasterCard** (www.mastercard.com) holders should call ☎ 800/307-7309 in the US, or ☎ 0800 96 4767 in the UK.

Warning: Take care when paying by credit card. Major venues and restaurants generally accept chip-enabled cards with a PIN number (if you don't have a chip card, you will be asked to sign a receipt); question anyone who wants to take your card away to make payment, as this might expose you to card fraud. In addition, overseas credit cards attract a 3 to 5% surcharge on many restaurant bills.

DOCTORS In case of emergency, doctors are on call weekdays 4pm–8am through **Lægevagten** (☎ 45 7013 0041). Visits cost from 250DKK. EU citizens are not charged if they have an EHIC card (see p 165).

ELECTRICITY Hotels operate on 220 volts AC (50 or 60 cycles) with two-pin plugs. UK and US visitors will need to buy adaptors, readily available in all airport shops.

EMBASSIES **Australian Embassy** Dampfærgevej 26, 2nd floor, 2100 Copenhagen (☎ 45 7026 3676); **Canadian Embassy** Kristen Bernikowsgade 1, 1105 Copenhagen (☎ 45 3348 3200); **British Embassy** Kastelsvej 36–40, 2100 Copenhagen (☎ 45 35 44 52 00); **US Embassy** Dag Hammarskjölds Allé 24, 2100 Copenhagen (☎ 45 3341 7100).

EMERGENCIES For police, ambulance or fire service, dial ☎ **112;** emergency calls from public phones are free.

GAY & LESBIAN TRAVELERS Denmark has a liberal tradition towards homosexuality, being the first country in the world to recognize same-sex marriage in 1989, and since 1999 gay couples have been able to adopt the children of their partners. Various gay festivals take place throughout the year and there are many gay and lesbian clubs and bars in the city (see p 111). The website **www.visitcopenhagen.com/gaycopenhagen** has lots of gay-specific information; **www.copenhagen-gay-life.dk** is another useful website with listings, transport, and cruising details.

HOLIDAYS Holidays observed include: January 1 (New Year's Day); March/April (Maundy Thursday, Good Friday, and Easter Monday); April/May – 40 days after Easter (Day of Prayer); May 1 (May Day); May/June (Whit Monday); June 5 (Constitution Day); December 25 (Christmas); and December 26 (Feast of St. Stephen).

INSURANCE Check your existing insurance policies before you buy travel insurance to cover trip cancellation, lost luggage, medical expenses or car rental insurance. For more information, contact one of the following recommended insurers: **Allianz Global Assistance** (☎ 866/884-3556; www.allianztravelinsurance.com); **Travel Guard International** (☎ 800/826-4919; www.travelguard.com); **Travel Insured International** (☎ 800/243-3174;

www.travelinsured.com); and **Travelex Insurance Services** (☎ 800/228-9792; www.travelex-insurance.com). For travel overseas, most US health plans (including Medicare and Medicaid) do not provide coverage, and the ones that do often require payment for services upfront. If you require additional medical insurance, try **MEDEX Assistance** (☎ 800/732-5309; www.medexassist.com) or **Travel Assistance International** (☎ 800/821-2828; www.travelassistance.com); for general information on services, call the company's Worldwide Assistance Services, Inc. at ☎ 800/777-8710.

European travelers can apply for an **EHIC** card (pick up an application form from main post offices or apply online at www.ehic.org.uk). This lasts 3-5 years and entitles holders to reduced or free emergency healthcare across the European Economic Area.

INTERNET Internet access is plentiful, both in cafes and hotels, most of which now offer Wi-Fi access. Free Wi-Fi is also available at the centrally located Copenhagen Visitor Service (Vesterbrogade 4A, ☎ 45 70 222 442, www.visitcopenhagen.com) where you can also charge devices.

LOST PROPERTY The main lost-property office is in the police station at 113 Slotsherrensvej, 2720 Vanløse, ☎ 45 3874 8822. Mon, Weds, Fri 9am-2pm, Thurs 9am-5:30pm. Closed Sat-Sun. If you lose something on the train, call ☎ 45 2468 0960.

MAIL & POSTAGE Most post offices are open Monday–Friday 9am–5pm and Saturday 9am–noon. Closed Sunday. Mail boxes are bright red. Post offices in tourist areas are open longer hours and some open Sunday. Main branches are at Central Station (Carsten Niebuhrs Gade 6), 33 Købmagergade and Dronningens Tværgade 21.

MONEY The currency in Denmark is the **krone.** At press time, the exchange rate was approximately 1DKK = $0.14 or £0.10). For up-to-the minute exchange rates between the euro and the dollar, check the currency converter website **www.xe.com**.

OPENING HOURS Opening hours vary, though stores typically open Monday–Thursday 10am–6pm, Friday 10am-7pm, Saturday 10am-4pm and Sunday 12pm-4pm. Department stores and supermarkets are usually open longer. Liquor stores, kiosks, and the shops around Rådhuspladsen stay open until late at night.

PASSPORTS No visas are required for Australian, US, Canadian, or UK visitors to Denmark providing your stay does not exceed 90 days. If your passport is lost or stolen, contact your country's embassy or consulate immediately. See "Embassies" above. Before you travel, make a copy of your passport's critical pages and keep it separate from your passport.

PHARMACIES Pharmacies *(apotek)* have an illuminated "A" outside and operate during normal business hours (see above). A 24-hour pharmacy is found at **Steno Apotek,** Vesterbrogade 6C (☎ 45 3314 8266, www.stenoapotek.dk) opposite Central Station.

POLICE The national police emergency number is ☎ **112.**

RESTROOMS *Toiletter* or WC are available in most tourist areas of Copenhagen. Mens' facilities are marked as "Herrer" or "H", womens' as "Damer" or "D." It's not unusual to find unisex toilets in Denmark, even in public buildings.

SAFETY Denmark is one of the safest countries in Europe and violent crime in Copenhagen is extremely rare. However, take care around the Central Station at night; muggings have been known to happen, mainly by the junkies who hang around the old Red Light District at the back of the station.

SMOKING Smoking is banned in all indoor public places. This ban covers public transport and the interiors of restaurants, bars, and cafes.

TELEPHONES The country code is **45**; there are no city codes in Denmark. Local numbers have eight digits. **Pay phones** accept 1DKK or 5DKK coins and pre-paid Telecards, available from kiosks and post offices (see p 165). For national telephone enquiries, dial ☎ **118.** For international telephone information, call ☎ **113.** For collect international calls, ☎ **141** for the operator. Be aware that these calls are charged at 5DKK per call, with an additional fee of 7DKK per minute. International codes are: UK +44; US +1; Australia +61.

TIPPING Round up taxi fares to the nearest krone. Service charges are built into most bills in restaurants; always check the bill before you leave a tip.

TOURIST INFORMATION The excellent **Wonderful Copenhagen (**Nørregade 7B, ☎ 45 3325 7400, www.visitcopenhagen.com) and **Copenhagen Visitor Service** (Vesterbrogade 4A, ☎ 45 7022 2442, www.woco.dk) tourist information offices are open seven days a week in the summer months, closed Sundays in winter.

TRAVELERS WITH DISABILITIES Denmark is forward-thinking; all new public buildings are wheel-chair accessible, as are most of the museums, restaurants, larger shops, and the airport. Contact the **Danish Disability Council** (www.dch.dk) for details. For British travelers, **Disability Rights UK** (www.disabilityrightsuk.org) provides tips for planning holidays overseas. US citizens can contact the Society for Accessible Travel and Hospitality (www.sath.org) for travel hints and recommendations. **Flying Wheels Travel** (www.flyingwheelstravel.com) offers escorted tours and **Access-Able Travel Source** (www.access-able.com) has access information for people traveling to Copenhagen.

VAT TAX A value-added (VAT) tax (known in Denmark as *moms*) of 25% is included in the displayed price of all items. If you are traveling from outside the EU, you can obtain a tax rebate on purchases over 300DKK as you leave the country. Global Blue and Tax Free Worldwide offer 13 to 19% of your purchase price back. Shop where you see their sign and ask for a tax-free refund form at the till. Show your purchases, receipts, and passport at customs and the company will refund your money straight into your bank account. For more information, go to www.globalblue.com or www.taxfreeworldwide.com.

Copenhagen: **A Brief History**

810 First recorded Danish king, Godfred, dies.

800–950 Vikings plunder England, Russia, and France.

940–985 Harald Bluetooth brings Christianity to Denmark.

1013–43 England and Denmark united.

1160–67 Fortress built on the isle of Slotsholmen by Bishop Absalon to protect the new settlement of Copenhagen.

1240–1400 Rapid growth of the city due to its position on the natural harbor of the Øresund.

1254 Copenhagen given a charter as a city by Bishop Jakob Erlandsen.

1369 Absalon's fortress razed to the ground by the German Hanseatic League.

1397 Queen Margrethe I (1353-1412) founds the Northern Alliance between Denmark, Norway, and Sweden, formalized as the Union of Kalmar.

1410 First Copenhagen Castle built on site of present Christiansborg Palace.

1417 King Erik of Pomerania is first resident of castle.

1443 Copenhagen replaces Roskilde as Danish capital.

1449 King Christian I, the first of the Oldenborg dynasty, crowned in Copenhagen.

1471 Sweden breaks away from Union of Kalmar.

1479 University of Copenhagen founded by Christian I.

1536 Lutheran preachers bring Reformation to Denmark.

1583 The world's oldest amusement park established at Bakken.

1588–1648 Reign of principal architect of Copenhagen, Christian IV. Canals, Rosenborg Castle, Børsen, Kastellet, and Rundetårn built.

1658 The Peace of Roskilde hands Malmö back to the Swedes.

1675–79 Skåne Wars, in which Denmark loses territory to Sweden.

1700–1810 City grows in wealth due to taxing of maritime traffic through the Øresund.

1711 Bubonic plague wipes out third of Copenhagen's population.

1728 Much of the city destroyed by fire.

1731–37 City rebuilt under Christian VI, including Copenhagen Castle, which becomes Christiansborg Palace.

1746–66 Frederiksstad and Amalienborg developed under Frederick V.

1775 Royal Porcelain Factory opened.

1794 Christian VI's palace at Christiansborg burns down. Royal Family moves to Amalienborg.

1801–07 British bombard Copenhagen, with heavy loss of life, to prevent Denmark siding with Napoleon.

1813 Denmark bankrupted after Napoleonic Wars. Cedes Norway to Sweden.

1810–30 Golden Age of Danish literature; luminaries include HC Andersen and Søren Kierkegård.

1814 First free compulsory primary schools.

1830–40 Copenhagen recovers from bankruptcy and extends beyond city walls to Vesterbro, Nørrebro, and Østerbro.

1843 Tivoli opens under auspices of Georg Carsten, friend of HC Andersen.

1847 Founding of Carlsberg Brewery. Central Station opens.

1849 Monarchy becomes constitutional; reforms signed in Copenhagen.

1863 House of Glücksborg succeeds the House of Oldenborg through King Christian IX (1863–1906).

1880 First wave of immigration to the US.

1890S A time of many liberal social reforms.

1914 Denmark retains neutrality during WWI.

1928 Third Christianborg Palace becomes seat of government.

1930S Economic depression.

1940–45 German occupation of Copenhagen during WWII.

1949 Denmark joins NATO.

1967 Copenhagen celebrates 800-year jubilee.

1972 Denmark joins EEC. Margrethe II becomes queen.

1992 Denmark votes against Maastricht Treaty.

1993 Accepts the Treaty and leads the European Union for six months.

1996 Cultural Capital of Europe.

2000 Øresund Bridge opens, connecting Denmark and Sweden.

2002 Metro opens.

2004 Operaen opens.

2005 Muhammed cartoons set off worldwide Muslim protests.

2008 Copenhagen is ranked as the best city in the world to live in.

2009 The city hosts the United Nations Climate Change Conference.

2012 The first of several Cycle Super Highways opens.

2013 Drilling commences on the Metro Cityringen (circle line), set to open in 2018

2016 Geranium becomes Denmark's first restaurant to win three Michelin stars.

Copenhagen's **Architecture**

Although the building of Copenhagen began in the 12th century with Bishop Absalon's fort on Slotsholmen (see p 39), much of what we see today is the result of the vision of the Royal Family. The present-day city began to take shape during the 52-year reign of Christian IV between 1596 and 1648.

17th-Century Town Planning

Under the auspices of King Christian IV, many of the buildings we see today were built. As money and riches began to pour into the city, he went on a building spree only equalled by the development of the past 100 years. Rosenborg Castle, the Dutch Renaissance Børsen, and the Rundetårn, complete with its observatory, all appeared during his reign, as did the canals to ease transport and the defensive walls of Kastellet.

18th-Century Rococo

The Danish Royal Family vast castle complex at **Amalienborg,** in aristocratic Frederiksstaden, was laid out 1746–66 according to the visionary and ultimately over-ambitious plans of Frederik V. The castle's rococo-style buildings are some of the most impressive in northern Europe, offset by the waters of the Øresund and the domed majesty of the **Marmorkirken.** For further examples of Frederik's ambitions for his city, look at **Det Kongelige Teater,** with its arched balcony encrusted with mosaics, built at a time when Copenhagen was increasingly wealthy due to maritime trade and taxes.

19th-Century Romanticism

Copenhagen's civic pride of the Golden Age is exemplified by the enormous **Rådhuset,** genius of architect Martin Nyrop and finished in 1906. He was inspired by the Palazzo Pubblico in Siena, wanting to create a building that dominated its surroundings with a massive tower and symbolic carvings, pinnacles, and mini-turrets on all corners. A black-and-gilt figure of Bishop Absalon appears above the main entrance, meters away from the two symbolic *lur* (horn) players perched atop their giant brick pillar.

20th-Century Modernism

The century of Arne Jacobsen, Georg Jensen, and Hans J. Wegner. Jacobsen's Egg, Ant, and Swan chairs, Jensen's silverware, and Henningsen's lamp shades can be seen in hip bars, hotels, and museums throughout Copenhagen. Jacobsen is the godfather of Danish design; his greatest work is the **Radisson Blu Royal Hotel** (see p 132), Copenhagen's first skyscraper. The late 20th century was a time of great innovation in Copenhagen, as illustrated by the splendid French Wing at the **Ny Carlsberg Glyptotek** (see p 14). Designed by Henning Larsen and opened in 1996, it is masterly in its use of light and space. Two years later saw the opening of the magnificent glass-and-concrete extension to the **Nationalmuseet** by Anna Maria Indrio.

21st-Century Minimalism

Ground-breaking contemporary designs include **Paustian,** the trend-setting furniture store and acclaimed restaurant in the docklands (p 100), designed by the architect of Sydney Opera House, Jørn Utzon (1918–2008). American Daniel Liebeskind designed the **Dansk Jødisk Museum** (p 19) in 2004. Iraqi Zaha Hadid designed the new wing of **Ordupgaard** Art Museum (p 31), which opened in 2005, and in 2008 Norman Foster designed the Elephant House at the **Zoo** (p 87). The modern jewels in Copenhagen's architectural crown, however, have to be its series of waterside public spaces, **Den Sorte Diamond** (Black Diamond, p 29), the **Operaen** (p 119), and **Det Kongelige Teater Skuespilhus** (Playhouse, p 121). Exciting buildings continue to appear with the redevelopment of Ørestad (p 31). In 2015, Danish-Icelandic artist Olafur Eliasson created the visually striking **Cirkelbroen**, a pedestrianized bridge spanning Christianshavn canal.

Useful Phrases & Menu Terms

Useful Words & Phrases

ENGLISH	DANISH	PRONUNCIATION
Hello	Hej	[hai]
How are you?	Hvordan går det?	[vaw-dan gawr day]
Fine, thank you	Godt, tak	[got tahk)
What is your name?	Hvad hedder du?	[vah hith-er doo]
My name is...	Jeg hedder...	[yigh hith-er]
Where are you from?	Hvor kommer du fra?	[vohr komm-er doo frah)]
How old are you?	Hvor gammel er du?	[vohr gahm-el er doo]
Thank you	Tak	[tahk]
Yes	Ja	[yah]
No	Nej	[nay]

ENGLISH	DANISH	PRONUNCIATION
Excuse me	Undskyld	[oon-skewl]
I'm sorry	Undskyld	[oon-skewl]
Goodbye	Farvel [formal) or Hej	[fahr-vell] or [haj]
Help!	Hjælp!	[yelp]
Good morning	Godmorgen	[goh-morn]
Good day	Goddag	[goh-day]
Good evening	Godaften	[goh-afden]
Good night	Godnat	[goh-naht]
I don't understand	Det forstår jeg ikke	[day for-stawr yigh igg-ih]
Do you speak English?	Taler du engelsk?	[teh-ler doo eng-elsk]
What time is it?	Hvad er klokken?	[vah er klok-en]
It's o'clock	Klokken er	[klok-en er]
Morning	Morgen	[morn]
Afternoon	Eftermiddag	[eft-er-mih-day]
Evening	Aften	[ahf-den]
Night	Nat	[naht]
Noon	Middag	[mih-day]
Midnight	Midnat	[mith-naht]
Today	i dag	[ee day]
Yesterday	i går	[ee gawr]
Tomorrow	i morgen	[ee morn]
Week	Uge	[oo-ih]
Entrance	Indgang	[in-gahng]
Exit	Udgang	[ooth-gahng]
Open	Åben	[aw-ben]
Closed	Lukket	[loog-et]
Left	Venstre	[vehn-strih]
Right	Højre	[hoy-rih]
Police Station	Politistation	[pol-ih-tee-stah-shohn]
Police	Politiet	[pol-ih-tee-it]
Toilets	Toiletter	[toy-let-er]
Men	Herrer	[heh-rer]
Women	Damer	[dah-mer]
Tourist Information	Turistinformation	[too-reest-in-for-mah-shohn]
Post office	Posthus	[post-hos]
Cathedral	Domkirke	[dom-keerk-ih]
Church	Kirke	[keerk-ih]
Main square	Torvet	[tor-vit]
Street	Gade/stræde	[gah-thih]
Castle	Slot	[slot]
Garden	Have	[hah-vih]
Square	Plads/torv	[plahs] [torv]
Bookshop	Boghandel	[boh-hand-ihl]
Delicatessen	Delikatesse	[dehl-ih-kah-tess-ih]
Laundry	Vaskeri	[vask-er-ee]
Market	Marked	[mar-kith]
News agent	Aviskiosk	[ah-vees-kee-osk]

Numbers

NUMBER	DANISH	PRONUNCIATION
1	en (en)/et (ed)	En [ayn] et [ayt]
2	to	[toh]
3	tre	[tray]
4	fire	(fear]
5	fem	(fem]
6	seks	(seks]
7	syv	[sewh]
8	otte	[awd-ih]
9	ni	[nee]
10	ti	[tee]
11	elleve	[ell-vih]
12	tolv	[tawl]
13	tretten	[trat-en]
14	fjorten	[fyort-en]
15	femten	[femt-en]
16	seksten	[sigh-sten]
17	sytten	[sewt-en]
18	atten	[aht-en]
19	nitten	[nitt-en]
20	tyve	[tew-vih]
21	enogtyve	[ayn-oh-tew-vih]
22	toogtyve	[toh-oh-tew-vih]
23	treogtyve	[trey-oh-tew-vih]
30	tredive	[trahll-vih]
40	fyrre	[fuhrr]
50	halvtreds	[hal-tres]
60	tres	(tres]
70	halvfjerds	[hahl-fyers
80	firs	[feers]
90	halvfems	[hahl-fems]
100	hundrede	[hoon-er]
150	hundrede og halvtreds	[hoon-er oh hahl-tres]
200	to hundrede	[toh hoon-er]
300	tre hundrede	[tray hoon-er]
1000	tusind	[too-sin]
2000	to tusind	[toh too-sin]
1,000,000	en million abbr: en mio	[ayn mil-ee-ohn]

Days of the Week

ENGLISH	DANISH	PRONUNCIATION
Monday	Mandag	[mahn-dah]
Tuesday	Tirsdag	[teers-dah]
Wednesday	Onsdag	[ohns-dah]
Thursday	Torsdag	[tors-dah]
Friday	Fredag	[frigh-dah]
Saturday	Lørdag	[luhr-dah]
Sunday	Søndag	[sewn-dah]

Months

ENGLISH	DANISH	PRONUNCIATION
January	Januar	[yahn-oo-ar]
February	Februar	[feb-roo-ar]
March	Marts	[mahrts]
April	April	[ab-reel]
May	Maj	[migh]
June	Juni	[yoo-nee]
July	Juli	[yoo-lee]
August	August	[ow-goost]
September	September	[sept-ehm-ber]
October	Oktober	[ok-toh-ber]
November	November	[noh-vehm-ber]
December	December	[days-ehm-ber]

Menu Terms

ENGLISH	DANISH	PRONUNCIATION
Breakfast	Morgenmad	[morn-math]
Lunch	Frokost	[froh-kost]
Supper	Aftensmad	[af-dens-math]
Chicken	Kylling	[kew-ling]
Beef	Oksekød	[oks-e-kewth]
Fish	Fisk	[fisk]
Ham	Skinke	[skin-kih]
Cheese	Ost	[ohst]
Eggs	Æg	[eg]
Salad	Salat	[sa-laht]
(fresh) Vegetables	(friske) Grøntsager	[frisk-e gruhnt-say-er]
(fresh) Fruit	(frisk) Frugt	[frisk froogt]
Bread	Brød	[bruhth]
Toast	Ristet brød	[rist-et bruhth]
Noodles	Nudler	[nood-ler]
Rice	Ris	[rees]
Coffee	Kaffe	[kah-fih]
Tea	Te	[tay]
Juice	Juice/saft	[dyews] [sahft]
Sparkling water	Danskvand	[dansk-vahn]
Water	Vand	[vahn]
Beer	Øl	[ool]
Red/white wine	Rød/hvid vin	[ruhth veen/vith veen]
Salt	Salt	[sahlt]
Black pepper	Peber	[pay-wuhr
Butter	Noget smør	[noh-ith smuhr]

ENGLISH	DANISH	PRONUNCIATION
May I have a glass of...?	Må jeg bede om et glas __?	[maw yigh bay-thih om ayt glas]
May I have a cup of ...?	Må jeg bede om en kop __?	[maw yigh bay-thih om ayn kop]
May I have a bottle of ...?	Må jeg bede om en flaske __?	[maw yigh bay-thih om ayn flask]
May I have some ...?	Må jeg bede om ___?	[maw yigh beh-thih om]
It was delicious	Det var lækkert.	[day vahr lek-ert]
Excuse me, waiter?	Undskyld! or Tjener!	[oon-skewl] [tyeyn-er]
May I have the check, please	Må jeg bede om regningen?	[maw yigh bay-thih om righ-ning-en]

Index

See also Accommodations and Restaurant indexes, below.

H

I

J

K

L

M

Accommodations

Restaurants

Photo **Credits**

p viii: © S-F; p 3, bottom: © Chris Peacock; p 4, top: © S-F/Shutterstock.com; p 4, bottom: © Chris Peacock; p 5: © Copenhagenmediacenter.com/Anders Bøgild. Tivoli; p 7, bottom: © Audrius Merfeldas/Shutterstock.com; p 8, top: © Copenhagenmediacenter.com/Christian Alsing; p 9, top: © Chris Peacock; p 10, bottom: © Holly Hughes; p 13, bottom: © Chris Peacock; p 14, top: © Chris Peacock; p 15, top: © Chris Peacock; p 16, bottom: © Chris Peacock; p 17, top: © Chris Peacock; p 19, bottom: © Leonid Andronov; p 20, top: © Chris Peacock; p 20, bottom: © Holly Hughes; p 21, bottom: © Arndale/Shutterstock.com; p 22, top: © Chris Peacock; p 23: © Andrey Shcherbukhin/Shutterstock.com; p 25, bottom: © Chris Peacock; p 26, top: © Chris Peacock; p 26, bottom: © Chris Peacock; p 29, bottom: © Chris Peacock; p 30, top: © She/Shutterstock.com; p 31, bottom: © alarico/Shutterstock.com; p 33, middle: Courtesy of Tivoli Gardens/Fotograf Peter Nørby; p 34, top: © Chris Peacock; p 34, bottom: © Copenhagenmediacenter.com/Ty Stange; p 35, bottom: Courtesy of Experimentium City/Jesper Rais; p 36, bottom: © Mikkel Bigandt/Shutterstock.com; p 39, middle: © Chris Peacock; p 40, top: © Chris Peacock; p 41, top: © Chris Peacock; p 41, bottom: © Chris Peacock; p 42, top: © Andrey Shcherbukhin/Shutterstock.com; p 43, bottom: © Didriks; p 45, middle: © Chris Peacock; p 47: © Copenhagenmediacenter.com/Ty Stange; p 49, bottom: © Copenhagenmediacenter.com/Ty Stange; p 50, bottom: © Copenhagenmediacenter.com/Visit Carlsberg; p 51, top: © Chris Peacock; p 52, top: © Mikkel Bigandt/Shutterstock.com; p 52, bottom: © Chris Peacock; p 53, top: © Morten Jerichau; p 55, bottom: © Copenhagenmediacenter.com/Tuala Hjarnø; p 56, bottom: © Oliver Foerstner/Shutterstock.com; p 57, top: © Chris Peacock; p 58, top: © Chris Peacock; p 58, bottom: © Frank Bach; p 59, top: © Mordechai Meiri/Shutterstock.com; p 61, middle: © Chris Peacock; p 62, top: © Eugene Kim; p 63, top: © Chris Peacock; p 63, bottom: © Aalborg Stift/Christian Roar Pedersen; p 64, top: © Chris Peacock; p 64, bottom: Courtesy of Café Wilder; p 65, top: © Holly Hughes; p 67, bottom: © Chris Peacock; p 68, top: © Alan Kraft; p 69, top: © Chris Peacock; p 70, top: © Chris Peacock; p 71: © Copenhagenmediacenter.com/Tuala Hjarnø; p 75, top: © Chris Peacock; p 76, bottom: © Holly Hughes; p 77, top: © Chris Peacock; p 78, top: © Chris Peacock; p 78, bottom: © Chris Peacock; p 79, top: © Chris Peacock; p 79, bottom: © Chris Peacock; p 81, top: © Chris Peacock; p 82, top: © Chris Peacock; p 83: © Copenhagenmediacenter.com/Ty Stange; p 85, bottom: © Copenhagenmediacenter.com/Ty Stange; p 86, bottom: © Copenhagenmediacenter.com/Christian Lindgren; p 88, top: © Chris Peacock; p 89: Courtesy of Fiskebar/Mira Arkin/Spiseliv; p 92, bottom: Courtesy of Bistro Royal; p 93, bottom: Courtesy of Andersen Bakery; p 94, top: © Chris Peacock; p 95, bottom: Courtesy of Cap Horn/Kristian Brasen; p 96, top: Courtesy of Geranium/Claes Bech Poulsen; p 97, bottom: Courtesy of Le Le; p 98, bottom: Courtesy of Nimb/Anders Hviid © HVIIDPHOTOGRAPHY; p 99, top: Courtesy of Pluto; p 100, top: © Thanh Nguyen; p 101, bottom: Courtesy of The Standard/Signe Roderik 2015; p 102, top: © Chris Peacock; p 103: Courtesy of Wallmans/John Resborn; p 106, top: Courtesy of Ruby/Uffe Weng; p 107, bottom: Courtesy of BrewPub København/Michael Nielsen; p 108, bottom: Courtesy of Curfew; p 109, top: Courtesy of Tivoli Gardens/Nimb; p 110, top: © Chris Peacock; p 111, top: Courtesy of Bakken; p 111, bottom: Courtesy of VEGA/Peter Troest; p 112, top: © Copenhagenmediacenter.com/Magnus Ragnvid; p 112, bottom: © Torben Christensen; Scanpix; p 113: Courtesy of Tivoli Gardens; p 116, bottom: Courtesy of Amager Bio; p 117, bottom: Courtesy of Det Ny Teater; p 118, top: Courtesy of Tivoli Gardens; p 119, top: Courtesy of Tycho Brahe Planetarium/Rune Johansen; p 119, bottom: © alarico/Shutterstock.com; p 120, top: © Laust Ladefoged; p 120, bottom: © Dave Messina; p 121, top: Courtesy of Det Kongelige Teater/Christian Als; p 123: Courtesy of Nimb; p 126, bottom: Courtesy of Central Hotel & Café; p 127, bottom: Courtesy of Hotel Alexandra; p 128, bottom: © Copenhagenmediacenter.com/Lisbeth Michelsen; p 129, bottom: Courtesy of The Copenhagen

Admiral Hotel; p 130, top: © Copenhagenmediacenter.com/Hotel Twentyseven/Søren Dam; p 131, bottom: Courtesy of Hotel SP34; p 132, top: Courtesy of Nimb; p 133, bottom: © Copenhagenmediacenter.com/Radisson Blu Royal/Henning Hjorth; p 134, top: © Copenhagenmediacenter.com/Wakeup Copenhagen; p 135: Courtesy of ARKEN/Hanne Fuglbjerg; p 139, bottom: © Chris Peacock; p 140, top: © Chris Peacock; p 143, bottom: © Chris Peacock; p 144, top: © Chris Peacock; p 147, bottom: © Chris Peacock; p 148, bottom: © Chris Peacock; p 151, bottom: Courtesy of Malmö Tourism; p 152, top: © Malmö Tourism/Werner Nystrand; p 157: © olgite.

Notes